West Point Admiral

"*West Point Admiral* is a fitting follow on and expansion of Mike's contribution to my *Profiles in Success* book series in 2013 entitled <u>Making The Decision</u>, which dealt with the problem of individuals who treat every decision as having the same importance. The military crucible has shaped some of the most transformative leaders. He is a prime example as illustrated in his handling of amphibious doctrine and creation of the Seabee Division. Lessons in this book go far beyond the military enterprise. Anyone who wants to extend and improve their leadership influence will benefit deeply by reading and applying its nuggets."

—**Gordon J. Bernhardt,** Author and Podcaster,
Profiles in Success book and podcast series

——✇——

"RADM (Ret) Mike Shelton offers in detail his insights on a myriad of military service and intra-Navy cultures he encountered during his decades-long Seabee and Navy tours of duty. He provides "hard talk" on leadership—good and bad—that he encountered, and how that impacted mission accomplishment and troop welfare as he negotiated a varied set of career challenges. Although his time on watch was a good while ago, many of the lessons are timeless."

—**Edwin P. Smith,** Lieutenant General, US Army (Ret)
Former Commanding General, US Army Pacific

Acclaim Press
— Your Next Great Book —

P.O. Box 238
Morley, MO 63767
(573) 472-9800
www.acclaimpress.com

Editor: Randy Baumgardner
Book & Cover Design: Frene Melton
Front cover photo credit: USMA Public Affairs Office

ISBN: 978-1-948901-98-7 | 1-948901-98-6
Library of Congress Control Number: 2021940143

First Printing: 2021
Printed in the United States of America
10 9 8 7 6 5 4 3 2 1

This publication was produced using available information.
The publisher regrets it cannot assume responsibility for errors or omissions.

CONTENTS

DEDICATION

My reflections in this memoir are dedicated to my fellow Americans who fought in the Vietnam War; especially those who died, including my West Point classmates and fellow Seabees of Naval Mobile Construction Battalion Nine (NMCB-9) listed below (chronologically). They, like the Light Brigade in the Crimean War described so eloquently by Lord Tennyson, rode "into the valley of death" because someone had "blunder'd." They did their duty. They did not fail but were failed by their leaders and their country.

SWF3 J. R. Couch, USN

EONCN H. G. Hodges, USN

BUH3 F. G. Goelz, USN

CMHCN J. F. Galati, USN

2LT J. R. Adams, USA

BUL3 G. R. Deshurley, USN

BULCN M. E. Hodel, USN

BUL3 J. F. Peek, USN

BUHCN J. R. Retzloff, USN

BUL3 A. L. Mair, USN

2LT J. P. Brown, USA

2LT R. L. Frazer, USA

1LT H. B. Brown, USA

1LT D. L. Neuburger, USA

1LT J. M. Pena, USA

1LT M. L. Nathe, USA

1LT J. T. Corley, USA

1LT R. J. Enners, USA

1LT R. A. Fulkerson, USA

1LT R. O. Bickford, USA

1LT M. G. Parr, USA

1LT J. K. Brierly, USA

1LT T. D. Thompson Jr., USA

1LT L. L. Preston Jr., USA

1LT T. Emerson, USA

CPT W. K. Schaltenbrand, USA

CPT K. W. Mills, USA

CPT G. W. Carlson, USA

CPT H. A. Etheridge III, USA

CPT J. E. Kelly, USA

CPT F. A. Hill, USA

CPT N. L. Nesterak, USA

CPT D. W. Dietz, USA

CPT D. T. Gray, USA

CPT G. B. Robinson, USA

CPT T. L. Ketter, USA

CPT E. D. Greene, USA

Two roads diverged in a wood, and I—
I took the one less traveled by,
And that has made all the difference.
                              —Robert Frost, *The Road Not Taken*

PREFACE

Jean Norton Cru was an author and critical analyst of World War I memoirs, having analyzed three hundred eyewitness accounts written by French combat veterans of that war. Cru believed that a genuine eyewitness account should be subjective—what they saw, what they felt, and what they were told.[1] This effort contains what I saw, what I felt, and what I was told at each stage of my career. My thoughts on leadership developed with each stage of my career as part of my evolving understanding and exercise of it. Key was the realization of the vital role of *empathy*—not only for subordinates but also for peers and superiors. I came to understand that factoring these competing empathies appropriately into directed action is the mark of true leadership.

The confluence of historical and cultural events reacting with my upbringing propelled me forward in my career as a leader and as an observer of the human condition. Despite the creeping encroachment of "political correctness," the constancy of the characteristics of good leadership based on ethical decision-making, mutual respect, shared risk, and empathy for the troops remained a constant. So many of the failures I observed could be traced to a deficiency in one or more of these characteristics aided by insufferable egotism to the exclusion of reality. Leadership cannot be taught—despite the efforts of the cottage industry of leadership and management gurus who avow it can. Good leadership skills, however, *can* be taught—but they cannot be imbued. It is up to the student to transform words into action.

As I wrote this book and discussed my experiences with lifelong friends, fellow veterans, and others whose opinions I respect, a topic kept coming up. How could the changes that have so radically changed the defense establishment, the armed forces, and the ability of the United States to successfully conduct military operations overseas have happened? This subject requires its own discussion, separate from this story of how I grew up around, worked in, and dealt with the armed forces as these changes were taking place. I am completing a book on that topic as a sequel to this book, but it is important to mention this project now as it will perhaps answer questions that might arise as to why this book does not expand on many of the more controversial issues touched upon herein.

Any of my achievements over the last forty years would not have been possible without the constant love and support of my wife, Mary. She completed a twenty-year career as a Navy nurse while raising three children. She took jobs that were available rather than desirable from an unsupportive Navy Nurse Corps so the family could be together. Her insights into being a married female officer in the Navy at a time when there were not many—let alone with children—helped develop my perspective on the integration of women in the military. Experiencing the changes and struggles associated with the expanding role of women in the Navy with her was vital to any success I had dealing with women's issues during my military career. This is really *our* story.

ACKNOWLEDGMENTS

Acknowledgments suffer from a distinct possibility of overlooking someone who should be included. This is particularly true of a memoir covering a lifetime. Some influences on one's life are stark, but many are subtle. I was an observer of the people I came in contact with through my life's experiences and learned from all—good, bad, or indifferent. I therefore say in the broadest terms possible, "thank you" to all I have interacted with. You have made me what I am.

My parents and my wife, Mary, have of course been a huge influence on me, but my extended family on both sides also provided a great deal to my life understanding and emotional maturation. The same is true of my children—Michelle, Jessica, and Tom. They are unique individuals who taught me as much as I taught them. They suffered from my frequent absences as they grew up, and I missed events that were important to them. They (and their children) have all made me extremely proud. I love them dearly.

Three flag officers were of particular importance in my career: Adm. Vern Clark, my friend since we were aides on the E-ring together as lieutenant commanders and when he was serving as chief of naval operations (CNO) when I retired; Rear Adm. Mike Marschall, my first flag mentor when he was chief of civil engineers; and Rear Adm. Jack Buffington, my friend, mentor, and Seabee's Seabee for most of my career, through his tenure as chief of civil engineers, and on to this day. Vern Clark's comments and insights on my draft manuscript were especially helpful and greatly appreciated.

The feedback I received from those I asked to read my draft was invaluable and greatly improved my effort. My classmates Woody Held, Kenn Harris, Bob Libutti, and Paul Kern provided reflections on our bonding long ago and my observations of the changes in the military. My fellow CEC officers Peter Marshall, Kate Gregory, Chuck Kubic, Jim Corbett, Brian Estes, and Jim Rispoli provided insights into events that transpired over our overlapping careers. My neighbor Ron McManus gave me the "honest broker" view as a published author and someone who was not familiar with the events I was describing. This was extremely valuable. Ken Weckstein, who I came to know as an exceptional Washington lawyer during my post-Navy career and remained a friend, also gave me an arms-length appraisal that was sorely needed, as did my stellar executive secretary in my last flag position and later when I was completing my post-Navy career with EMCOR Government Services, Holley Bell.

My editor, Aden Nichols, has guided me through the painful process of cutting down a long draft to the finished work. While it was important for me to write it all down as a catharsis, he made me realize that once I had done that, I could edit the results into something that could provide insights to those dealing with leadership and management issues and the state of the armed forces today. His advice was expert, logical, and sound, including his own observations from his days in Army Special Forces.

Finally, I must acknowledge the debt I owe the thousands of military men and women I engaged with over my lifetime. The vast majority have provided selfless service to our country and suffered the indifference of its general population, especially since the advent of the All-Volunteer Force. Any successes I have achieved were accomplished by their efforts on my behalf. They are the nation's most valuable resource upon which our way of life depends.

INTRODUCTION

Most of us are asked questions concerning some aspect of our lives that others find curious. The frequency of these questions usually determines the type of response, the amount of thought we give, and our desire to end further discussion. Responses become rote and we move on, hoping to go no further. For me, the question asked was, "How can you be a West Point graduate and a Navy admiral?" I had answered many times, but one time my answer led to a chain of events ending with this book. I was playing in a fundraiser golf outing at the West Point golf course with Dan Rice, USMA '88, when he asked me the question. He found my answer interesting and mentioned that he was working on a book about West Point graduates and leadership. We enjoyed the round and went our separate ways.

Subsequently, Dan contacted me and asked if I would like to contribute a piece for his book. I agreed. His efforts produced *West Point Leadership: Profiles of Courage*, the preface of which states: "This is a book about leadership. Its purpose, however, is not to catalogue a set of rules to follow that will guarantee a successful outcome; rather, it is to reveal how leadership manifests itself through the incredible and unique life stories of 180 West Point graduates and two of America's Founding Fathers."[2]

This ego-inflating statement started working on me. I had never thought about myself in terms of having an "incredible and unique life story" illustrating leadership abilities. The more I thought about it, however, the more this seemed plausible, as my life experiences were a series of apparent contradictions that kept pushing me onward. This memoir is my answer to the question I had answered by rote concentrating on the "how" it could happen from a bureaucratic standpoint rather than the "why" it happened because of my life experiences. Clearly, my West Point and Navy experiences refined and built upon something central to the person I became—my ancestry. Wilbur Wright said: "If I were giving a young man advice as to how he might succeed in life, I would say to him, pick out a good father and mother, and begin life in Ohio."[3] I was born to wonderful parents, Wayne

(Bill) and Nellie (Vicki) Shelton, who ensured that when I left home, I was equipped to deal with the world as I found it through the lessons they tried hard to pass on to me. I was also fortunate enough to be born in the greatest country in the world. This I say unapologetically and unabashedly, as I have traveled the world extensively and can say that even though it is not perfect, America is the best the world has to offer. My path contained elements that formed the foundation of my military experiences, and I took them with me to West Point and into the service with the Navy. A brief review of some of these essentials might be helpful.

The Sheltons are of Scotch-Irish[4] heritage, having arrived in colonial Virginia before the American Revolution. I commend James Webb's superb history of this unique group, *Born Fighting*, to those interested. He chronicles them as a people with a strong sense of individualism and common sense. These early immigrants did not believe wealth or education proffered special privileges or superiority to anyone. These traits were embodied in my father and grandfather, whose relationship developed in the cauldron of the Great Depression on a small farm in Illinois. It was a tough life and my father opted to join the Navy to escape. He became a career enlisted man, retiring as a master chief. A combat veteran of Pearl Harbor, Midway, the Santa Cruz Islands, and numerous other actions, the war left its mark on him.

My mother descended from a Swiss immigrant, who arrived in Illinois before the Civil War. His son served in the 2nd Illinois Volunteer Cavalry in the western campaigns of the Civil War, including the siege of Vicksburg. Afterward, his descendants owned small farms in the same county as my father's farm. My mother's ancestors passed along many of the same traits as those of my father's family, revolving around the attributes of hard work, independence, religious and moral values, and love of family and country. Mother became a beautician after high school and worked during the war in a shop near Chanute Field, an Army Air Corps training site. The impact of the war was intensely personal to her, as many of the young men she knew there were sent overseas and killed in combat or training accidents.

The basic Scotch-Irish characteristics I inherited, leavened by my mother's influence, meshed with my childhood experiences. Virginia Woolf's observation that "growing up is losing some illusions, in order to acquire others" applied to me. The lessons that came of being a military dependent traveling widely in the United States and overseas in the years after World War II made this happen. The loss of my younger brother when I was seven affected my entire family significantly. It focused my parents' attention even more on trying to ensure I learned life's lessons by not being overprotective or sheltering me from the world. The trust and independence I was given is hard to imagine today in a world of "helicopter" parents who smother their children with overprotection and dependency.

The building blocks of my leadership foundation were many, but beyond my parental influences, three were especially important. First, there were the omnipresent effects of World War II on my parents, their contemporaries and friends, and America. Dad's personal experiences highlight the vagaries of combat. At Pearl Harbor, where he was serving on the USS *Nevada* (BB 36), he initially did not understand what was happening, but it all became all too clear as the General Quarters alarms sounded. A Japanese torpedo plane that crossed over the stern of the ship and dropped its torpedo into the water had the canopy back. Dad said he and the Japanese pilot, complete with the head wrapping sporting the red rising sun, had "eye lock" for those brief seconds, adding, "The son of a bitch smiled at me!" Then he dashed away to his damage control station below decks. The rest of the time until the crew was told to abandon ship was a confusion of noise, screams, terror, death, and frenzied laboring to save the ship.

While he and his shipmates were in a compartment trying to stop the flooding from a torpedo hit, a bomb exploded on the deck above causing fist-sized rivets to pop and zip around the confined space. "It was like someone fired a machine gun into the compartment." Four of the eight men there were killed instantly by the ricocheting rivet heads, the compartment's hatch sprung closed and wouldn't budge, and the small space continued to fill with water. The survivors beat on the hatch with their tools, and another damage control party was able to force the hatch open and free them before they drowned.

While this was going on, the crew got the big ship underway under its own power, the only battleship that was able to do so. As this was happening, Japanese Val dive-bombers concentrated their bombs on the *Nevada* to sink her in the channel leading in and out of Pearl Harbor and block it. The *Nevada* was ordered to beach itself across from Hospital Point to prevent this from happening. There the crew was ordered to abandon ship. Dad's clothes had been blown off, leaving him clad only in his underwear; he lost everything he owned in the debacle. He and the survivors took refuge in a sugar cane field that night while wild rumors spread of the Japanese landing on the other side of the island. Everyone was afraid to move for fear of being shot by a jumpy security patrol. The following morning the real horror of the devastation became apparent. The men moved cautiously out of the field and were able to survey Pearl Harbor. Dad never forgave the Japanese for their treachery, and he hated them until the day he died, the only ethic group I ever heard him say a disparaging word about.

He did not have long to reflect on how this would affect him. He was initially assigned to a pool of sailors whose ships were out of action and then moved to the USS *Enterprise* (CV 6) as it prepared for the highly classified and dangerous Doolittle Raid on the Japanese home islands in April 1942. The *Enterprise* accompanied the USS *Hornet* (CV 8) that carried the raiders and their B-25 aircraft; the "Big E" provided fighter aircraft to protect the task force. He remembered watching Doolittle lead his attack group off the heaving deck of the *Hornet*, the bombers taking off in heavy weather after a Japanese picket boat had spotted the task force. Doolittle's heavily laden bomber—known only as #40-2344—had to time the rise and fall of the deck and started rolling forward while the deck was pointed straight into the water; by the time the plane launched off the deck, it was pointed toward the sky. Despite this maneuver, the plane dropped precipitously and those watching thought it was going to crash into the sea and be run over by the carrier. Fortunately, it was able to gain enough airspeed and pulled up just in time. The remaining raiders all managed to take off safely and fly into history.

The Doolittle Raid was soon followed by the sea battle that proved to be the turning point of the Pacific War—Midway. Dad was there again on the *Enterprise* as a communications relayer for the landing signal officer (LSO), who was stationed on the deck of the carrier to launch and land the planes safety. As the pilots approached the carrier, the LSO evaluated their approach and corrected it, so they could hit the deck of the carrier at the appropriate point. Dad's recollections centered on the bravery and tremendous losses of the pilots and crews, particularly the torpedo planes, whose slow speed and straight-line approaches to the enemy ships made them easy targets for the Japanese fighter pilots. Their sacrifice drew the Japanese fighters away from protecting their carriers against U.S. Navy dive-bombers that came in high and in just a few minutes inflicted mortal wounds on four of the Japanese carriers which only months before had sent their planes to Pearl Harbor. As my dad stood on the deck of the carrier forlornly waiting for the planes to return, he had no way of knowing that the loss of the Japanese carriers and the cream of the Japanese carrier pilots spelled a defeat that the Japanese navy could never recover from, but he did know the price that had been paid for this victory. He simply said: "No quarter asked or given." That was the Pacific War.

Perhaps dad's most insightful revelation came from an action called the Battle of Santa Cruz Islands, in which enemy dive-bombers heavily damaged the *Enterprise*. He was running to his battle station when he looked toward the antiaircraft guns flanking one side of the ship and saw a high school classmate, Max Lee, sitting in a gun mount looking at him while smiling and waving. He returned the wave and ran through a hatch to go further down that side of the ship. After a few steps, he was knocked down by the shock from an explosion nearby. Looking back, the entire area where his friend had been was gone without a trace except for smoke and twisted metal. Despite many such close encounters throughout the war, dad was never wounded, though men around him were killed. He lived to ask himself the question that still haunts all combat survivors (including me): "Why him and not me?"

I grew up listening to these stories of not only the Pacific War but also the war in Europe through the eyes of Army, Navy, and Marine Corps senior enlisted personnel in all specialties—from infantry, armor, and artillery to communications, submarines, surface ships, and aviation. One friend had been a POW of the Japanese. My high school classmates' fathers supplied additional stories from officers' perspectives.

There was the combination of the era of my adolescence in the late '50s and early '60s coupled with the insular military community in Naples, Italy, where I finished junior high school and started high school. Coming of age in the postwar era was growing up in a different American culture that demanded more from its children in terms of maturity, respect, moral judgments, conduct, and achievement. This was magnified as a military dependent in a time when a dependent's misbehavior could have career-ending results for the parent. Today that culture is gone, replaced by concerns over sensitivity, safe spaces, and entitlements. That earlier cultural imperative had an immense effect on my contemporaries and me; it made us what we are today. We did not feel entitled to more than we had. My father told me many times: "No one owes you anything. You must earn what you get and not expect life to be fair." I found this to be accurate advice.

My father's transfer to Naples when I was thirteen immersed me in two new worlds. The first was obvious. I was in a foreign country and would be living in the local neighborhood since there was no military housing. The second was less obvious but no less significant. The American community I was joining was entirely composed of military members and their dependents. Most of my classmates were the children of officers, as there were few senior enlisted billets and only a handful of this group had older children. My contemporaries were born during World War II when restrictions on marriage in the enlisted ranks were imposed by wartime duty. To be sure, I did have classmates whose fathers were enlisted men, including one girl I had gone to first grade with in South Carolina, but we were in the minority. That made all the difference. Up until that time, my family had lived almost exclusively in the civilian community. I went to the community schools where there were few military dependents. This reinforced my parents' teachings that no one was inherently better than us; people should be judged by their accomplishments, not their status. With a couple of exceptions, all my friends were officers' kids, and I was not intimidated in the least by the difference in rank between my father and their fathers.

Additionally, there were my extensive travel experiences in post–World War II Europe. The cultural experience of living and traveling in Europe and throughout the Mediterranean was huge. This was only thirteen years after the end of the war. There were plenty of reminders of that conflict—from little things like having to watch the change you received to be sure you did not get any fascist coins (that were no longer any good) to using military scrip instead of standard U.S. currency and coins because of the ongoing black market since the war. Driving through the countryside, there were many reminders of the combat that had taken place, such things as concrete bunkers and a forlorn German military cemetery located not far from the beach. In other parts of Europe—most notably Germany—destroyed buildings, bridges, and factories were ever-present. Added to that were my dad's friends' stories of combat in Europe. Some had served in the aircrews that had bombed it, some were infantrymen who had fought for every inch of ground as they passed across it, and some were sailors whose ships had blasted it from the sea. As we took our family camping trips throughout Europe, my dad struck up conversations with Europeans, principally Germans, who had fought in the war. I listened intently. I took away several lessons from these anecdotes. Aside from a somber appreciation of what the war had done to Europe, there was the realization that America was not the center of the universe. There were many interesting things to see and do outside my country, and they were leavened by different viewpoints.

There was an expectation that I would do well in school and any extra-curricular activities I was involved in and never bring disgrace on the family. Academics were easy for me, and I concentrated on sports, becoming an Eagle Scout, hanging out with a variety of boy and girl friends, and experiencing just about everything a teenage boy could in those days. I did not think much about my future after high school as dad had pronounced that I should go to the Naval Academy and directed my efforts that way. Fate intervened.

The physical I took at the Navy hospital included a thorough vision test. Up to that point my eyesight had always been better than 20/20, but it had apparently deteriorated. During the examination, the doctor asked me where I wanted to go to college. I replied that I would be trying to go to the Naval Academy. He simply said, "That's not going to happen. You can't pass the vision test." When I inquired why, he informed me that the requirement was 20/20 vision uncorrected, and there were no waivers. When I went home and told my dad of this development, he thought for a few minutes and then said, "Look at the other academies and see what their requirements are." In the end, the only one that I could pass the vision test for was West Point, as the Army allowed corrected vision to 20/20.

As I went through my senior year in high school, getting into college became the first order of business. My dad decided I needed a "plan B" in case I did not get into West Point on the first try, so he wanted me to apply to The Citadel in Charleston, South Carolina. A term spent at this prestigious military school would give me a leg up when I applied to West Point again the following year. I was admitted to The Citadel as the West Point admissions process took place. I had applied for one of the presidential appointments reserved for sons of career military members of the armed forces.

In February of my senior year, there was an article in the local paper that our new congressman, Robert McClory (who went on to serve on the House Judiciary Committee during the Watergate fiasco), had an appointment available for West Point and those interested should apply, which I did. In due course, I learned that I was short listed for an appointment, and I had to then undergo the academic, physical, and athletic aptitude tests to see if I would emerge as the best candidate for the appointment.

I received instructions to report to Fort Sheridan, Illinois, for testing. The academic test was the easiest part since it consisted of taking the college board tests I had already been through once. The physical went smoothly since I did not have to worry about the eye test. I had practiced the skills to be demonstrated in the athletic aptitude test and passed with a score just a little above average. The most important thing that happened at Fort Sheridan was that I stayed in an army barrack, so I was in constant contact with others who were taking the tests, some of whom would be my classmates in a few months. It was my first opportunity to measure myself against the competition, and I came away convinced I did not stack up well for several reasons. First, a number of those I met were "college boys" with one or two years of college that seemed to validate my dad's thought that college would make me more competitive. Second, the athletes that were being recruited for the various sports teams at West Point who were taking the tests—particularly the athletic aptitude test—were just plain intimidating. I came home and told my parents and friends that West Point was not going to happen this time, but the entrance process was a very enlightening experience.

As my last year of high school was progressing, my father received orders to assume the post of supervisor of bands for the commander, Cruisers Destroyers Pacific (COMCRUDESPAC) in San Diego, California, with a reporting date not long after I was scheduled to graduate. One day in April, I came out of the dressing room headed for the bus that was waiting to transport the baseball team, when I looked out in the parking lot and saw my dad running across the lot. I rarely ever saw my father this excited and could not imagine what had happened or why he was waving a piece of paper. Breathlessly, he ran up to me and said, "I'm sorry, but I just couldn't stand it. This letter came for you from West Point, and I had to open it. You're going to West Point on the first of July!" My life had changed in an instant; to say I was shocked would be an understatement, as I never thought this was going to happen. I had received a congressional appointment from Congressman McClory and qualified to receive a presidential appointment.

The next thing I knew I was saying goodbye to my parents at Los Angeles Airport before I boarded a red-eye flight to Idlewild Airport in New York City. I was ordered to report to West Point in two days. My mother was sobbing uncontrollably as her only child left home to join the Army and become a man at seventeen. Dad was emotional (for him), trying to comfort my mother, offer last minute advice, and handle the obvious pride he felt without being gushy. I remember not really understanding why they were so upset as I would be home from time to time while I attended West Point. It was not like I was leaving forever, but it was a most profound rite of passage that I did not understand until much later. My mom and dad were not "helicopter parents," and they had prepared me to leave home as best they could. They had provided me two essential things besides love: guidelines to live by and independence—along with association with warriors who led by example.

Leaders are born with the inherent capabilities that are nurtured through their observations and experiences as they grow to adulthood and beyond. These character traits make them what they become—good or bad leaders. My experience taught me that while good leadership traits can be pointed out in classes or by example, a bad leader or person with no leadership skill cannot be made a good leader simply by being exposed to what have been deemed "good leadership traits." Leadership requires understanding of human nature and perhaps, more importantly, empathy with not only subordinates but also with peers and superiors. I have never believed empathy can be taught. Leadership capability is not developed in a vacuum. It requires constant feeding through life experiences and exposure to the gamut of personality types of both sexes. If it could be taught effectively, the world would be overrun with good leaders. Clearly, it is not. My exposure to senior enlisted men and officers with profound World War II and Korean War experiences was critical for my further development at West Point and in the Navy. I had data points to compare during those years, and those vicarious imprints helped guide me in evaluating the people and situations I was exposed to.

This started when I was very young in Guantanamo Bay, Cuba. One of my dad's friends was at our home frequently. I remember him as a huge, kindly man who liked to romp around with my brother and me. My father subsequently told me, when I was much older, that he was the only survivor of his part of the crew of the USS *Houston* that was sunk in the Java Sea in 1942 after a no-quarter fight with a much larger Japanese force. He swam nearly four miles through shark-infested waters at night to reach the nearest land—only to be captured by the Japanese. He spent the rest of the war in a prison camp in Thailand; indeed, he was among the POWs featured in the largely fictional war movie, *The Bridge on the River Kwai*.

I mention him for two reasons. First, the men who were my father's friends tended to be combat veterans like him. I heard many of their stories as I grew up. One of the men who lived in our building had been on a landing ship, tank (LST) that was sunk off Anzio. Another friend was a gunner on a B-24 bomber that had made the raid on the Ploesti oilfields in Romania where they came in at less than 500 feet for the bombing run. He had seen the planes on both sides of him go down with all aboard killed. Their social gatherings always involved a lot of drinking, which many times led to tales about the lighter side of their war service. Quite frequently, they were stories about some "son of a bitch" officer that made an impression on me. Second, I developed an admiration and respect for these men who had braved so much yet expected so little in return. They were not all very well educated, and some talked funny, but they were not unintelligent. In fact, they were cunning problem solvers when left to their own devices, as many of their anecdotes illustrated by demonstrating how they had gotten around bureaucratic rules and martinet officers.

The magnitude of the losses in World War II and the ramifications of chance became apparent—not only through my father's stories of Pearl Harbor, Midway, and the rest but also from stories I heard from a girl-friend's father, an Air Force colonel who had been a fighter pilot in North Africa and Europe. In 1961, he mentioned that he had been a full colonel for seventeen years, having been promoted to that rather lofty rank after just three years in the service. He elaborated,

Mike, luck was the key. When I reported to my first combat squadron in North Africa as a first lieutenant, I was immediately promoted to captain because I was the senior lieutenant of those reporting. There was a vacancy because a pilot was missing and believed killed in action that week. I flew combat missions for several months and the captains senior to me were either lost in combat, wounded and sent home, or transferred to other units. One day, the squadron executive officer, a major, was shot down. I was called in and promoted to major and assigned his job. After more combat missions in the Mediterranean, our squadron was transferred to England to prepare for the invasion of Europe. Shortly after arriving in England, my squadron commanding officer [CO] was lost and I was promoted to lieutenant colonel and became the CO. We continued combat missions from England until relocated to France after Normandy. The colonel who was our air group commander was lost and I was selected from among the squadron commanders to be his replacement with a promotion to full colonel at the age of 24. Pretty lucky huh?

I saw even then that there had been more than luck involved. There was no doubt that his skill as a fighter pilot and leader had made him the best candidate for promotion after he got through the attrition ranks at the bottom. The fortunes of war gave him the opportunity to demonstrate these traits. In my various command positions, I recalled his story when I put contingency plans in place for the casualties that might and did occur. The compelling stories shared with me by combat-seasoned officers and enlisted men were important leadership lessons I took with me when I left home.

I have one final comment regarding leadership development: leadership capabilities are constantly being sifted through screens and tested as an individual is promoted. At each stage, there are new requirements for success. Some cannot adjust and should move no further up in leadership responsibilities. (Unfortunately, unqualified candidates are often promoted, particularly micromanagers and people with questionable ethics.) Achieving success in diverse organizations of increasing scope and responsibility requires empathy for realistically evaluating not only subordinates but also peers and superiors, while continually assessing their tasking to understand what is achievable and at what cost. Successfully blending inherent leadership traits with these acquired people skills is the mark of a true leader.

AUTHOR'S NOTE

To understand these reflections and observations, it is necessary to provide some background reference information and a glossary of terms. The jargon, acronyms, military ranks, and microcosms of military and defense terms and structures can be overwhelming even to those with a solid acquaintance with the subject matter. I apologize to those who find this tutorial too basic, but given the lack of familiarity of the general public with things military since the advent of the All-Volunteer Force (AVF), I felt some basic information necessary. Among other things, this covers the structure and organization of the United States Military Academy (USMA) when I arrived in 1963; the Department of Defense and the United States Navy when I joined it in 1967; the Naval Construction Force (NCF) over the course of my career; and roles, equipment, and missions of the Navy Amphibious Forces when I joined that organization in 1983.

I should also note that I will not be using a lot of names in my account, as there is no need to identify people who are well known by those who were there and do not need to be identified to those who were not; the circumstances I will describe might prove embarrassing or upsetting to them or their families. That is not my intent. Others might have perceived events I describe differently. I really do not care. It is history now, and I see no need to sugarcoat it.

West Point Admiral

Leadership Lessons from Four Decades of Military Service

Chapter One

METAMORPHOSIS IN THE GRAY WOMB

Metamorphosis is the most profound of all acts.
—Catherynne M. Valente, *In the Night Garden*

Many cultures have rituals to mark the passage from child to adult. The military culture is no exception. Starting at the bottom of an organization and learning what it is like to have no power and few rights has always been important in the acculturation of military personnel. To lead, it is necessary to understand what it is like to be required to obey orders from a position that requires unquestioning obedience.

A favorite story my father told me of his days in the "old Navy" was about his job as the lowest ranking enlisted man on the battleship. His task was to clean and polish the spittoons on the ship, no small job. It was gross and unpleasant, and it taught him the meaning of being at the bottom of a military organization—as well as the importance of seniority and advancement. Likewise, my plebe (first) year at West Point was designed to teach the important lessons that my father had learned as the lowest-ranking sailor on his ship—that is, what it is like to be at the bottom and yet held to high standards with little or no opportunity to protest or change one's lot. Those who have never had the experience of being on the bottom of such a power structure are not likely to understand what it means and the ramifications of directing people to do things that they have not done themselves.

Beast
West Point, which is about sixty miles north of New York City, is nestled in a mountainous highland valley situated along a ninety-degree bend in the Hudson River. It had served as a strategic defensive position during the Revolutionary War. "The Plain," as the parade ground is called, is located

on an elevation above this bend. It was hemmed in on two sides by austere nineteenth-century cadet barracks reeking of "Black Jack" Pershing, "Old Blood and Guts" Patton, and countless other ghosts of the Old Corps. It was also bordered by a road that meandered along on a roughly north–south track that connected the post to Newburgh. Across this road was Trophy Point. Its phallic marble column known as Battle Monument—massive, majestic, and masculine—served as a constant reminder of the cost of war: it was emblazoned with the names of Union regular army personnel killed in the Civil War. Dominating the Plain was the medieval-looking Cadet Chapel on the hill behind it—detached, defining, driving home the academy motto of Duty, Honor, Country. The footprint of the academy's stark granite buildings, monuments and statues, and wandering paths seemed encapsulated in a time warp harkening the visitor back through the glorious history of West Point.

"Beast Barracks" accurately describes how the cadets viewed the new interlopers arriving in their world—beasts in need of taming. New cadets were not worthy of even being called plebes until accepted by the Corps of Cadets at the end of the Beast Barracks initiation. On the morning of July 1, 1963, I met the Beast Detail in the space between the Old North Barracks buildings, a location known as "the Area." No one who ever attended West Point and made it through the first day will ever forget it, whether they went on to graduate or not. For those not familiar with the socialization process designed to turn young male civilians into soldiers and more specifically Army officers, it was severe by design (in those days before "sensitivity" became the watchword of American society and women were admitted to the country's military academies). It was the same at all the academies as each sought to weed out those who were not suitable either by motivation or capability to stand up to the stresses they could expect to face in their new calling.

While there was some oversight of Beast Barracks by the uniformed officers known as "tactical officers" (or "tacs") and the staff under the command of a colonel, the ratio of these officers to new cadets was low (say twenty officers to a thousand cadets). It was impossible to monitor what was really going on. Should the Beast Detail target a new cadet for removal, much could be and was done beyond the view of the tacs to "encourage" the individual to resign; these incentives included physical hazing in addition to verbal abuse. What constituted physical hazing was in the eye of the beholder. Physical beatings were a rarity; more common were excessively demanding physical activities such as repeatedly running up and down the stairs in the four floors of the barracks in a variety of uniforms that had to be changed in impossibly short time, doing countless push-ups and chin-ups, and sitting in the "green chair." This was no chair at all but a requirement to maintain a sitting position with one's back pressed against the wall with his weight supported entirely by flexed legs while reciting whatever was demanded of him. When the victim inevitably collapsed from muscle fatigue, he would be ordered to assume the "dead cockroach" position: lying on his back while attempting to hold his arms and legs up in the air.

Sometime during the first week we were all brought into the auditorium in Thayer Hall, one of the main academic buildings, and told several things. We were told to look to our right and left as one of those two new cadets would not make it through to graduation because they were not dedicated enough, smart enough, physically fit or strong enough, or maybe even lucky enough. Some would be unable to meet the requirements of the Honor Code that stipulated that a cadet would not lie, cheat, or steal or tolerate anyone who did. Those who flouted the code faced a Cadet Honor Board (since the Honor Code was maintained by the cadets, not the Academy), and the punishment was almost always "voluntary" resignation. Should the offender elect not to resign, the board would submit a recommendation for a court-martial to the superintendent. It rarely went that far. This code of conduct was strikingly like the unwritten rules I had been raised on; my parents would not tolerate this type of behavior, so I had no issue with living under the ironclad Honor Code. Sadly, there have been two honor scandals at West Point since I graduated, and the enforcement of the Honor Code has moved from cadets to the administration, with negative effects in the view of many graduates on the code and current graduates.

The prediction proved remarkably accurate as 583 of us graduated— around 68 percent. About a third resigned, as predicted, for a variety of reasons. Another, perhaps more interesting, number that I remember is that after plebe year there were 658 of us left, meaning 166 had departed due to the weeding-out process that year, whether for academics, Honor Code violations, hazing, bad luck, or whatever. The attrition over the next three years was around 75, including one classmate who died of cancer. It always seemed to me that the purpose of a demanding system had been served to the benefit of West Point and the Army.

One of the most important aspects of the training was to cement the bonds between classmates so that they worked together to make it not only through Beast Barracks but also plebe year, the four years at West Point, and their military careers. At first, it was the plebes against the upperclassmen and officers, but upon becoming an upperclassman, that morphed into a fraternity of the top three classes against the officers who were there to enforce discipline. While each class had certain privileges based on tenure, to my mind, there were just two groups: upperclassmen and plebes. The upperclassmen did not generally dump on each other; rather, they worked together within their relative positions. This was a significant difference between West Point and the Naval Academy, as I discovered later.

There was an aptitude evaluation system that made each cadet rate his peers and cadets in subordinate classes in his company in numerical order from first to last. This was a significant factor in cadet ranks during the last two years of the program and, if the rating compilation was bad enough, could result in separation from the Academy for lack of aptitude for the service. This happened to one of my classmates in my company at the end of our second year and was thought justified by the classmates who knew him.

The first classmates that a new cadet's life depended upon were his roommates. At the most basic level, there was a shared responsibility to make sure each roommate looked out for the others, helping to ensure they were all ready for whatever evolution was about to happen and that the room was in the proper order, ready for inspection at any time. Punishment for any infraction was generally levied against all the occupants of a room, so roommates shared the penalty for one roommate's carelessness or offense. The same went for the whole squad, platoon, or company depending on the nature of the offense. Looking out for each other was the desired outcome of this training and it worked. The bonds cemented that summer, through plebe year, and through the remainder of the four years at the Academy have lasted a lifetime for most of the class, with a closeness that cannot be articulated adequately. My two roommates were at opposite ends of the continuum of military aptitude with me somewhere in the middle (at least that's how I saw it). One, Mike Andrews, went on to graduate and become a hero of the Vietnam War. In fact, he was one of the chief architects of the Army reforms instituted to address the failures of that conflict. These changes paved the way for the decisive victory in the Gulf War. My other roommate didn't fare as well; he was separated from the Academy.

Our socialization that summer was left to the gentle graces of the upperclassmen, and they understood their task well. First, they were not inhibited by the later demands to keep as many new cadets from leaving as possible as a money saving effort for the taxpayer. In fact, they jealously guarded the Corps membership and sought to get rid of those they thought did not fit in; hence, physical hazing, verbal abuse, and limiting the food intake of new cadets who were slow in correcting their mistakes. If you did not want it bad enough, you should leave. That was the attitude. My chief difficulty was that I found a lot of what went on funny and was forever getting in trouble for smirking. This resulted in copious push-ups, chin-ups, the green chair, and ultimately the dreaded "laughing bag" that required the individual to dump out his laundry bag, place it over the upper part of his body while standing in a corner, and forcibly laughing out loud until given permission to stop. This is difficult despite the apparent humor involved and, in my case at least, finally produced the desired result. I stopped smirking.

The upperclassmen did their job well and made Beast Barracks hard for us. I only saw two things that I considered real abuse during that summer; they both resulted in a classmate being rendered unconscious. The first was a new cadet being run up and down the stairs in the barracks with progressively more and more clothing added on in the heat and humidity until he collapsed and had to be drug back into his room and revived. In the second case, I witnessed a classmate get punched in the face and knocked down a set of stairs by an upperclassman who had reached his limit for whatever reason. Neither of these occurrences was reported, and both new cadets lived to go on. They were, however, permanently fixed in my mind as poor leadership practices proving that "the ends do not justify the means."

Plebe

Beast ended with the Acceptance Parade and our assignment to our regular company. Approximately twenty-four hundred cadets were organized into a brigade commanded by the first captain (whose rank was signified by six chevrons) and a staff. The brigade was subdivided into two regiments, each commanded by a five-chevron cadet captain who had a similar staff. Each regiment was further divided into three battalions of four companies. A five-chevron cadet captain, again with a staff component, commanded each battalion. The companies were designated with letters—so A-1 to M-1 and A-2 to M-2. The company, led by a four-chevron cadet captain and supporting staff, was the basic organizational unit of the Corps of Cadets. It was composed of four platoons of approximately twenty-five cadets each.

A cadet's assignment to his company—which was entirely random— played an important part in his experience at the Academy after Beast Barracks. What was most important, however, was the regiment's reputation regarding the severity of the treatment of plebes. I was assigned to H-1, and of course the First Regiment was deemed to be the hardest, while the Second Regiment was regarded as being a bit less stringent. My old comrades still kid each other that the classmates who were lucky enough to be in the Second Regiment "did not have a plebe year."

The socialization within the lettered company was by necessity done quickly since once the academic courses started most of the upperclassmen did not want to be bothered by dealing with plebes. This was left to the cadets in the second class, who were the squad leaders for the plebes. Third-year cadets were called "cows," a term derived from the time when cadets did not receive any leave for their first two years and returned from an extended leave after the second year "as fat as cows." The squad leader was responsible for monitoring the performance and conduct of the plebes under his supervision and training them to be acceptable cadets.

The most significant interaction with the other upperclassmen was at mealtimes. Two or three plebes and two or three of each of the other classes under the supervision of a first-class cadet, or "firstie," represented each class at the ten-man tables. Food was served family style and passed from the head of the table down though the classes to the plebes. One of the basic tenants of leadership in the Army is that the leader is responsible for the well-being of those under them. Food was generally evenly distributed on the table with plebes getting their share. Whether they got to eat it all was another matter. Plebes were required to eat "square meals," maintaining a rigid posture and lifting a utensil straight up to mouth level and then carrying it back to the mouth. Upperclassmen frequently interrupted this process, ordering the plebes to recount information from "the days," a recitation of all the major events until the firsties' graduation date. This included the number of days left for the firsties, any upcoming sporting events (including naming the opponents), movies playing at the theater, and so on. Failure to know the answers led to further grilling and less food and perhaps an invitation to some upperclassman's room for more opportunities to recite. Depending upon the members of the table, a plebe's meal experience could be good or bad, despite the official Academy policy that all plebes should get an adequate meal. I observed—and learned—many lessons in leadership in this dining hall.

As the academic year started, we settled into our roles at the bottom of our company organizations, and the importance of being invisible became apparent. If a plebe went about his duties without drawing attention to himself, life was bearable. Those who were not able to do this became a magnet for attention, resulting in having opportunities to perform such punishments as "sweating pennies to the wall," in which the transgressor assumes a position with his back braced up against a wall in the position of attention with the back of the neck laid flat against the wall. The sweat produced from this stress-inducing activity was enough to allow a penny to attach itself to the wall.

The academic load was heavy and grueling, and all graduates received a bachelor of science degree. West Point was the first engineering school in the country; it was designed to produce engineers for the Army. There was an abundance of math and engineering courses rounded out by humanities subjects. Classes were five-and-a-half days a week. The "Thayer System," imposed by Sylvanus Thayer (the superintendent credited with formalizing and systematizing the curriculum and policies at West Point during his tenure from 1817–1833), required cadets to be graded in each subject and assigned a ranking within their class. This class standing (by subject) was revised every week, so everyone knew exactly where they stood nearly all the time, as did the company tactical officer, who would ensure those doing poorly received help, either from cadets who were doing well or instructors. As an added incentive, privileges were suspended if a cadet was falling behind in his studies. Class standing in the form of general order of merit (GOM) was extremely important; it included not only the academic grade point but also a physical fitness achievement component and a leadership aptitude component based upon the peer ratings and officer ratings. Cadets were given their choice of branch assignment based on their GOM, with the premier choices for both branch assignment and first station being awarded to those at the top of the class. There were quotas in the five combat arms branches: infantry, artillery, armor, signal corps, and the Corps of Engineers. This became a major factor in my decision to go into the Navy. A significant number of my classmates were assigned to the infantry whether they liked it or not due to their low GOM and increased quotas for infantry officers, as we graduated at the height of the Vietnam War.

Few elective courses were allowed—one each semester of the last two years. The only other variable was one's desired foreign language, with input requested but choice not guaranteed. In theory, everyone had an equal chance. I ran up against a "catch 22" situation in language. I wanted to take French (as I had taken it in high school), but I was found to be too qualified for beginning French and not qualified enough for advanced French. I was given Russian. The well-known difficulty of this language, coupled with my lack of facility for languages, cost me at least several tenths of a point from my GPA. That, coupled with my close encounter with the English department in my second year, cost me my opportunity to be high enough in the class rankings to make the cut for the prestigious Corps of Engineers.

Over time, one would likely get to know most of their classmates in the same regiment; we all had the same classes on the same days, while the other regiment had those classes on alternate days. It was during summer training that we were all mixed together in different companies so that we were able to meet and get to know classmates in the other regiment. Still there were some classmates whose paths never crossed for whatever reason during the four years at the Academy. For me, these were mostly Second Regiment guys. Later reunions and military service provided the first opportunity to get to know some of them. For the moment, I logged away that there were some smart people around that I had not really appreciated before. As I watched classmates across the breadth of cadet life, it slowly started to dawn on me that academic or intellectual capabilities and good common sense were not necessarily intertwined and, in some cases, were incompatible. My Beast Barracks roommate (who was eventually to leave the Academy) was a prime example—he had a photographic memory and a sharp mind but no common sense. This led to problems he could not surmount.

In addition to the academic courses that made up the curriculum, we also had physical education courses. For plebes this was not the PE we had known in high school but an introduction to "manly" skills that presumably had direct applicability to being an Army officer. During plebe year, we were required to take swimming, boxing, wrestling, and gymnastics in rotation each semester. No cadet could graduate who could not swim, and the "rock squad" of the least proficient went through their own private hell in the pool trying to meet the minimum standards.

All the athletic endeavors we were subjected to had a key component of winning individual or team contests or attaining the highest score in tests.

Participation was not enough; the Army wanted officers who understood that winning—not just participating—was paramount. Quitting because one was hurt or exhausted was not an option. Another leadership lesson: leaders are generally not wimps, and they need to overcome the fear of physical failure.

Our time was filled with academics, mandatory sports participation (either on varsity squads or intramural teams), and military training that took the form of three parades a week during parade season (fall and spring). Both intramurals and parades were after classes most days, with a regimental parade and brigade parade during the week and a brigade review on football Saturdays. If we were lucky, we had two days a week when nothing was scheduled—Sunday and one other day. Study was basically pursued after dinner, and cadets could stay up knowing they would be outside at reveille formation at 0600 every morning except Sunday. Time management was the key to a cadet's success, particularly a plebe. Since everything could not be done in the time allotted, prioritization and value-weighting became key. Days were long, but time passed quickly.

The major and most important entertainment available was going to athletic events, specifically football games. A winning football team meant a happier atmosphere on campus with plebes receiving the benefit. A losing football team contributed to a sour atmosphere, which in turn led to negative consequences for plebes despite their inability to influence the outcome of games (freshmen could not play varsity sports in those days).

Much has been said about the Army-Navy rivalry and most see it as just a football game; it really extends across all the varsity and club sports in which the two schools compete. Call it bragging rights, service pride, or whatever, the outcome of these contests had great importance to both schools, and the overall tally at the end of the year of which academy had won the most was important to us all. Both schools have gone through ups and downs in their sports programs and reaped the criticism of alumni for losing to their archrival more than fifty percent of the time (winning fifty percent seems a realistic metric to most given the emotion involved in the contests). During the four years I was at West Point, Army won nearly two-thirds of the contests with Navy across the board, including two winter seasons that registered 7–0–1 records. I would add that although the Army–Air Force and Navy–Air Force contests are important to cadets and midshipmen, they take a back seat to Army-Navy.

Monastic Life

We had the opportunity to date girls on the weekend, with dances and movies available. We had to either be fixed up by a trusted classmate's girlfriend or go over to the office of the cadet hostess and choose from the many girls who wrote to her volunteering to be a date for a cadet. The results of both adventurous methods were all over the map, with some cadets meeting great girls who they might even end up marrying after graduation, while others almost gave up dating altogether after encounters that I would diplomatically say were less than satisfactory. My experience was mixed over the four years, but plebe year it was awful; however, in retrospect, I am not sure that I was much of a prize either. I struggled to adjust to this type of dating and could not figure out "city girls" (as in New York City) that I had little in common with.

There were few opportunities to leave West Point during the eleven months of plebe year. By tradition, the plebe class was not allowed to go home for Christmas and spent "Plebe Christmas" at West Point. My class was the last class to have this restriction. Although there were no upper-classmen around, no classes, many events were planned, and relatives came up to spend the holidays, it felt more like a parole than a holiday, with the final examinations for the first semester just around the corner. On top of that, it was bitterly cold that holiday period with significant snowfall contributing to the isolated atmosphere. The only other times we could leave either focused on sporting events or participating in some event of national importance, two of which happened that year—President Kennedy's assassination and a subsequent funeral parade in Washington, DC (that a select company of cadets marched in), and General MacArthur's death and funeral parade in New York City (for which my battalion was chosen as the honor battalion to march behind the caisson transporting his body). For me, there was a total of about nine days away in eleven months that drove home to me the meaning of the word "cloistered."

Discipline

Dealing with discipline issues is a key component of leadership in the military. At West Point there was a larger disciplinary system that applied to all cadets beyond the plebe system. This was largely administered by the Army officers responsible for maintaining military discipline in the Corps of Cadets and adherence to regulations. Each cadet was allowed a specific number of demerits each month—as I remember, thirteen for upperclassmen and twenty for plebes. Exceeding that number for the year could lead to dismissal from the Academy.

Rooms were inspected, as were personnel in formation, at any time the tactical officers got the urge. How these Army officers perform this function would become another lesson in leadership. Some were quite straightforward, giving notice of inspections, such as the traditional Saturday morning room inspection while we were at class and personnel inspection in formation after that. They were fair and not chicken. Others made it their goal to be as nitpicky as possible, awarding demerits for the pettiest of infractions using white gloves to inspect the remotest corners of shelves in the closet or even to search through laundry bags in hopes of finding some item they deemed contraband. I recall one officer (later a four-star general) who would wear a tennis shoe along with his regular uniform shoe when he was acting as the officer in charge (OC), a duty officer responsible for discipline at night. The sound of the single leather-soled shoe created the auditory illusion that he was coming up the barracks stairs slowly, when in fact he was running, hoping he could catch cadets engaging in unauthorized activity. Upperclassmen would give plebes demerits for failing to meet standards, but this tended to diminish over the year as plebes became more invisible and knew and carried out what was expected. The real attention-getting flaps that came up were when upperclassmen put other upperclassmen on report when it was perceived they did not have to—that is to say, when they were not ordered to do so by an officer. This type of petty behavior could have significant consequences as I saw a classmate deck another during our first-class year for reporting him on a Saturday evening for some particularly chicken reason. The idea was upperclassmen should not dump on each other; rather, they should work out their differences and band together against the officers.

Plebe year ended with the graduation parade, after which there was the traditional Recognition Ceremony during which all the upperclassmen in the company, starting with the firsties, shook our hands in recognition of our having made it through the year. We were plebes no longer. As I look back on plebe year, there were three significant emotional events that rose above the frenzy of just being a plebe and making it through the year. The first was the assassination of President Kennedy. Little did I know until much later how much that event directly affected me, personally, as well as my classmates and all those in the military. Jack Kennedy had resisted placing any combat troops in Vietnam despite the advice and forceful recommendations of his cabinet, military staff, and the vice president, Lyndon

Johnson. The book *Lessons in Disaster* by Gordon M. Goldstein should be required reading for every aspiring politician and military person. Goldstein makes the case that it is more than a logical conclusion that Kennedy would never have introduced ground combat troops into Vietnam. He would have likely withdrawn the advisors serving there, due to the inability of the Vietnamese to form a viable government and military in the face of the united enemy that had coalesced under the leadership of Ho Chi Minh.

Supporting this view was David Halberstam in the introduction of the twenty-fifth anniversary publication of his seminal work on the origins of the Vietnam War, *The Best and The Brightest*. He wrote:

> Because I saw him as cool and skeptical it always struck me that he would not have sent combat troops into Vietnam. He was too skeptical for that: I believe that, in the last few months of his life, he had come to dislike the war, it was messy and our policy there was flawed and going nowhere, and he was wary of the optimism of his generals. In 1964 I think he wanted to put it on the back burner, run against Goldwater, beat him handily (which I think he expected to do) and then negotiate his way out.[5]

Lyndon Johnson's ascension to the presidency guaranteed the Americanization of the war and ultimately led to more than fifty-eight thousand deaths for no good reason; hence, the "blunder" referred to in the dedication of this book.

The second event was when one of my classmates and company mates in H-1 was "found," or convicted, of an honor violation and withdrew from the Academy. The company was called together and informed that the individual had been caught cheating on a test, given an honor hearing, found guilty by unanimous vote, and had resigned the night the verdict was delivered. It was a gut shock, as it was unexpected and indisputably final in the world of an eighteen-year-old, a world seemingly without limitations. The third event was, oddly enough, the loss of the Army-Navy football game because of what we thought was questionable officiating at the end of the game. Up until that point in my life, I had believed that playing by the rules would be rewarded fairly, and doing the right thing was the most important thing. The realization that "no one ever said life was fair" came like a glass of cold water dashed in my face after that game and has been a key guideline for me ever since. I have dealt with many individuals, like the official in that game, who made subjective judgments without merit and learned how to deal with them as I moved forward. In the end, plebe year had changed my surviving classmates and me forever, and I went home on leave a vastly different person from the one who boarded that plane from Los Angeles eleven months before.

Yearling

The second year of a cadet's tenure at West Point is called yearling year. It starts with two months of specific indoctrination into the business of being in the Army. This phase is conducted at Camp Buckner located on the West Point reservation about ten miles from the main campus.

While there, cadets undergo familiarization training in the five combat arms branches of the Army. For me, the highlight of the training was a week of intense field training called "Recondo," based on the Army Ranger School that provides advanced infantry training and survival skills under an arduous 24/7 schedule.

Buckner provided more leadership lessons. An understanding of discipline was of immense importance. I performed my first punishment tours on what passed for the Area at Buckner—a parking lot, if I remember correctly. I had made it through plebe year without a disciplinary breach that merited this type of punishment. I received seven demerits plus three punishment tours for the "crime" of leaving my footlocker unlocked. The severity of this punishment boggled my mind: Why require I secure my footlocker in a barracks full of cadets who embraced the Academy's Honor Code and with little to no access by anyone else? Further, we kept little in the way of valuable personal property in our footlocker. What lesson this punishment was supposed to teach was not clear, but it started me thinking about the relationship between disciplinary measures and their purpose, an inner conversation that continues to this day. The exercise of power in the form of dispensing punishment/reward is a key ingredient of leadership and one, in my observation, that is rarely handled well for a host of reasons.

There were several memorable occurrences during yearling year. Despite a disappointing football season, the team defeated Navy to end a five-year losing streak and beat Roger Staubach to boot. Yearling year also marked the high point of my relationship with my girlfriend from high school, Barbara. I am not sure if "relationship" is the right word since I only saw her once during my entire plebe year, when she came to the Army–Air Force game in Chicago. We spent the handful of hours after the game together until I had to catch the train back to New York that evening. I saw Barbara four times during yearling year. Since she had a life and I was not really part of it, she moved on the next year. My observation was that West Point tended to be the burial ground of high school romances. Relationships generally did not survive the long separations or, more likely, the maturing of both parties. That is not to say that some of them did not survive those four strenuous years. Barbara and I are still friends, renewing our friendship after she tracked me down to try to convince me to attend our thirtieth high school reunion.

Changing Companies

Toward the end of yearling year, we were notified of our new company assignments for cow year, in accordance with the mandatory shuffle of companies conducted after two years. This was a somewhat more complicated reshuffling than those in the past because the Corps was expanding to accept classes of more than a thousand cadets in 1968 and 1969. This necessitated reorganizing the Corps into four regiments (the old First Regiment becoming the First and Third Regiments and the old Second Regiment becoming the Second and Fourth Regiments) of nine enlarged companies. I was assigned to D-1 that was quartered in Old South Barrack across the Area from H-1.

Leaving my classmates, roommates, and friends as we dispersed from H-1 to our new companies left me with mixed emotions. From the original plebes who reported to H-1 out of Beast Barracks, we had lost two, one to the Honor Code and the other to the Aptitude Board. No one had quit of his own volition. We had helped each other through the two years. Out of the twenty-nine original H-1 plebes of the class of '67, twenty-seven went on to graduate, defying the attrition predictions we heard in Beast. Of that group, sixteen completed a military career and retired, four were medically retired or discharged for medical reasons, and seven served their military obligation and resigned from the service. Three of us became flag officers, with Monty Meigs and Paul Kern being two of the three four-star generals our class produced; two others became army doctors and medical specialists; two became army dentists and one a civilian dentist; two became lawyers; one earned a doctorate in nuclear engineering and went on to be one of the Army's nuclear experts; one became a PGA golf professional; and the others completed successful careers across the spectrum of military and civilian occupations. None was lost in combat in Vietnam or subsequent combat actions, although Doug Pringle was so severely wounded he was retired for medical reasons.

The common denominator was that we all came to West Point through winning a competition, whether academic, sports, or a prep school slot that ended with us being awarded appointments to the Academy. Many of us came from blue-collar families and were the first in the family to ever go to college, while others were sons of military officers and enlisted personnel or enlisted military personnel themselves. This seemed to fulfill President Jefferson's desire when he established the U.S. Military Academy in 1802.

I was puzzled by the fact that Jefferson had been the prime mover in founding West Point, as he had no military background and often clashed with the prominent men of his time who did have military service on their resume, men like Washington and Hamilton. As reported by Theodore Crackel in his book, *Mr. Jefferson's Army*, Thomas Jefferson personally had no problem with the existence of a professional army, but he objected to the leadership of the American army at that time, as it was predominantly composed of his political opponents, the Federalists.

> He wanted the cadets who would be there [West Point] at public expense to be drawn not from the wealthy big-city political elite of the Federalist Party, but rather to be the sons of men from across the land whose political ideas were more those of the common man.... . In Jefferson's eyes, West Point was a key agency through which he could help politically reform the army from within.[6]

The appointment system that evolved—having congressmen across the country recommend candidates principally through competition—accomplished the goal of making selection merit based rather than political. It provided a means for bright young men with no financial means to rise above the class in which they were born, acquire a university education, and join a cadre of officers who would serve the country in a variety of ways. While the Federalists are long gone, Jefferson's apolitical plan of meritocracy became the foundation for all the service academies.

Becoming a "Cow"

Yearling year ended with a whimper as we immediately moved into the summer period before cow year. After indoctrination trips to Air Force and Navy bases and leave, I reported to Fort Bragg in August for an enlightening look at the real Army. I was assigned to the 36th Signal Battalion—which was not my choice but what I got as the fruits of my class standing at that point. While I was there, the Army (including several units based at Fort Bragg) was involved in the intervention in the Dominican Republic. For the first time I saw how the defense budgets since the Korean War had shortchanged our military in the buildup of the nuclear deterrent to confront the Soviets. The Army could not support the relatively minor forces deployed to this operation without robbing from all the units stationed at Fort Bragg. The communications and motor pool equipment that was in the table of organization and equipment (TOE) of the signal battalion to which I was assigned was part of the robbery. During the month I was there, the battalion did virtually no training that required communications equipment or vehicle assets because all that was left was broken equipment awaiting parts. Additionally, many of the most experienced soldiers had been assigned temporarily to deploying units so that vital military occupation specialties (MOS) could be covered. This was not the lesson that the Army wanted this cadet to learn, but it was one of the more important lessons I learned that year.

Fort Bragg was a busy place not only because of the Dominican Republic crisis but also because of the ongoing conflict in Vietnam. Despite the Army's important mission, most of its facilities were of World War II–vintage supporting a draft-based Army with low pay and benefits. The paratroopers of the 82nd Airborne Division were a mix of volunteers and draftees, but the supporting units did not require volunteers and relied on draftees to handle the more menial of the tasks assigned. Relying on good advice given by my father, I kept my mouth closed and did what I was told and got along fine. As always, I enjoyed being with the enlisted men, particularly the few sergeants still left in the unit. There were some World War II and Korean War vets among the noncommissioned officers who viewed imparting their knowledge to cadets as a duty to ensure they were ready to lead when the time came. I left Fort Bragg with an understanding that taking care of one's charges was a key ingredient in a leader's performance. Lousy facilities, poor pay and benefits, and aging and poorly maintained equipment was little inducement for convincing good men they should stay in the Army.

With Fort Bragg behind me, I started cow year in D-1. The new company brought with it a new group of classmates in addition to the other classes that made up the company. The first classmate I really got to know was my new roommate, Woody Held, the tallest guy in the class at six feet eight inches and the son of a senior FBI agent. He was on the practice squad for the basketball team and was run ragged by Coach Bobby Knight guarding the star of the team, Mike Silliman (who went on to captain the '68 Olympic team to a gold medal). We roomed together throughout cow year and developed a lifelong friendship. We shared our first leadership opportunity at West Point. Woody was the squad leader for the first three months. He had three plebes assigned to his squad who had to report to our room at various times to ensure they were ready for whatever evolution was about to transpire. Should one of them screw up somewhere, that offense would be brought to Woody for corrective action. He was exactly the kind of leader the school was trying to produce—a thoughtful, caring mentor, who had a sense of humor while instilling the necessary discipline in these impressionable plebes. He also had a girl back home, Sally, who informed me that it was my job to keep him on the straight and narrow. That really was not hard, and they are still a loving couple after over fifty years of marriage.

In the academic world, two things happened that turned my mediocre performance around. The first was the introduction of an incentive for better grades. An extra long weekend pass was granted if a cadet was on the dean's list (top thirty percent academically) at the end of the semester. The second was a change in the curriculum to engineering subjects that I really liked. We also had to take two semesters of legal studies that I found easy. I did extremely well, making it into the rarified air of the First Section. This started a lifelong fascination with the law and a desire to understand the legal implications of actions I might take. Important among the lessons were that justice and right and wrong are not synonymous. To the surprise and sometimes chagrin of classmates, I started progressing up through the academic sections in these classes and ended up in the higher sections as my class GPA continued to rise. The result, to the shock of my parents along with everyone else, was by the end of the semester I was on the dean's list and was rewarded with my extra long weekend. Never one to overexert myself in those days, I did not see any benefit to working any harder than it took to make the dean's list, so I remained just above the cut line for the rest of my time at USMA.

From the Army to the Navy

My road into the Navy started during the Christmas break when I went home to California. Out of the blue, my dad asked what I knew about the Seabees and the Navy Civil Engineer Corps (CEC). Other than having seen *The Fighting Seabees* (starring John Wayne and Susan Hayward) as a kid, the answer was, "Nothing." I had mentioned in passing that it did not look like I would be able to go into the Corps of Engineers (COE) because I would not be high enough in the GOM to get one of the small number of available slots. Dad's logic was simple and profound: "Seabees build and fight in constructions battalions, usually with the Marines, and don't go on ships. CEC officers take care of the bases for the Navy and oversee the Navy's construction program. Isn't that what the COE does for the Army?" That sounded right to me. He continued, "Under the rules, you can go into the Navy if you want because I have served a career in the Navy. Why wouldn't you do what you want in the Navy rather than what you don't want in the Army?" I really did not have an answer when the question was put that way.

Among the things that occurred during cow year that would make a lasting impression on me was an event called "Exchange Weekend." This was a practice carried out principally between the Naval Academy and USMA, although there was limited participation by the Air Force Academy (AFA), Coast Guard Academy, and Merchant Marine Academy. Almost every third-year cadet at the Academy would spend several days at the other school to see the similarities and differences firsthand. The exchange program was conducted over the winter months, and in the case of West Point and Annapolis, we were hosted by and hosting a midshipman, or "mid." They called us "woops" or "woo poos." We both called the Air Force guys "zoomies." Those of us who went to the Naval Academy were billeted, went to class, ate meals, and so on with our host mid. In my case, the mid was a high school classmate who had been appointed to the Naval Academy at the same time I received my acceptance letter to West Point. I was impressed by the size of Bancroft Hall, the immense barrack building that housed all the mids under one roof—all 4,400 of them. The building contained the mess hall as well, so there was no need to leave for meals. It was an interesting arrangement. One thing my classmates and I did not like was the sadistic practice of turning on all the room lights at reveille when we were not required to do so. For their part, they did not like the fact that we went outside for a reveille formation, something they did not have to do.

While there were many small differences between the schools, there were several stark distinctions. A significant difference that we cadets liked was that mids could go into the town of Annapolis (unless they were under some restriction based on duty or poor academics). They had places where they could go and drink, socialize with girls, and just get away from the school. Not so at West Point where no one could leave the post like this until they were a firstie. All underclassmen had to have a weekend pass or some other special authorization to leave the school or go into the town of Highland Falls. There were also restrictions regarding how close a cadet could be to the post while consuming alcohol. While drunken behavior brought disciplinary consequences at both schools, the ability to at least get a beer on the weekend without sneaking it and worrying about being caught made the mids' system seem much better in our eyes.

There were two other significant differences that I observed and did not like; I felt that they played a significant part in the culture of the school and the subsequent culture of the officer corps in the Navy. They involved the "Honor Concept" and the class system. The Naval Academy Honor Concept reads:

Midshipmen are persons of integrity: They stand for that which is right. They tell the truth and ensure that the full truth is known. **They do not lie.**

They embrace fairness in all actions. They ensure that work submitted as their own is their own, and that assistance received from any source is authorized and properly documented. **They do not cheat.**

They respect the property of others and ensure that others are able to benefit from the use of their own property. **They do not steal.**[7]

The Cadet Honor Code is simpler, stating: "A cadet will not lie, cheat, steal or tolerate those who do."[8] The key difference between the two is the "toleration" issue. At USMA, anyone knowing of a violation of the Honor Code and not reporting it is guilty of an honor offense and can be dismissed from the Academy. Many of those who were dismissed from West Point in the 1951 and 1977 honor scandals were tagged for tolerating cheating rather than participating in it. At the Naval Academy, there is no requirement to "bilge" a classmate (turn him in) if they know about a violation *so long as* they do not participate in a cover-up and questions regarding the situation are answered truthfully. The AFA Honor Code is nearly the same as that of West Point and has led to similar major cheating scandals involving the toleration issue. Scandals of this type have not occurred at the Naval Academy because violations of the Honor Concept can be and are tolerated by the mids; there is no penalty attached to doing nothing. Peer pressure not to rat out a fellow mid apparently carries more weight than loyalty to the Honor Concept. The phrase I heard while I was there was: "You rate what you skate." Translation: "If you can get away with something, there's no harm/no foul." I did not understand this until I went on the Exchange Weekend, but I took that observation with me and remembered it when I joined the Navy.

There were basically two classes of cadets: upperclassmen and plebes. While each class received more perks than the lower classes, the more senior classes did not lord it over the junior ones nor use their seniority to take advantage of the junior classes. The example of how the food was shared on the meal tables perfectly illustrates this dynamic. This was not the case at the Naval Academy. I observed each class seemed to relish dumping on the classes below them because that's how *they* had been treated. This was confirmed in conversations with the mids I stayed with. Seniority was everything and within the first class there appeared to be little hesitation in putting lower-ranking mids on report, even classmates. This practice was especially frowned upon at West Point. There was no faster way to get a poor reputation than to write up a classmate unless ordered to do so by an officer.

During the first evening meal I had in Bancroft Hall I noticed that as at West Point, there were representatives of each class at every table. The food was also served family style, starting with the first-class mids. The difference was that instead of ensuring that everyone received an equal share—including the plebes—those at the head of the table took as much of everything as they wanted. This resulted in some items being completely gone before the platter got to the lower classmen. This was apparently a regular occurrence with favorite meats and desserts. I was told the justification for this behavior was that mids had to put up with it when they were in the junior classes, so it was right to get payback when they moved to the two senior classes. The concept that "rank has its privileges" was reinforced in this manner, driving home the concept that if you are senior, your subordinates must put up with your actions. The missing part of the "rank has its privileges" saying is "and its obligations." This insight proved valuable when I went into the Navy.

Firstie

I received my summer assignment: I would serve as the supply sergeant for one of the new cadet companies during Beast Barracks after the first class trip.

The first class trip took up most of the rest of June, during which we were flown around to representative elements of the five combat arms branches so each could give us their best sales pitch. We stayed in barracks on the army posts, saw impressive demonstrations of the skills employed in each area, were fixed up with blind dates with the local girls for a formal dance at the officers' club, and were generally treated like we were important. The trip reinforced my desire to be an engineer versus the other choices I had, but I knew with certainty that that path was not open to me in the Army with my class standing. I resolved to write a letter to the Navy CEC and ask if I could join it upon graduation. I decided that could wait until the beginning of the school year.

After the first class trip, we headed to our summer assignments. There was not a great deal of time before the new cadets arrived, and I had to organize the supply function and make sure everything was properly laid out in each room in accordance with instructions on the first day they reported. My two classmate roommates for first Beast were John Brown and Ron Frazer, who were both in D-1 with me, but I did not know either that well. We got to know each other well during that high-pressure month.

The disappointing reality that was brought home to me was how the standards and fundamental character of Beast Barracks had changed in the three years since I had experienced it. The upperclassmen in our Beast cared little if a new cadet wanted to resign because they saw their function as to weed out the unsuitable, yet we were lectured by the officers in charge of Beast that our job was to retain the maximum number of new cadets possible because of the expense involved in getting them to West Point. Our company tactical officer—who happened to be a new exchange Navy officer—told us we would be measured on our ability to retain the newbies. We were to let them eat in peace and not be harsh with them, even if we thought they should not be army officers. That was not our decision. Since this kind of prescriptive leadership always flows downhill, the burden of this new direction fell heaviest on the cow squad leaders whose aptitude ratings would reflect how successful they were in keeping their charges at the Academy. It got to the point that when a new cadet indicated he wanted to leave, he had to talk to practically everyone in the chain of command before he could resign.

The notion that some of these young men did not want to be army officers, did not want to be at West Point, and perhaps never did seemed to be completely ignored in the quest to have the statistics reflect what the great analyst Secretary of Defense Robert McNamara believed to be "cost effective." We would see more of this type of statistical goal and achievement methodology very soon in the form of body count being applied as an indicator of success in the Vietnam War. For that moment, however, it just made us angry because we knew we were keeping future problems for the Army by not weeding out those who did not have the will, or ability to be good cadets or, ultimately, officers.

Vietnam's Shadow

There was a backlash building up on college campuses across the country to our involvement in Vietnam. We were somewhat isolated from it except through the newspapers and radio. President Johnson had sent combat troops to Vietnam, and the results were starting to be felt at West Point. One of the first graduates killed in action, Clair Thurston (KIA November 8, 1965), had been in H-1 as a firstie when I was a plebe. Even though he graduated as a star man (academically distinguished, as represented by gold stars on the collar), he chose the infantry as his branch because he wanted to be a soldier's soldier. He died a hero's death and was posthumously awarded the Distinguished Service Cross (DSC), second only to the Medal of Honor (MOH). More deaths followed, and we started to talk about this reality. Others were "unlucky" and got killed, but it would not happen to us. John Brown, Ron Frazer, and I spoke in this manner. Ron was the most troubled by the war and the thought that he might have to participate in it even though he had doubts about its justification.

In his book *Sacred Ties*, Tom Carhart (USMA '66) outlines the situation perfectly as it applied to our class. He describes the cadets who were at West Point as the Civil War loomed on the horizon: "This unwillingness to accept one's own mortality is not uncommon among young soldiers. It seems fair to say here that the more idealistic and confident these cadets were in their aspirations toward greatness, the more oblivious they would have been to any real possibility of their own deaths."[9]

Permit me to share my opinion of the cadet aptitude ranking system that culminated in the awarding of cadet ranks from first captain (the highest cadet rank) down to what were called file-closing sergeants (my category). The file-closing sergeants were the lowest-ranking firsties and marched at the back of the formations closing the files or columns in the formation. I got what I deserved. I had determined early in my West Point experience that the day we graduated all of us would be the same rank; we would depart from the Academy for assignments where we would all be addressed as "lieutenant." Cadet rank would mean nothing to my classmates or me, except perhaps the first captain, of whom much would be expected.

The second thing that was obvious to me was that leading a group of like-minded over-achiever cadets of nearly the same age and motivation was markedly different from leading enlisted personnel who varied widely in age, education, and motivation—never mind the draftees, whose motivation was minimal or nonexistent. Growing up with an enlisted father and hearing the stories about officers they respected and did not respect, the self-important, control-freak attempts at leadership exhibited by cadets with no real experience in the leading of troops irritated me. Worse still was the fact that a few cadet officers seemed to take their selection for higher cadet ranks as a personal validation that they were better than those of lower rank. It would be different in the service, where real rank merited respect or at least the appearance of respect.

Finally, as the years rolled by and my classmates and I pursued our careers, there really was truly little correlation between being a high-ranking cadet officer and successfully achieving high rank in the military or the private sector.

I was assigned a room with Bob Libutti. He was from Westchester, New York, and has been my friend ever since. He has a unique sense of humor and sly intelligence that belies his class rank that was very near the bottom of the class. Bob was my opposite: where I enjoyed engineering subjects and tolerated the humanities, Bob disliked the engineering subjects and liked the humanities courses that were, unfortunately for him, not the bulk of the last two years of academics. But he accepted his fate stoically and made it through to graduation.

Several significant events occurred during that last year that I have never forgotten. The first was the day in September that I heard that my second Beast Barracks squad leader, Doug Davis, had been killed in action in Vietnam. He had been out of West Point just over a year. He had not only been my squad leader in Beast but had also spent his last two years at West Point in H-1 with me. He and his roommate in Beast, Tony Livic, had been tough on us, vowing to run us out for not meeting their standards; however, when they both went to H-1, they treated me fairly and forgot my smirking and other offenses in Beast. Doug was a track star with numerous gold stars on his letter jacket for beating Navy. While we never were really friends, I respected him and thought he would make an excellent officer, and I was proven right: he was awarded a Silver Star for the action that cost him his life. His death, along with an increasing number of other recent graduates' deaths and burials at West Point, made the war real and death a possibility. For the first time, I really thought about how I would perform my duty in the face of death with others depending upon me. Just like other young men, I did not believe I would be killed, but failing under fire might be a possibility, and I, of course, resolved that I would not let that happen.

Second, there were two different programs that the Army had introduced at West Point for what we would now call mentoring firsties. The first involved bringing the most senior sergeants major (the highest enlisted rank in the Army) for a final assignment at West Point before they retired so they could pass on their knowledge to the firsties. I don't remember exactly how this was done, but I do recall an extensive conversation that I had with one of these men who had been the sergeant major of the 1st Infantry Division. While I can no longer remember his name, I will never forget his story of his actions in World War II. Seeing him for the first time, I could not miss the rows of decorations on his chest that included a Silver Star, multiple Bronze Stars, and a Purple Heart with so many oak leaf clusters (each indicating a subsequent award) that it was difficult to see the ribbon. What my eyes were drawn to, however, was a European theater campaign ribbon with three arrowhead devices on it, meaning he had participated in the initial amphibious landings on three different assaults. He later told me they were for North Africa, Sicily, and the D-Day invasion in Normandy. He had sure beaten the law of averages! What struck me was he did not talk about himself except in a tangential manner; rather, he spoke of the deeds he had seen other soldiers perform, often giving their own lives for their comrades in a selfless manner. He spoke about wasting lives through bad planning and not taking care of your soldiers who expect that from you. Leading from the front was a consistent theme, and as my father had said, those officers who shared danger with their men and led them into battle were the most revered leaders. This old soldier had obviously been a leader from in front and the kind of senior noncommissioned officer that made up the backbone of the Army.

The other mentor program consisted of a high-ranking Army officer, usually a three- or four-star, having an intimate off-the-record conversation with a relatively small group of firsties that allowed an interchange. I have always considered it my great good fortune to have been lucky enough to be selected to attend a discussion with Gen. Creighton Abrams, who was then the vice chief of staff of the Army. Three things struck me about this man: his frankness, his professionalism, and his honesty. He wanted us to understand the tremendous responsibility of leading soldiers in combat and the exceptional devotion and courage those soldiers displayed in the worst of human situations. As a highly decorated tank battalion commander under General Patton, Abrams described witnessing and subsequently writing up MOH recommendations for two of the men in his battalion. To do this, he had to be right in the middle of the heavy combat he was describing, leading his men. He talked about the soldiers, not himself. When it came to question time, someone asked him what it would take to win in Vietnam.

His view of winning was defeating the enemy and breaking his will to fight. Since it was obvious that the United States would not invade and destroy that will in North Vietnam, he said it would take at least sixteen Army divisions to control all the borders of South Vietnam to prevent resupply and reinforcement of the Vietcong and to achieve their ultimate destruction. For political considerations, that number of divisions was not going to happen. The conclusion was obvious even to us lowly cadets: the United States was not fighting to win in Vietnam. His honesty and frankness have always stayed with me; I treasured his example of a soldier faithfully doing his duty despite his own opinions. He was ordered to relieve General Westmoreland as commander of forces in Vietnam executing a strategy he considered to be flawed.

The final intimate bonding experience with my classmates, especially my roommates and company mates, had a significant and lifelong effect on me. We were all now young men, over twenty-one, getting ready to go into the service and probably into combat. We had shared a common experience that would not be replicated by anything we would do in the future. We knew things about each other that no one else could ever know and which could not be passed along verbally. These things permeate the atmosphere when we get together at gatherings such as reunions or more frequently in smaller groups where we live or share a common interest. A truly special relationship is reserved for one's roommates. To lose a roomie in combat is a particularly devastating experience, but that was yet to come. My roommates from D-1 (Woody Held, Bob Libutti, and Kenn Harris survived the Vietnam War—Dan Neuburger, John Brown, and Ron Frazer did not) and I have remained close in that manner ever since that time together. I have a special relationship with a few other classmates

I roomed with—John Kuspa and Cal Delaplain from H-1 come to mind. There are others who I only have gotten to know well since graduation and my retirement from the Navy since we were not in the same regiments at West Point. I did not serve with them and only saw them occasionally, but the bond exists nonetheless. The common experiences we shared while not really knowing each other at West Point created an instant empathy when we met again, and the bonding came naturally without a thought. The profound effect of our experiences at West Point is well described in *Sacred Ties*, when author Carhart talks about the transformation of the cadets before the Civil War—it applied equally to my class:

> In an effort to strengthen cadets, the academy intentionally sub-jected them to great duress, so much so that many of them analogized their cadet life—as we will see, not unfairly—to "prison" or "slavery."
>
> While the hardening was no doubt realized, the perhaps more important impact on them, at which we will look, was what occurred after they had been stripped naked psychologically and found they could only depend on each other for succor and solace. Through the most harrowing of disciplinary experiences, then, they became the closest of friends and quickly learned to lean on their fellow cadets in ways they had never before experienced. So I believe their denomina-tion as "brothers," as will be seen, is a more appropriate and meaning-ful usage of the term than those of either Shakespeare ("Henry V") or Ambrose (Band of Brothers).[10]

I should also mention the girlfriends who became wives and have remained with these sometimes tough guys; they have lived with and loved together through wars, separations, and single parenting, many times at the cost of a career they wanted to pursue. They are also part of this fabric of intimate bonding. They patiently listen as we repeatedly tell our same old stories of cadet days. Added to this roster of fine women are those, like my wife Mary, who did not know us in those days but patiently attend our class functions and have developed relationships with the other wives and classmates, with all the details that such a task invokes. It has been said that true friendship consists of having a relationship in which, despite the duration of separation, the moment of reuniting brings a feeling that you are picking up a conversation right where you left off. Such is it with all of us.

My decision to go into the Navy was a game changer. It was the culmination of weighing the options that lay in front of me when I graduated. In a sense, I would be abandoning my classmates and the Army that had paid for my education, but in the end, my father's question of why I would do something I did not want to do if I had the chance to do what I really wanted carried the day. Early in firstie year, I wrote a letter to the Navy CEC Officer Assignment Office in the Bureau of Naval Personnel relating that I had been told that as the son of a career Navy serviceman, I could choose to be commissioned in the Navy if I wished. I then stated that I had investigated the CEC, and more specifically the Seabees, and was interested in signing up for them. I asked if what I had heard was true. Would the CEC take me? I had no interest in any other part of the Navy, so I further inquired about what I could expect as a duty assignment if I was accepted coming out of West Point. In due course, I received a letter back saying what I had heard was true, and I was eligible to be commissioned in the Navy. Further, the CEC would be delighted to accept me upon graduation. I would be assigned to any Seabee battalion on either U.S. coast and deploy with them to Vietnam. When I completed that assignment, I would be sent to any civilian graduate school I wanted for two years to get a master's degree in any engineering field I wanted. I was astonished and overjoyed. I did not get much grief from my classmates, as the quotas for everything but infantry filled up quickly, and the guys at the bottom of the class, including Bob Libutti, were given no choice but the infantry. I wrote back to the CEC and accepted its offer, requesting assignment to a Seabee battalion on the West Coast since my parents were still in San Diego.

Firstie year sped quickly by as I looked forwarded to the Seabees and Vietnam. After Bob Libutti, I roomed with Kenn Harris, an Army brat from Oklahoma with whom I hit it off very well. The combination of Woody, Kenn, Bob, and another company mate, Bill Cusack, and I produced an almost continuous search for a laugh, either at just our own expense or someone else's. Practical jokes became a normal occurrence. Bob Libutti turned out to be a master jokester. We all tried to torment the high care factor classmates who were so full of themselves.

Final Days

My last roommate was Dan Neuburger, from Ellis, Kansas. Dan was a short, muscular man built like a fireplug. Although he was not part of the clique I mentioned, we got along well and shared our plans. He was going into the air defense artillery that was responsible for manning the Nike missile air defense sites around the country, which he thought would delay him being sent to Vietnam for a while. Dan's hopes for a delay in being deployed to Vietnam were not realized. He deployed there in late spring of 1968. Sadly, he was killed in action, leaving a young wife and baby daughter that he never saw.

Graduation came on June 7, 1967. My parents and aunt and uncle came, and we had a great time. I do not remember much about graduation day other than that we were sworn into the Navy—that is, I, Rick Rice (who was also going into the CEC), and Jim Reilly (who was assigned to Navy line)—before the graduation ceremony. Then we were all throwing our white caps into the air and it was over. Next, I was saying some goodbyes and promising to be on time to John Kuspa's wedding in Dearborn, Michigan, so I could be his best man. Later I was to meet up with Woody Held at his fiancée's house in Lansing, Michigan, before finally meeting up with Kenn Harris and Bob Libutti for a trip to my house in California during graduation leave. In my hands were my orders to report to Naval Mobile Construction Battalion Nine (NMCB-9) in Port Hueneme, California, after completion of the CEC Officers School Basic Class that was to start the end of July. My family members and I went to New York City that evening and had a wonderful and memorable dinner. The dinner was memorable for two reasons—first, my dad and uncle joked with each other the entire evening over good food, and we laughed with relief that the four stressful years of separation were over. I would be going back to something I was familiar with— that is, moving around with the Navy. Second, in the next booth in the restaurant was Dan Neuburger and his family and girlfriend enjoying the laughter from our booth. It was the last time I ever saw him.

West Point taught me that leadership is really understanding human nature and making quick, accurate appraisals of individuals, situations, and tasking. To lead, one must understand those to be led. To follow or not, one must understand one's superiors. While I never thought there was an option of not leading those entrusted to my supervision, I realized there was a choice of whether I followed or not and how well I followed. The ramifications of decisions in either situation are the real benchmarks of leadership. I had learned this lesson at West Point, and I am grateful for it, but the impact of this lesson was still awaiting me in Vietnam.

Chapter Two

FROM KAYDET GRAY TO NAVY BLUE

We've not much longer here to stay,
For in a month or two
We'll bid farewell to Kaydet Gray,
And don the Army Blue.
　　　　　　　—Lucius O'Brien, *Benny Havens, Oh!*

In my case, it was the Navy blue I would be donning as I left West Point. Graduation leave lasted nearly two months, the welcome prize for making it through those four challenging years on the Hudson. Never again in my military career would I have that much time off at once until I went on terminal leave after my thirty-four-year tenure.

It was a pleasant way to make the conversion from the Army to the Navy, with John Kuspa's wedding, a trip home to San Diego with Kenn Harris and Bob Libutti, and a visit from Woody Held before all of us went on to the next phase of our lives. This was a different world in a different time.

Universal Military Service

Military service was dramatically different in the summer of 1967. First and foremost, it was based on universal military service administered through selective service—the draft—and had been so since before World War II. It has now been nearly fifty years since the peacetime draft was abolished in favor of the all-volunteer military. Those growing up since really have no idea what that meant to those young men coming of age between 1940 and 1974. The assumption had to be that one was going to serve in the military—absent some vocation like the ministry, a physical disqualification, or an exemption of some kind (endless college deferments, for example). It became a decision of when, under what conditions (officer or enlisted), and for how long. For the nation, this situation provided a cheap military force in terms of pay and allowances, facilities, and dependent care, allowing greater amounts to be spent on weapons systems and hardware. The military, particularly the junior enlisted and officers, was intended to consist of single young men who lived on military bases or ships and were supported almost entirely in those locations. A common notion among those in the service was that the public liked the military to be sequestered, as popularized by the famous sign in Norfolk, Virginia: "Dogs and sailors keep off the grass."

Family life in the military was more difficult during this period. Limited support for dependents was provided with an understanding that it was the individual's choice to marry and not the military's responsibility to deal with the problems that marriage and family life might present. Indeed, for many years, enlisted personnel were required to ask permission to marry. If they did so without permission, marriage benefits could be and often were withheld. Looking at today's military, in which single parents are acceptable, it is almost impossible to believe this situation could have been so dramatically reversed. Childcare centers, privatized housing, and many other perks have now become requirements the government must furnish at great expense to maintain a voluntary military force.

Another major difference was the disciplinary system. The military has always been synonymous with discipline. As a predominantly male organization that was expected to obey orders instantly and without question, the penalties for failing to do so were severe, and few outside the military cared very much what "severe" meant. Our fathers had put up with this during their service and understood the necessity of obeying orders in combat, so they saw nothing wrong with the system as it existed and, in fact, complained that the services had "gone soft." Discipline did not just consist of the Uniform Code of Military Justice (UCMJ), which laid out the offenses against "good order and discipline," but also total control of the living environment and off-duty freedom in the form of off-base/ship privileges. There was a thing called a "liberty card" in the Navy or a "pass" in the Army that was required in order to leave the military jurisdiction. Senior officers, noncommissioned or commissioned, could simply withhold these documents for just about any reason, and the individual would be confined to base or ship without further due process. It was an attention getter, and it worked without the necessity of criminal charges for minor breeches of discipline or poor performance of duty. The concept of rights to all the things that are now taken for granted did not exist and would have been thought incompatible with military service.

The purpose of the military justice system was to enforce discipline with little thought of rehabilitation of the offender. The point was to teach him he did not want to make the same mistake twice. Marines ran the Navy brigs (correctional facilities); they were tough on the prisoners to reinforce the point. The Army also had specially trained guards in their stockades for the same purpose. Oversight was sometimes lax and bad things happened, but their purpose was clear. The motion pictures *From Here to Eternity* and *The Last Detail* paint a picture of what the system was like in the Army and the Navy that is not too far off the mark. Courts-martial or administrative boards readily handed out discharges for undesirables and troublemakers, usually after some punishment at hard labor in the brig. These black marks affected the former soldier or sailor's civilian employment for the rest of their life and brought disgrace to the family. Nonjudicial punishment—called "captain's mast" in the Navy, "office hours" in the Marines, and an Article 15 in the Army—was used for minor offenses and could result in fines, the loss of rank, restriction to base, and extra duty. Lawyers were not involved in every aspect of what was going on as discipline was viewed as a command function. Lawyers were consulted for advice and to prosecute or defend "the guilty" if the offense was severe enough. Officers appointed by the commanding officer conducted special courts-martial (SCM) and the less serious disciplinary methods; these proceedings were conducted without the involvement of legal counsel. The officers acting as judges were not lawyers or legally trained specialists. Lawyers were reserved for general courts-martial (GCM) for the more serious offenses. This was the culture, and it was understood and accepted by those participating in it from top to bottom.

Welcome to the Navy

The starkness of the change from Army to Navy did not take long to hit home when I reported to the huge Seabee base in Port Hueneme, California, for the Civil Engineer Corps Officers School (CECOS) on a Sunday afternoon late July 1967. In the parking lot of the Bachelor Officer Quarters (BOQ), I met a guy who claimed to be a lieutenant (we were in civvies); he informed me that he was transferring from the Navy line to the CEC after serving at sea on destroyers. He would be the senior person in my basic class. He "suggested" that we have a chat over dinner so he could begin my education in the Navy since it was obvious that someone who had just graduated from West Point would need a lot of help. He was not a Naval Academy graduate but still made it clear that my education was clearly lacking. After I had found my room in the World War II–vintage junior officer BOQ—which lacked air conditioning, featured gang toilet and shower facilities, and sported a most uncomfortable bed—I met up with my self-appointed mentor in the same parking lot at the appointed time.

We walked into the officers' mess and were greeted by a steward (enlisted man responsible for serving officers as a kind of majordomo). These men were predominantly from the Philippines or other South Pacific islands, as well as some blacks. Some of the older ones were Chinese, men who had signed contracts to serve as stewards before World War II. There may have been some white stewards, but I do not remember any. "Steward" was synonymous with servant and had been a part of the Navy from its earliest days, being inherited from the Royal Navy.

There were things officers did not do for themselves, and that was the way it was. Naval officers learned this as midshipmen since there were stewards at the Naval Academy and on board the ships they embarked in on summer training. This steward pointed at a table, indicating we should sit there. My companion surprised me by screaming at the man, chewing out the steward and informing him that we would sit wherever we wanted, and demanding he get the chief out here *now*. The chief was the senior steward responsible for the mess. Another ugly scene followed in which my new acquaintance verbally abused the chief for his lack of leadership, noting that his subordinates did not show the proper respect by attempting to order officers around. This ended with a threat that any repetition of this type of thing would lead to disciplinary action. The meal that followed was anticlimactic, filled with more counseling on the role of a steward. Apparently, he felt that they were basically lazy and had to be watched all the time since they were always trying to get away with the least work possible. This had my head swimming. I had seen plenty of cadets dressed down at West Point (myself included), but I had never witnessed such a blatant, racially motivated spectacle in my brief military career. The anecdotes my father's friends had related about despised officers came flooding back, and I resolved to try to keep as far away from this officer as I could.

The next day our basic class convened. Several things became apparent. First, most of the class members were older than I. They were either lieutenants transferring into CEC from line billets or ensigns who had come into the CEC after exhausting their education draft deferments by completing graduate school—they had applied for the CEC to avoid being drafted into the Army. Second, there were a few recent NROTC graduates and my classmate Rick Rice from West Point, but by and large they were Officer Candidate School (OCS) graduates, who were called "ninety-day wonders" to describe the length of time required for their conversion from civilian to officer. They were generally looking to serve their military obligation and go home. The exceptions were a few of the transferring lieutenants who were Naval Academy graduates with three or four years of service under their belt. Third, there were some married officers, even a few with children. Fourth, although it did not register at the time (as no one was concerned about such things at that time), there was little diversity in the class that was all white males as I recall. All the unmarried officers were required to live in the BOQ and eat in the officers' mess. We were told what the regulations were, as well as the conduct expected of us. Following all this, we were briefed on the course we would be taking. Those who did not yet know what their first duty assignment would be were told the assignment officer would be coming in a couple of weeks to tell them. The majority would be going to Vietnam in some capacity, whether with the Seabees or in some construction-related job or staff billet, so we should all get used to it.

The Basic Course

The officer's introductory instruction was broken into two parts: the basic course and a specialty course that was geared to prepare the individual for his first duty station. I was going into the Seabee option as opposed to public works or contracts. The courses were taught by the faculty, which consisted of a mixture of active-duty CEC officers, retired CEC officers, and a few civilians. It became apparent this was not going to be much of a challenge. I could revert to the previous study habits since there was nothing they were going to teach in the military section I had not already done or learned. The same was true of the Navy culture stuff. It was apparent this course was for the OCS ensigns and not the NROTC or USNA graduates. I just wanted the basic course to be over and get on to the Seabees-related stuff that interested me.

By and large, everyone got along well enough among the academy graduates, having a natural affinity for each other regardless of how long it had been since they had graduated. The NROTC graduates pulled closer to them than the OCS ensigns. The predictable differences between these groupings were the result of the length of exposure to the military. Some of the OCS folks still couldn't figure out how to wear their uniforms, leading to laughable inspections.

The other area of general ineptness that I suppose we were all meant to correct through osmosis had to do with social behavior with the officers' wives, especially the senior officers. This is another area that has changed so markedly in the last forty-plus years it is hard for the current generation of officers to imagine. To begin with, most wives did not work and were expected to participate in the various functions put on by the officers' wives' club and the wives' organization of their husbands' unit. This, in turn, forced a hierarchy within the wives based upon their husbands' rank and position, making the senior officers' wives the leaders of this social world. Given that most of the ensigns were unmarried and new to the military, this was not a well-understood reality. It led to some funny and painful lessons, not only for the single ensigns but also for the young wives of the few that were married. Among the painful ordeals then in vogue was an official call on the commanding officer and his wife at their quarters. These were social in nature and designed to be relatively short affairs where the new officer and wife would meet the CO and his wife in a social setting. I always supposed this was so the CO's wife could look them over and see how much guidance was required. Most of the time this requirement was met by the CO hosting an afternoon "at home," during which the new officers would be cycled through at precise intervals so that it could be done as painlessly and efficiently as possible. Everyone was supposed to dress up, and that could mean that the young wives were expected to show up with outfits including gloves and calling cards, which were put in a small silver tray for the purpose. The better and more popular COs dispensed with this formality and had more casual affairs like barbeques with no expected cycling. The self-important CO and wife pairs seemed to really enjoy being treated regally and expected it. This led to some spectacular gaffs. I was soon to be introduced to that world when I reported to my battalion.

Beyond the basic school, the giant Seabee base at Port Hueneme was a hive of activity as it rocked with a wartime tempo unseen since World War II. Half of the total Seabee force of nineteen battalions was homeported there, and they were rotating through Vietnam deployments. Additionally, the school for training the enlisted Seabees in their skill areas was also there, as was the huge equipment maintenance and shipping facility that supported the battalions, together with all the logistics support. As opposed to other military units whose personnel rotated on twelve-month tours, the Seabee battalions rotated in and out of Vietnam as units. The rotation was nine months deployed and three months in homeport preparing for the next deployment. Specific groups from the battalion left and returned home early or late for various reasons, such as equipment turnover, that could make their rotation ten and two. This might seem like a good deal initially over the twelve-month tour except that the battalion tour for junior enlisted was forty-eight months, meaning they could make at least three deployments to Vietnam during their time in the battalion before they were rotated to shore duty in the United States or overseas. Senior enlisted had thirty-six-month tours, and officers generally rotated after twenty-four months.

All this activity was carried out with long days broken only by the stand-down period, when the battalion returned for leave prior to commencing the training cycle for the next deployment. NMCB-9, my next home, was in homeport getting ready to deploy shortly before I joined it in Vietnam. I was able to observe some of what they were doing as they communicated to me expectations of how I should prepare for my assignment. Mostly this was ensuring that I qualified on my personal weapons, an M16 rifle and a .45-caliber M1911A1 pistol. While the M16 was light and easy to fire (compared to the M14 rifle I had qualified with at West Point), the M1911 pistol was unwieldy and difficult to become proficient with. I qualified but often thought I would be better off throwing it at the enemy than firing at them.

I was invited to a pre-deployment party at my new CO's quarters to meet the wardroom, as the complement of officers assigned to the battalion was called, and their wives. For good or bad, I had experienced a sense of foreboding in several situations in my life, most recently several times during my West Point experience. This party was one of those times. I was struck instantly by the persona of the two senior officers in the battalion, the CO and executive officer, better known as the XO. The CO was an Annapolis grad (from the late 1940s), and he wore it with all the trappings of an officer of that era in formality and status. He did not appear to be a troop guy, but I assumed he must be competent since he was in command. The XO seemed strange to me for undefined reasons that fall under the foreboding category. The rest of the officers were a duke's mixture, but I noticed the other ensigns all seemed older than I was, like the situation I encountered in my basic class. I don't remember much about the wives.

The basic course plodded along, and I kept myself entertained the way young men did in those days: sports, girls, and drinking. I had never smoked since I watched my father cough and hack as long as I could remember from the two to three packs of unfiltered cigarettes he smoked a day. This eventually sent him to an early grave from cancer. My mother never smoked. Similarly, drugs appeared just plain stupid. At that time, the services had robust club systems that were broken down by general rank categories; that is, officers' clubs, chief petty officers' clubs, NCOs' clubs, and enlisted sailors' clubs. The good things about them were they were on base, cheap, and kept those who had too much to drink under surveillance. To provide access to women who lived off base, there were open gate events that allowed women on base to go to the clubs for entertainment purposes. Happy hour was a cultural thing in the services and commands were expected to turn out on Friday after work to socialize with even lower priced drinks and floor shows that sometimes included strippers. No one seemed to mind, including the wives or the women from off base. These shows paled in comparison with those held in frat houses or movies shown in dorm rooms—or so I was told by those who had attended civilian colleges.

Even though the BOQ was a pit, I had, for the first time in the military, a room that I did not have to share. The fact that it had no private bathroom and I had to walk down the hall to shave and shower in a gang shower was the way I expected it to be in the military. I had my first new car, a '67 Mustang that I bought a few months before I graduated from West Point and drove across the country. I could get around on the weekends, including driving down to San Diego to see my parents. At night, some of the basic students would go out to such colorful entertainment as the world's fattest topless go-go dancer in the many questionable bars around the base. There was safety in numbers, as one could never really know what might happen in one of these places. We were young and stupid, so we went. All in all, this experience was a lark compared to West Point, so I just enjoyed myself and graduation finally came. The overachievers who studied garnered the coveted "Distinguished Graduate" on their diplomas, the kind of thing that I did not care about.

Learning the Law

I am not sure what I expected from the Seabee option course, so I had not adjusted my sights accordingly. As it turned out, it was very basic and went back over most of the stuff I already knew from the Army like what a battalion organization is, its weapons, communications equipment, construction equipment, and so forth. Once the realization that I was not going to learn much in this course sank in, the only thing to look forward to was the much-anticipated trip to the Naval Justice School (NJS) Detachment in San Diego for the course in the Navy justice system. This was important because battalion officers carried out much of the disciplinary action at the battalion level without lawyers, and junior officers were frequently assigned as prosecutors or defense counsel in a SCM. That, however, was not why the trip to this school was so eagerly anticipated. San Diego was a wild wartime town with its large concentration of Navy ships and aircraft deploying to and returning from Vietnam. It was a magnet for women looking for men, and the open gate policies made meeting them easy for those eligible to use the clubs. Those who had gone before us to the school put it simply, "If you can't pick up a girl you like at the Downwinds Club on Friday night, you are either dead or queer." The Downwinds was the junior officers' annex to the North Island Air Station officers' club at the tip of the Coronado peninsula across from San Diego. It was an unadorned cinder block building separated from the main club to confine the activity that took place there from getting to the main club. There were shore patrol (military police) personnel who worked between these two facilities to ensure the more senior officers and their wives would not be annoyed by the rowdiness of the junior officers.

What made my visit to the Downwinds even more momentous and memorable was that a couple of days before, a carrier air wing had flown in from one of the carriers that had just completed a deployment off the coast of North Vietnam. When I walked in, it was something wilder than the scenes of debauchery in the familiar films *Animal House*, *Revenge of the Nerds*, and similar comedic romps. To say these young airmen were letting off steam would be a gross understatement. This should be remembered in the context of today's more politically correct world in which combat troops are not allowed to have beer in an Islamic country because it offends the populace that they are fighting for or go on R&R (rest and recreation) to overseas locations that provide a needed release from their stressful vocation. They are expected to just come home and adjust to their PTSD. The noise was unbelievable, and there were pitchers of beer flying. As promised, there were young women to suit almost any taste available in copious numbers. Some were in shock, some drunk, some in various stages of undress, and others just taking it all in while surveying the young men to see if there was someone they might be interested in. This was the group I concentrated on, as I got my beer and went to a location I felt had protection from the various things that were flying and afforded me an opportunity to do some surveying myself.

There were about six weeks left after I completed this course until I got on a plane for Vietnam to join my battalion. I was not looking for the love of my life but someone I could have fun with over that time and not leave anything serious behind me as a distraction. While I realized at some level that life happens, and one cannot always control these things, this seemed like a good game plan. The other thing I had already learned was I was not looking for the most beautiful girl in the room, as there were plenty of others doing that. My experience on dates with girls in love with themselves had not been good, so there were other things that were more important to me. Armed with all this, I talked and danced with a few girls and found one with a personality that seemed to mesh with mine. We talked about me leaving for Vietnam soon, so she understood that from the start, and it apparently fit in with her plans at that time. Around us, the mayhem continued, and we finally left since the noise inhibited conversation. We had both accomplished what we had set out to do in finding someone to share some time with.

The real pluses with this girl were that she had her own apartment, car, and job, so she was "liberated," in the parlance of the time. She had her own rule book, and I respected that. She was funny and fun to be with, and we went out almost every night I was in San Diego and on weekends until I left for Vietnam.

The NJS was interesting and gave me a good overview of what to expect when dealing with disciplinary problems in the battalion. It reinforced the fact that the legal system was about enforcing discipline and not rehabilitation of wrongdoers. My only complaint was that it was over too soon, and I was back in Port Hueneme to finish the remainder of the Seabee course before leaving. It was unremarkable and plodded along while my thoughts concentrated on my upcoming adventure. Every weekend was spent in San Diego now, as my parents were also anticipating my departure date from a different point of view.

Off to War

It seemed incredible, but after all the anticipation, my departure date finally arrived. I found myself checking in at Norton Air Force Base (AFB), California, on October 25, 1967, for my flight on a Military Airlift Command (MAC) charter flight to Danang, Vietnam. I would be one of the first in my West Point class to go to Vietnam, as my Army classmates were still in the training pipeline going through airborne and ranger schools.

My parents had driven me up to the base, and we spent the day trying to pretend it was just another farewell like all the ones we had gone through before, though we knew better.

I kissed my mother goodbye; I told her not to worry and that I would write. I shook hands with my suddenly quiet father and walked through the door to the loading area. Soon the plane was airborne. There seemed to be some irony in flying off to war in a Boeing 707 replete with flight attendants, but that was the way it was. We made stops in Honolulu in the middle of the night and Okinawa for fuel and arrived in Danang about 6 a.m.

Chapter Three

SEEKING THE ELEPHANT

*The Civil War veteran described being in combat as having
"been to see the elephant." ... I now know that they
understood what every combat veteran since Caesar's
legions has known. War is an intensely personal experience.*
—Bud Campbell, *Seeing the Elephant*

While there were millions of servicemen and women who served
during the Vietnam era, fewer served in the Southeast Asia war
zone, fewer still were in-country in Vietnam, and only a fraction of those
were involved in combat. The accepted estimate of the ratio of support
troops to "trigger-pullers" was seven to one—meaning for every trooper
that was squeezing a trigger, firing artillery, dropping a bomb, and so on,
there were seven other troops to support him. Most of these support troops
were in rear areas and never saw any combat at all during their tour of duty;
however, some did by circumstance. REMF (rear-echelon motherfuckers)
was a popular pejorative applied by line troops to support personnel.

By any fair definition, Seabees are support troops, as are all engineer
troops except combat engineers, who are responsible for breeching obstacles
like minefields, enemy fortifications, and the like. Combat engineers were
often some of the first troops in action in an assault. Seabees are not combat
engineers by design; however, they are sometimes pressed into that role.
Their primary role was to support combat troops (primarily Marines) by
building fortifications, airfields, fuel storage depots, ammunition storage
facilities, roads, berthing, and other necessities so the combat soldiers could
do their job. This involved going where the soldiers were—and sometimes
becoming targets in the process. I understood this as I left for Vietnam
and had already reconciled myself to the fact that any combat I might see
would most likely be a matter of pure bad luck. Most probable would be

some glimpse of the action from afar, such as watching a bombing run or maybe some artillery firing. This thought had been confirmed in my discussions back in Port Hueneme with those who had already completed deployments to Vietnam. However, like most young men embarked for a war zone with no real idea of what combat entailed, there was a part of me that was seeking the elephant, so I could say I was a combat veteran like my dad, and we would have a new and stronger bond.

Welcome to Vietnam

My first impression of Vietnam was that it was hot and it smelled. Perhaps my olfactory impression had something to do with the way the wind was blowing since someone was always burning something somewhere. The Vietnamese used human feces to fertilize their rice paddies (a practice common throughout Asia), adding to the aroma no matter which way the wind blew. The heat I was experiencing was attributable not only to the tropical heat and humidity—even at 0700—but also to the stupid uniform I was wearing, complete with a coat and tie, as I lugged my bags outside the air terminal. I saw one of the ensigns I had met at the CO's quarters waving at me. We were soon on our way to the battalion location at Camp Hoover, named for SW2 William E. Hoover, the first Seabee killed in action in Vietnam. CM3 Marvin G. Shields, who was also KIA in this action, was the only Seabee to be awarded the Medal of Honor. The camp was on the west side of Danang on the way to the 1st Marine Division headquarters. To get there, it was necessary to cross Highway 1, the only north–south highway that ran the length of South Vietnam. It was not a long trip and featured my first trip through Dogpatch, the squalid shantytown of improvised shacks outside the gates of the airfield on the other side of Highway 1. I was told this was off-limits and filled with whores and thieves: "Don't drive through there by yourself." On the other side of Dogpatch were rice paddies and Camp Hoover. We drove through the camp gate, past the sentry, and straight to the Southeast Asia (SEA) hut I would be sharing with three other junior officers. I dropped my bags at my new home before I was deposited at the XO's office, my first stop for in-processing.

As I walked into the XO's office, I had no real idea of what lay ahead, only the same sense of foreboding I had when I left the CO's quarters several months before. The XO struck me as an officious, self-important, and affected man. My warning bells told me to be careful around him.

After welcoming me to the battalion, he inquired about my flight and my completion of the Seabee option at CECOS. Did I have my documentation showing that I had qualified on my personal weapons? I offered him the requisite papers. He told me that as the junior officer in the battalion, I was being assigned as the communications/ordnance officer, and if my performance was up to speed, I could move on to other jobs. My boss would be Lt. Bob Schroeder, the S-2 (training and intelligence officer). Schroeder was a veteran World War II Seabee who had moved up through the ranks and would be a good mentor. With that out of the way, he said he was giving me two especially important instructions to read and understand before I left his office.

This sounded serious, and I remember a feeling of apprehension as he handed them to me. This disappeared immediately when I saw the title of the first, which the XO had said was the most important, "Officers' Country Standards." Despite the circumstances, it was all I could do to keep from laughing out loud. I read this pompous, laughable, and to me, ridiculous description of the rules of the officers' mess intended for junior officers. Included were such gems as "rude and off color stories, especially concerning females, will not be told in the mess" and "junior officers are expected to listen to their seniors and gain the benefit of their experience." I took this to mean I was supposed to speak when spoken to. "Questions?" he asked flatly. "No, sir!"

Next, I was handed an instruction sheet entitled "Rules of Engagement" (ROE). These are essentially the rules of combat; they define when it is permissible to fire your weapon. Having read many books, seen many movies, and talked with many World War II veterans, these rules struck me as odd and scary. To begin with, we were not supposed to fire our weapon unless someone had already fired at us, and we were sure they had. This seemed to indicate that if we saw someone getting ready to shoot at us, we could not fire first to preclude that engagement from happening; this struck me as being counterintuitive. I asked if my perception was correct and was told that it was. I thought to myself, *fat chance!* Although I had not heard of it before, this was a clear case of the "Occam's Razor" effect—the idea that when confronted by seemingly opposing theories, the simplest explanation is probably the correct one. In this case, if someone is pointing a gun at you, he probably intends to shoot you. Since I could not understand the logic behind this policy, I decided I would not risk my life or those of the servicemen under my command because of rules that made no sense. "Any more questions?" Again I responded, "No, sir!" and was dismissed.

I went back to my SEA hut, a plywood building that had no interior walls except for the attached bathroom facility. It was roughly divided into four sections by lockers and some desks. In each section, there was a bed and a nightstand with a light. I unpacked my bags, took a shower, and donned my Seabee greens—the utility uniform, complete with combat boots and soft cap. I would be issued my personal weapons and combat equipment (helmet, flak jacket, web belt, canteen, combat first aid kit, etc.) later. I was then off to meet my boss and mentor and the men I would oversee.

First Day

Although I had briefly met him at the CO's quarters, this would be my real introduction to Bob Schroeder. Bob proved to be all that anyone could have wanted for a first boss. Although he looked like the proverbial schoolteacher, he was a professional who had forgotten more about the Seabees than most of the officers in the battalion would ever know. He worked his way up through the ranks after enlisting in World War II. His manner was quiet but firm, and he always had time to explain his directions to me. From my later observations, he was the only officer in the battalion that the CO respected to the point of accepting what he recommended without further justification. The XO had learned not to take him on by being proven wrong several times. Schroeder was not only my mentor but also my protector. Ours was a short first meeting with directions to meet my men, check out their work area and berthing areas, and give him my impressions when we got together next. As it was approaching the noon hour, Bob said we should eat before I headed off to begin my indoctrination.

Looking back at my arrival at the section of the mess hall that was partitioned apart from the rest of the battalion eating area for officers, I would say it was one of the most significant emotional events so far in my acclimatization to the Navy after West Point. The mess steward asked for my "lineal number" so I could be seated in the proper place. Every officer in the Navy is assigned a lineal number from the chief of naval operations to the most junior ensign. That number designated the officer's seniority in relation to every other officer in the Navy, the lower the number, the more senior the officer. The real lineal numbers were assigned to line officers; all staff corps officers like me had a running mate in the line to whom our number was tied. I was so new I did not have a lineal number yet. This meant I would be seated as the junior commissioned officer in the mess with only the warrant officers below me.

I understood why this was important: the tables were set up as I had seen in movies of shipboard wardrooms, with a small table at the head of the room where the CO and officers who were lieutenant commanders (XO, operations officer, and supply officer) sat. There were two longer tables perpendicular to that head table: one where all the lieutenants sat and the other for the lieutenants (junior grade), ensigns, and warrant officers. The tables were set with tablecloths, china, and silverware. There were stewards to take orders and serve the food, much like a restaurant. I had never seen the like when I was at my summer training signal battalion at Fort Bragg with the army and ate in the battalion dining hall. There was a segregated section for officers' tables, but that was just a place where we brought our trays from the mess line to eat without any ceremony.

Due to the varying schedules for the workday, breakfast and lunch were casual meals; officers just sat down and ate when they arrived after the meal period started and did not have to wait for the senior officers. Dinner I was told was formal, with each officer expected to be on time and standing behind his chair until the CO or whoever would be the senior officer for that meal was in place and gave permission to sit. If an officer was late, he had to ask permission to join the mess. Those who were going to be absent were to inform the XO of the reason in advance. Visitors had to be approved in advance by the XO. There was a new officers' mess being finished that would move the wardroom out of the general mess to its own building. It housed not only the dining area, but also a club with a bar, pool table, TV (for watching the Armed Forces TV network), a sofa and chairs, lamps, and coffee tables. This would truly set the wardroom apart from the men, I was told.

I was introduced or reintroduced to those who were at lunch. The CO was there and shook my hand, indicating we would have a formal appointment later. The meal menu contained several choices, and it was more food than I would ever eat for lunch, but it reflected that Seabees do hard physical work, so they were fed well. I noted that true to the "Officers' Country Standards" instruction sheet, there was not much conversation at my table of junior officers. Everyone pretty much just ate and left. My cue that it was time to leave was when Bob Schroeder got up, so I followed him out. He explained that most officers went back to their hooches for a little break before going back to work and to read their mail, which was distributed to individual mailboxes in the mess. After that, he had the senior enlisted man who would be working for me, Gunner's Mate (Guns) Petty Officer First Class Afalava, coming to meet me to take the tour he had recommended.

It was imperative that I draw my personal weapons and get outfitted with my 782 gear, the combat outfit we were required to wear in Condition 1. As I read in the ROE, there were basically two conditions of readiness: Condition 1, which meant attack was imminent or we were under attack, and Condition 3, or "normal" conditions. Although I was told there were three conditions of readiness, I did not learn what Condition 2 was until later. My battle station, the place where I was to go during an attack, was the command post bunker; the CO's battle staff assembled there. I was responsible for ensuring the CO had the necessary communications to do his job. All the attacks to date had been 122-mm rocket attacks on the Danang Air Base. The rockets flew over our camp from the west, and there was always the possibility of one landing short of its primary target and hitting us. Other than that, we were not really considered target worthy according to intelligence estimates. The airplanes and trigger-pullers were of more concern to the enemy. Nonetheless, when the sirens went off in the middle of the night, we all had to go to our posts until the all clear was given.

Afalava, a South Seas Islander, acted as my guide as we visited the armory spaces, ammunition bunkers, the communications and electronic repair spaces, and finally the battalion communications center located in the command bunker. I met the enlisted folks that would be under my supervision and got a general introduction to the equipment for which we were responsible. There were five gunner's mates, one electronics technician, two radiomen, and a seaman. Not a huge responsibility, but you must start somewhere. This was my real introduction into the odd composition of the Seabee battalion's personnel makeup. The construction and automotive functions of the battalion were the responsibility of the Seabee ratings that included equipment operator, construction mechanic, construction electrician, builder, steelworker, utilitiesman, and engineering aide. All the support functions were fleet ratings such as cook, personnelman, yeoman, gunner's mate, radioman, corpsman, dental technician, storekeeper, and so on. This set up a natural conflict between those who had signed up to be in the Navy (that is, on ships at sea) and Seabees, who had signed up for construction duty supporting the Marines. The fleet sailors had never expected to be ashore in harm's way with the Marines nor were they trained for shore combat until they joined the battalion and went through military training as part of the preparations to deploy. I often heard: "If I wanted to be a doggie or jarhead, I would have joined the Army or Marines." Still, Seabees were a tough bunch with muscles generated by hard construction work and not to be provoked lightly, as many fleet sailors, Marines, and, later, soldiers found out to their dismay.

Except for the M16 rifles and M60 machine guns, the weapons, ammunition, and equipment—especially the communications gear—was old. The recoilless rifles and mortars were Korean War–vintage, and the ammunition was old and of questionable reliability. The M1911 .45-caliber pistol had been a mainstay of the military since World War I, and our issue pistols looked like they had been in the inventory since World War II. The communications equipment was not much improved from the Korean War, with EE-8 hand crank field phones and walkie-talkies that looked like the World War II variety. The PRC-15 radios were heavy and required batteries that always seemed to die at the most inopportune time. My crew maintained all this equipment, and of course, they had not been trained on this antiquated gear until they received their orders to the battalion. Some had been sent to Army or Marine schools; the junior grades had gotten whatever training they had on the job. I found we had little training or experience to support what were life-or-death necessities in combat. This applied to my small crew across the board. It quickly became apparent that there were a couple of talented men I would have to rely upon to carry these functions. They were not the most senior men; rather, they were relatively junior in each of my two areas. I dutifully drew my two personal weapons and was assured they were the best by my gunner's mates.

I found that the battalion workweek was six-and-half days. Moreover, the workday was ten-to-twelve hours long, including transportation to and from project sites. We would get Sunday afternoon off if we were not assigned some other task, such as manning defensive positions, taking care of personnel matters, inspecting the camp, and so forth. If a Condition 1 was initiated during the night, it just cut the sleep period down, as everyone was still expected to work a full day the next day. Nights of repeated enemy activity, such as those we experienced during the Tet Offensive, took a serious toll on the men due to lack of sleep and strained nerves from anticipation of the unexpected.

While I could not imagine that the evening meal could be worse than the noon meal, I was wrong. The wardroom members, except those who were on detachments away from the base camp, gathered at the appointed hour and stood behind their chairs. The CO arrived, noted the attendance, and directed the chaplain to say grace. We were then ordered to "take seats," a directive I had last heard in the dining hall at West Point. There was, again, little conversation at our table, although there was somewhat more at the table where the lieutenants were seated. The reason for this became clearer to me as I got to know the members of the mess, their backgrounds, and their personalities. This process accelerated a month or so later when the new officers' mess facility was completed and we had more of an opportunity to socialize. At some point after the main course but before dessert, the CO made some remarks as was apparently his habit. I don't remember them, but I do recall looking at those at my table who seemed to be struggling hard to show any interest and hoping not to be asked any questions. The combination of all this, plus my body's physical state, made the whole episode seem to take an eternity. I finally got to go back to my hooch, where I talked briefly with my new hut-mates and then collapsed. My first day in the war zone was over.

Seabees

The next week or so was filled with learning about the battalion (its personnel, its mission, my job and responsibilities) and experiencing Vietnam. Between the base camp and the detachments in the field, there were over a thousand men in NMCB-9. The largest detachment was building Liberty Bridge south of Danang. It was in an area called "Arizona Territory" by the Marines because it was wild and dangerous like its predecessor in the Old West. Jim Webb's semi-autobiographical book, *Fields of Fire*, takes place in this area and even mentions Liberty Bridge. The battalion had a Seabee team operating somewhere in Vietnam—much like the one the namesake of our camp had been working with when he was killed. We had no contact with them as they deployed separately from the battalion. The composition of the thousand men in the battalion was interesting to me as I got to know it well over the next few months. The leadership was composed of a couple of dozen officers, mostly CEC, a couple of junior line officers, and the rest staff corps support, including two supply corps officers, a chaplain, a doctor, and a dentist. Within the CEC officers, there were four former enlisted men who had been commissioned as either limited duty officers (LDO) or warrant officers (WO) and whose main responsibility was to provide the technical expertise for construction and equipment operations.

My boss was one of the LDOs and was very competent but reserved. The other three were more vocal, taking the formality of the wardroom setting fostered by the CO less seriously; hence, more conversation took place when they were in the mess.

At the apex of the leadership of the battalion was the CO, a CEC commander (O-5). The unit reflects the CO's personality and leadership. It never stopped being demonstrated to me over the course of my career how a unit could change, for good or bad, almost overnight simply by the replacement of the CO. At the most basic level, everyone in a unit, particularly in a combat environment, understands that the CO's decisions can determine whether the individual lives or dies. This is not some dramatic exaggeration, as I saw in the succeeding months, but a fact. The competence, technical and military, and for that matter the ethical standards of this officer are on constant display. The lowest-ranking Seabee in the unit could form an opinion in a truly short time concerning these qualities and the amount of faith he has in this decision maker as a result. This faith is reflected as defined in the terms of morale and esprit de corps. The persona of the unit can reflect a pride, swagger, and excitement that cannot be generated by speeches or bribery. It may also reflect a sullen attitude that cannot be hidden by reluctant compliance with orders or, of course, something between these extremes. I had learned this from my father's experiences and my own observations at West Point and during summer training with active-duty units. Now I was about to really live it and put the lessons into practice. While there is a chain of command responsible for ensuring that the CO's orders are interpreted correctly and executed expeditiously, the CO alone is ultimately accountable for his actions. And that remains true whether he likes, believes, or even understands it.

In the briefest of time and before I had had my arrival call with the CO, the atmosphere in the wardroom and throughout the camp told its tale. This was not a high-morale unit, and I should be wary in my dealings with the senior officers. The XO was officious, opinionated, and had all the characteristics of a geek nerd. When it came time to have my official call on the CO, I came away with the same impression that I had of several of the more senior officers at West Point who formed the cadre responsible for cadet training. I would be working for a self-important martinet whose exalted station had been confirmed in his eyes by receiving the assignment of CO. It was not so much what he said but how he said it, together with the things he talked about.

Both the CO and XO had a low opinion of the enlisted personnel. I was warned to be constantly vigilant of them trying to "get away with something." Officers were to ensure proper discipline always and place those who broke the rules and did not follow orders on report. In a sense, the enlisted troops were like children in need of strict parenting by the all-knowing father and mother. The XO's nickname was "mom" behind his back. During my call, the CO remarked on my USMA background, and that evolved into a discussion of his days as a midshipman in the '40s. He had high expectations of me based on my background and did not want to be disappointed. He projected a certain aloofness that would become more apparent as time when on, but for now I was glad to be done with the meeting and hoped my contact with him would be limited.

The middle tier of the leadership pyramid was supposedly the rest of the officers in the battalion from the XO down to the junior warrant officer. While there is no doubt that the former enlisted component of this group, the LDOs and WOs, did provide their own brand of leadership that was vital to the battalion, it was different from that of the other officers and recognized as such by those who cared enough to observe. All the other officers were in training as far as leadership went, having been principally in technical jobs (if they were CEC officers) working with civilians or contractors prior to coming to the battalion. All were in their first assignment where they interacted extensively with enlisted personnel. This was also true of the line officers, who were very junior, and all the staff officers apart from the supply officer, who previously served on board ships and had enlisted folks working for him. This, together with the spectrum of personalities to be expected in a wartime wardroom of career officers and grudging volunteers avoiding the draft, made for unending leadership fiascos—some funny, many sad, and a few tragic. The characters in the TV show *MASH* and the movies *Mister Roberts* and *Catch-22* may seem unbelievable, but these dramatizations of wartime units show how fate throws strange bedfellows together. Such was the case in NMCB-9. The notion that one was an "officer and gentleman" by an act of Congress had a strange effect on not a few who felt their superiority to those below them in status made their decisions and orders unquestionable. If subsequently proven to be in error, then it was obviously those below them who had misunderstood or failed them in some way, not their own inadequacies. All of this placed a heavy burden on the base of the battalion leadership.

The backbone of the leadership in the battalion was the chief petty officer (CPO, or simply chief) contingent comprised of the senior enlisted personnel in the E-7, E-8, and E-9 pay grades. They numbered between thirty and forty in all, making the total battalion leadership numbers somewhere over fifty. The chief held a special position in the Navy back in the day; they made all things happen. They reacted best to general direction without micromanagement that had the immediate undesired effect of pissing them off. If they wanted advice, they would ask for it, but generally they wanted to know what you wanted done and by when. I recalled my father's admonition that the "how" of getting something done was the chief's province. The officer, in many cases, "did not want to know." The junior enlisted learned quickly to do what they were told and keep their mouths shut.

Chiefs took care of troublemakers in a variety of ways, including physical violence, the results of which were generally described as the individual "falling down a ladder" or "tripping." Accusing a chief of assault, absent eyewitnesses (of which there were remarkably few), resulted in more problems for the individual since the chief's explanation was always accepted as true for several good reasons that I understood. The chiefs' community varied in quality of leadership and technical skill according to the bell curve of probability, with the more astute officers and chiefs knowing who the top chiefs were, regardless of pay grade, and seeking their advice accordingly. I already knew that the chiefs could make a junior officer look good or bad and had resolved not to piss them off. I took advantage of the vast experience of the best ones to help me when I was unsure of what to do. I should also note that in addition to the chiefs, there was a Marine gunnery sergeant (E-8), or "gunny," usually with an infantry background, assigned to each battalion as a tactical advisor. This would be another asset I would avail myself of during this tour of duty.

Below the chiefs, the enlisted community consisted of petty officers (or PO, at the E-4, E-5, and E-6 pay grades) and nonrated personnel (E-1, E-2, and E-3), commonly called "nonrates." Aside from the obvious differences between the various Seabee and fleet ratings on technical skills sets, there was another interesting difference in how the Seabee petty officers had achieved their pay grade. There were those who had been promoted through the ranks from construction recruit (CR, E-1) by striking for a technical rating or requesting permission to learn a trade after showing some fundamental skills via on-the-job training and perhaps being sent to a Navy technical school to broaden the skill sets and acquire a unique skill such as welding, generator operations and repair, and so on. These Seabees had passed Navy-wide tests for advancement up the pay grade ladder to wherever they were after being recommended for promotion by the chain of command. Their performance evaluations had reflected satisfactory marks. Depending upon the manning of a rating and the existing vacancies, this kind of promotion could be slow or fast. The other way Seabees achieved PO status originated during World War II.

The Seabee ratings had been rapidly expanded in World War II using a recruiting method called the Direct Procurement Petty Officer Program (DPPO) that had been reinstated for the Vietnam War. Simply stated, an individual was tested on his technical skill set in a rating and provided a résumé of the jobs he had performed. Seabee recruiters familiar with the civilian construction industry and the trades evaluated that document. Based upon this evaluation, the individual was offered a pay grade commensurate with his demonstrated skill set. These POs were known as instant petty officers (IPO) and had one significant downside in many cases. They had been technicians in the civilian world but had not been required to become leaders commensurate with the PO level they were being offered. The brief military indoctrination training they received could not hope to teach them what others had learned as they advanced through the ranks. They were good technicians but sometimes laughable leaders. It was not an infrequent occurrence to go to a construction site and see a crew supposedly headed by an IPO E-6 being run by an E-3 who possessed natural leadership skills and just told the others what to do. They were accustomed to this in the civilian world. This strange marriage of POs from two backgrounds added yet another ingredient to the leadership equation for the officers and chiefs.

The bottom of the manpower pyramid was occupied by the nonrates. In the Seabee rating structure, they were called constructionmen (as opposed to seamen, as in the fleet). They were recruited without the promise of a particular school or the opportunity to strike for a trade they could qualify for. They were the laborers of the battalion system and generally were assigned to a menial job upon joining the battalion, such as a cook, a laundry worker, latrine maintenance, or some equally unpleasant, labor-intensive, thankless job. This was sure to instill in the individual exactly where he stood in the pecking order, as my father had discovered when he cleaned spittoons. Having the privilege to strike for a rating upon completing the initial scut job was carefully made clear to the new Seabee and the system worked well. Screwing up sometime later could result in that person being sent back to the scut jobs for additional time to consider the error of his ways; it served as an excellent deterrent for bad behavior.

One other occurrence during my tour with NMCB-9, that could have only been the product of individuals with no military experience driven entirely by political or bean-counter agendas, was the direction from the secretary of defense that the armed forces should recruit what became known as the Project 100,000 (or "McNamara's 100,000"), which involved drawing recruits from Mental Group IV. This was a group whose intelligence tests scores on the screening tests were the lowest and previously below the standard that had been required to enter the service for years. These men were drafted despite low IQ on the dubious premise that they could function at some level in the military and free up others for combat duties. The intense supervision this group needed to make sure they functioned at all far outweighed any possible contribution they might have provided. The whole idea was a joke and subject to ridicule by those unfortunate enough to have to deal with it.

The nonrates numbered around four hundred and, when added to the IPOs whose leadership capabilities were questionable, the fifty to sixty members of the leadership team had somewhere between eight hundred and nine hundred souls to supervise. The leadership team had to make sure this rather large group of men was productive and safe when working in a hostile environment. The many levels of hostile working environment varied from being in a combat zone with the constant possibility of enemy action (and the requisite access to live ammunition for their weapons) to the danger involved in working in the construction trades across a significant geographical area. Other related issues, such as excessive indulgence in alcohol and/or drugs, were also a concern, as were the prostitutes who prowled the roads and project sites, as "camp followers" had done for millennia. They would provide a quickie, with a significant possibility of a sexually transmitted disease, for a dollar if the oversight was not constant. The leadership lessons I learned with this unit have stayed with me for a lifetime, reinforcing the lessons I brought with me from my adolescence and those I was taught at West Point. Taking care of your people was a top priority.

Camp Hoover

Camp Hoover was our home. We enjoyed much more comfortable quarters than those of most of the trigger-pullers in the field, but not as luxurious as those of the Air Force personnel who lived on the air base. This was not a surprise; since the Seabees are builders, they should be expected to make their camp the best it could be. Clearly access to construction materials and the skills to use them made all the difference. We never apologized for our camp or the envy it generated, but our Seabees were generous with their time helping other units to improve their lot, often after regular working hours. They worked on Vietnamese orphanages and hospitals as well. The camp was largely made of SEA huts, some for berthing, some for offices, and others for shop spaces for the various trades and automotive repair functions. There were larger prefabricated metal or wooden plywood buildings that were used for storage, the mess hall, the clubs, and more equipment repair functions.

There was a lighted triple concertina fence with tangle foot around the camp, overlooked by elevated guard towers in the corners and gates, all manned by armed sentries to ensure no unauthorized personnel—U.S. or Vietnamese—got in. The streets were not paved, and the dust was bad despite a water truck that sprayed water to keep it down. When the monsoon rains came, there was mud. Everyone had a bed to sleep on, as opposed to the ground, and mosquito netting. There were fans, some air conditioning, and lighting since the berthing spaces were wired for electricity. There were gang showers and heads or toilet facilities that consisted of essentially outhouse-like structures with holes cut into the bench seating and halved fifty-five-gallon drums below each hole filled with diesel fuel to some depth. These were affectionately known as "shitters." They smelled and generated even more stink when they were burned-out to get rid of the waste. Since most field units used the same type of facilities, the stink harmonized with the chorus of other odors. The stench of decomposing fish was also common, as a favored—and pungent—Vietnamese sauce condiment called *nuoc mam* featured brined, fermented fish. At strategic locations throughout the camp, there were pee tubes (with minimal privacy screens) stuck in the ground over a leeching plot of sorts. There were a few flush toilets in the camp in "officers' country," the chiefs' berthing area, the clubs, and the medical/dental clinic. In the field or on project sites, the available facilities varied greatly and did not generate a lot of concern except in areas where there might be enemy activity because one's vulnerability when using them.

Since this was not a ship, the camp could have alcoholic beverages and clubs for off-duty recreational purposes. The clubs, which were segregated by pay grade, similarly had their beverage choices assigned as if by some divine determination. The E-4 and below personnel had the enlisted club, where only beer and soft drinks were served. The E-5 and E-6 personnel had the Acey-Deucey Club, where in addition to beer and soft drinks, they could also buy alcohol by the drink; they were not, however, allowed to have bottles of liquor. The E-7, E-8, and E-9 personnel had the chiefs' club, where they could have anything they wanted and were authorized to have bottles of liquor in their possession. All the officers in the wardroom were members of the officers' mess that had no restrictions on alcohol use or ownership. It should be mentioned that alcohol was cheap since it was not taxed, had minimal markup for profit generation, and no one worried about a "sin tax" to save everyone from their own inclinations. A beer was generally ten to fifteen cents, and a mixed drink might be as high as a quarter, depending on the markup. Quarts of liquor cost between one and two dollars for most types; something special might cost a little more. Since all were held accountable for their actions, there seemed to be little concern for the availability or cost of alcohol or the consequences. It was about the only diversion, other than movies, AFRS TV, or the occasional live show that might come through the camp. The long working hours did not leave a lot of time to indulge or for recovering from hangovers.

As the week progressed, I ventured around the battalion area with no set indoctrination schedule other than my boss suggesting that it would be a good idea if I did this or that. Being the "boot," or junior ensign, placed me in the category of both not being expected to know anything and being regarded as a pain in the ass for that crime since it meant I would ask stupid questions. My first stop was the motor pool to receive a military driver's license, so I could drive a jeep. A Seabee battalion is equipment-intensive with over four hundred pieces of construction equipment in its inventory. ALFA Company, as the equipment company was called, is where the rolling stock is located. The equipment operators (EO) and construction mechanics (CM) were assigned to this company. The equipment ranged from automotive equipment such as "ass haulers" like jeeps, buses, three-quarter-ton trucks, and two-and-a-half-ton "deuce-and-a-half" trucks to construction equipment: bulldozers, graders, roller compactors, transit mixers, tow truckers, rock drills, and the like. The battalion could also be assigned equipment to augment its assets, such as rock crushers to make aggregate and concrete batch plants to make concrete.

Equipment requires a never-ending supply of repair parts and maintenance supplies, together with the tools and trained construction mechanics to keep things running. A reliable source of diesel and gasoline fuel and lubricants is a given. Seabee battalions had a couple of fleet-rating machinist mates assigned who repaired broken parts or fabricated improvised fixes to keep things operating to the extent that it was possible. The major problem was that this equipment was old and worn out from almost nonstop use. Battalions that were rotating out at the end of their nine-month deployment turned over the equipment in place to the incoming battalion. To be sure, there was a process called the Battalion Equipment Evaluation Program (BEEP), under which each battalion's representatives inspected every piece of equipment and agreed on its condition. This did not fix or replace the equipment or magically produce the required repair parts. In some cases, parts for aging equipment were not available because they were not made any more. Looking at the line of broken equipment in the motor pool, officially called "deadlined awaiting parts," reminded me of newsreels I had seen of World War II and Korea since some of the equipment looked that old. The logistics support problems associated with Seabee equipment from procurement to maintenance to repair would be a continuing theme throughout my career. It was a limiting factor on the utility of any battalion; hence, their ability to support the trigger-pullers.

In the construction companies, I saw lots of toolboxes of every type to support the construction companies. These contained everything from hammers and wrenches to tape measures, screeds, and trowels to electrician's wire cutters and test gages—and on and on. It was apparent that replacement was slow. There were a significant number of tools that were past their useful life but were still in service. The procurement system did not provide state of the art products anywhere; rather, they procured equipment based on the lowest bid for government contracts. Bravo Company was the home of the utilities trades of utilitiesman (UT) and construction electrician (CE). It served as subcontractor to Charlie and Delta, the construction companies, to whom the builders (BU) and steelworkers (SW) were assigned. They were responsible for the project management of the various construction projects, except for utilities projects that were assigned to Bravo Company. It became very apparent to me that the technical skills and leadership of the chiefs and skilled senior POs under the watchful supervision of the LDOs and WOs were the keys to success in completing projects. What the other CEC officers did was not clear to me after my first week in the battalion.

The construction companies' chiefs complained about construction materials availability and problems in obtaining repair parts and maintenance supplies. This again would be something I was to hear throughout my Seabee tours. Getting the right material or parts to the correct site at the correct time is a monumental task that has been underappreciated by military and civilian leaders throughout history, and Vietnam was no exception. A pipeline that was thousands of miles long from the United States to Southeast Asia had an almost infinitely many number of opportunities for the material to go missing or to be ordered incorrectly, packed poorly, or stolen. This made completing projects or repairs to meet a time schedule extremely difficult and required constant checking and follow-up. It did not help that our supply department was manned by fleet storekeepers and supply officers (albeit with Seabee ratings augmentation in the key positions) who were unfamiliar with the non-fleet equipment, parts, and construction materials that were the life's blood of the battalion. Most of this stuff could not be ordered through regular Navy supply channels, as it was not in that system.

Most of the time the battalion that was constructing the project was not the one that had designed or planned it. There was a lead time required for planning, designing, or adapting the design to the location, making material lists, and so forth that usually stretched beyond a single battalion deployment. While this problem had been recognized to some extent and a separate Seabee logistics system slowly evolved to address the problem, it did not solve it. The issue of competing demands for limited capability led to continuing problems. These problems were many times solved strictly by the ingenuity of the chiefs and senior enlisted personnel in finding what was required when the system could not. They regarded the problem as one of poor distribution of material that sent things to the wrong units or warehouses. Those units in turn did not receive the things their senior enlisted cadre knew were needed. The solution was simple: trade to solve both problems or steal what was required. The ability to solve a logistics problem one way or another, inside or outside the system, has always been among the many valuable characteristics of the good senior enlisted personnel in all the services.

One other oddity that a Seabee battalion had as a Navy unit in a land warfare environment was its own medical and dental personnel. The Army and Marine Corps had dedicated medical and dental units assigned to handle casualties through a sorting and evacuation process. NMCB-9 had its own doctor and hospital corpsmen, together with a dentist and dental technicians. As it turned out, I became good friends with "Doc" because of our mutual interest in sports. The battalion also had a chaplain. There were two junior line officers who were assigned to administrative functions such as special services or running the administrative office. Special services encompassed overseeing the clubs, any sports activities, or special events, like live shows, to boost morale. This rounded out the support functions.

The function of the other CEC officers became apparent when I was briefed in the battalion's operations department. They were charged with managing the construction projects assigned, preparing for future projects, and reporting our accomplishments to higher headquarters via battalion operations reports monthly. The operations officer (S-3) was also tasked to oversee the tactical disposition of the battalion with advice from the Marine advisor and make recommendations to the CO. There were several CEC officers in the operations department headed by the third-most senior officer in the battalion (behind the CO and XO). CEC officers oversaw the battalion's activities and adjusted as necessary while reacting to direction from outside the chain of command. Clearly, this function was highly personality and experience dependent as I would see play out in time.

The Wardroom

The formation of my impressions of the wardroom of officers I would be serving with rounded out my first week of war zone experiences. Other than my boss and one other officer who worked for him sharing an office with us, my contact with the other officers was limited to mealtimes, social events, and the briefings that I had received. I had always been able to size up individuals very quickly. While I did not have a perfect track record in this regard, I was not often wrong. This ability served me well throughout my personal, military, and business life. It was a key to my trust determination and the selection of those whom I had to place in key positions working for me later. For now, it was just the trust factor that was important as I needed to quickly ascertain whose advice, friendship, and assistance would be helpful to me and whose might be detrimental. The wardroom itself was typical of the type depicted in movies, novels, and other media. And this applies across the board to ships, aircraft squadrons, or rifle battalions—particularly in the days before the AVF military. There was a diversity of backgrounds, education, motivation, personality, and personal value systems that can only be created by the artificial environment caused by mandatory military service. Even my experiences at West Point had not fully prepared me for this world since all my classmates were volunteers for that experience and had roughly similar motivations (with minor variations on a theme).

What came out of this impression formation is not surprising in that there were those I determined I would not trust because they seemed self-promoting, egotistical, incompetent, or just stupid. Then there were those who were competent and trustworthy but not really candidates for close friendship. Finally, there were those who could be good friends and fun to be around. There was one officer who could be a mentor, and I was lucky enough to be working for him. Unfortunately, the leadership of the battalion in the form of the CO and the XO fell into the first group, and that was not a good thing.

Warfare is prone to long periods of boredom punctuated by short, intense episodes of frightening chaos, fear, reaction, and death. That was my experience. What follows are anecdotal memories of significant emotional events I still carry with me.

My World

The focal point of my assignment as communications/ordnance officer was the limited area of the armory, the command bunker (which housed the communications center), the ammunition storage bunkers, the communication storage and repair spaces, and finally the office that I shared with my boss, a yeoman clerk, and a third officer who served as the security officer for the battalion. This last man was responsible for the security platoon entrusted with perimeter security and reaction to enemy action. I quickly ascertained what was important, which again wasn't extensive. Keeping the radio and landline communications flowing plus the security and readiness of the weapons and ammunition topped the list of what was important. This entailed knowing the status of the equipment, weapons, and ammunition and ensuring that the appropriate repair parts, replacement equipment, and ammunition were in the logistics pipeline. Unfortunately, due to the age of the equipment, it was a long pipeline, as was the queue for ammunition for the older weapons. I was not responsible for the naval message traffic that flowed from the battalion to the outside world. This had to be carried to a message center outside the battalion to be sent and received.

My officemate the security officer belonged to the first group I described above under the category of incompetent. Literally from the time I met him, he commenced to tell me what a highly qualified warrior he was because he had enlisted in the Seabees during the Korean War. Although he had not been involved in the actual war, he had remained in the Seabee reserves after he left active duty. After college, he received a commission in the CEC reserves and was assigned to a reserve Seabee battalion. He felt it was his patriotic duty to volunteer for active duty in the Vietnam War even though reserves were not being called up. His physical presence detracted from the image he was attempting to portray as he was overweight and out of shape. The term "blowhard" came to mind. It was clear why he had been assigned to report to my boss even though they were both the same pay grade. What was not clear to me then was why such an individual would be assigned to what I felt was an important job with responsibility for the security of the battalion base camp.

The Neighborhood

It would be tedious to describe in detail the environs surrounding Camp Hoover. It was sandwiched between the air base and the headquarters for the 1st Marine Division, with several individual unit camps dispersed around us. The major landmark was the Hill 327 Exchange, the department store that provided essentials and "luxury" items. How they decided what would be sold, I was never quite sure, as the merchandise included uniform items, alcohol, stereo gear, and condoms. There was even a small section for women that looked like a man had incorrectly guessed what a woman might want. Then there was the air base that, like all Air Force facilities, was better than what everyone else had. The Air Force never saw the need to rough it, so they did not; they always had posh barracks, clubs, and even a swimming pool. There were always two F-4 Phantom fighters on hot standby at the end of the runway ready to scramble if a MIG came down from the north (which never happened) or some unit came under attack and needed help quickly. Out in the Danang harbor floated the USS *Sanctuary*, the Navy's big, white hospital ship emblazoned with red crosses. It supported our area together with the hospital at China Beach. The facility was a naval hospital until the Navy pulled out with the Marines in 1971. Then it transferred to the Army's 95th Evacuation Unit.

The most important place I had to navigate to and from in a jeep was Red Beach. It was the home of the Seabee command in Vietnam, the Third Naval Construction Brigade (3NCB), commanded by a CEC flag officer. Our immediate operational commander, a CEC captain, commanded the 30th Naval Construction Regiment (30 NCR). It was located generally north of us and was on the beach of the bay that formed Danang harbor.

Also located there were two sister Seabee battalions, the large logistics facility where construction materials were issued, and a large motor pool.

One of the major challenges we faced being so far from our direct operational boss was communicating with the regiment. The landline telephone system required us to go through so many different switchboards, the likelihood of being cut off was great. Conducting business through radios was too hard. In many cases, it was just easier to set up a meeting to work things out or send a messenger to carry a message to someone with whom we wanted to communicate. The degree of independence of the field commands was significant as was the accountability of the CO. There was no effective real time method of communicating with their superior, and COs were expected to make decisions and back-brief their boss. Severe mistakes might result in the CO being "relieved for cause" or fired. Lesser failures were reflected in fitness reports (evaluations of performance) and could lead to being passed over for promotion. Because of this, perhaps my most frequent trips out of Camp Hoover were to Red Beach to deliver messages, attend meetings, and inquire about something that someone thought was important.

The one facility that is most imprinted in my memory stood by itself at the end of the runway that we had to drive by when we were crossing the air base. It was the morgue, where every individual who died (regardless of cause) in our part of Vietnam was processed before being loaded on a plane and sent back to the United States. There were large stacks of big silver containers for that purpose outside the building. Knowing what was going on there became part of a vivid, horrific scene if one happened to be passing when body bags that had been transported in were being unloaded. Words cannot adequately impart those moments of the finality of "giving the last full measure" in a faraway land. This cost was made abundantly clear several months later when the Tet Offensive was underway. This was the highest casualty period during the entire war, and the results were there to see. Through this facility passed the Seabees of my battalion who died, the greatest number of any Seabee battalion during the entire war in one deployment.

My last general background observation, aside from the smell that would be impossible to convey, is that two things are most frequently deficient in media portrayals of Vietnam. These are the constant noise of all types that was necessarily assessed for danger and the atmosphere at night. There was a synergy of sound from the sky that was constantly filled with all manner of aircraft, the roads jammed with military vehicles, and the air rent by sirens, artillery shell and bomb explosions both near and far, weapons discharges, and so on. The camp's loudspeaker announcements were much like those that punctuated the TV show *MASH* with their unintelligible, garbled directives. Background music of every genre from rock to country to classical blared from tinny radios and robust stereo gear. This cacophony blended with fragments of thousands of conversations in all manner of languages and dialects conveyed through screams, yells, and normal conversations. Collectively, Vietnam was an auditory assault. The nighttime magnified this sensory overload, which was compounded by the eeriness of the constant flares soaring into the sky for all manner of reasons, from signals of various types to illumination used to identify suspected enemy troops lurking in the dark. Our illumination flares were fired via mortars, either 81 mm or 60 mm, and they descended to the earth slowly, oscillating under their small parachutes. The pendular movement of the flickering light bathed all below in an unnatural light and dancing shadows that made the imagination difficult to control. Fear brought constant requests to fire illumination without any real justification other than supposed things going bump in the night, and I became very aware of this. I was responsible for the illumination rounds being fired and having enough of them on hand for real emergencies. Managing the use of illumination rounds has always been a problem in combat zones.

The Deployment

In retrospect, my Vietnam deployment was divided into two parts: pre–Tet Offensive and Tet Offensive (until I rotated back to the States). The first significant event after my acclimatization to the battalion, camp, and immediate surroundings was my first convoy/visit into the "Arizona Territory" south of Danang. The purpose of the trip was to familiarize me with the detachment at Liberty Bridge and meet the officer in charge, a warrant officer. It would also acquaint me with the adventure involved in traveling on the roads in contested territory and subject to enemy action. This trip took place about two weeks into my tour and was my first real taste of the pucker factor—the anticipation, fear, and uncertainty that could range from boredom to death at the extreme. Convoys from our battalion had been ambushed and triggered mines on this route. Marine units were regularly attacked both along this road and in their various strong points along it. This was contested territory where the Vietcong (VC) moved freely at night and could mount daylight attacks if it suited their purpose and the probable cost from artillery and air attack was offset in some manner. The convoy I joined was carrying materials to be used in the construction of the bridge and supplies for the detachment camp, along with mail, movies, and other necessities of life. As I look at a picture of me taken as I completed this trip, I looked more like a Mexican bandito than an American fighting man, with my bandoleer of M16 stripper clips, flak jacket, and steel pot, but in the moment, it was a big deal to me.

I arrived at the appointed time in the motor pool to climb on board a deuce-and-a-half. Since I had no leadership role or any role at all in this convoy, I assumed the position of a rifleman in the bed of the truck, ready to add whatever firepower I could to any firefight we might get into. My mind reverberated with the instructions of the Army sergeants at Camp Buckner about how to react in an ambush: "Attack into the fire or you will die where you are!" It seemed counterintuitive to me, but years of experience had proven this to be the best course of action. The communications and weapons checks were made, along with several comments about the state of the vehicles in the convoy and the hopes they would not break down in the middle of the trip. This happened regularly. Sometimes tow trucks were part of the convoy, if it was large enough, so that broken vehicles would not be abandoned and subject to destruction or booby trapping. Ours was not large enough to merit this investment of a valuable resource.

The first part of the journey was like being on a tour bus, as we left Danang passing through the secure areas with military cantonments and Vietnamese villages along paved roads. There were Vietnamese soldiers and Marines along the way and reassuring checkpoints, but the level of alertness and readiness reflected a low threat condition. This all changed when we crossed a pontoon bridge that had been put across a stream (the permanent structure had been blown up). The result of the fight that led to the destruction of the bridge was evident in the form of a defensive position that lay in ruins. As we climbed the embankment on the far side, a sign greeted us. It read:

AMBUSH ROW
Last Ambush __1__ Days Ago
LOCK AND LOAD

Got my attention right away. We had been told that between this sign and Liberty Bridge, there were no friendly forces outside the defensive positions we would be passing through. The area was a "free-fire zone," meaning anyone we saw was likely the enemy, and we could shoot first and ask questions later (despite the ROE). No one needed to tell me twice, as this was becoming real to me.

While the remainder of the trip down and back was uneventful from an enemy action point of view, it provided me with good insight into the various Marine positions along the way, dominated by Hill 55, along with numerous smaller outposts. The positions were generally well dug in, surrounded by wire entanglements in the form of concertina wire and tangle foot barbed wire with or without M18A1 Claymore mines set to blunt assaults. There were observation towers in strategic points, cleared fields of fire for sandbagged and dug-in machine gun positions, firing pits containing mortars in the center of the position, bladders filled with water or fuel and similarly protected, and antennas for radio communications, many sporting state flags. Helicopter landing pads, numerous slit trenches to jump into to escape incoming fire, and underground command posts completed these points. Fighting positions (foxholes), were spread around the perimeter. The positions were manned at various levels based upon the threat condition. Most of the action took place at night with patrols and ambushes being set up by the Marines hoping to throw off the VC movement and prevent concentration for an attack on Marine positions or any Vietnamese village in the area. The troops on the perimeter and anywhere outside the camps were in full battle dress and armed for combat. Inside the positions, they were less decked out, but still close to their weapons, flak jackets, and steel pots as they carried out camp duties or rested for the night's activities.

At last we came to the compound our detachment shared with their Marine protectors at Liberty Bridge. There was a platoon of Marines assigned to guard the Seabees, who had weapons and would join any fight that broke out but needed to concentrate on their construction tasks during the day. Immediately the dichotomy of the situation was evident as the Marines on the perimeter of the camp in full battle dress were juxtaposed to the Seabees working on the bridge, who were in cut-off fatigue trousers and bare-chested due to the heat. What became apparent during my deployment was that the VC rarely targeted Seabees, as they were no threat to them and many times were building things that might be of value to them at some point. I also thought that they felt there would be a greater psychological effect if they waited to destroy something until after the Seabees finished it rather than waste time attacking while it was being built. The result of this situation was that most Seabee combat was collateral to VC action against the Marines or Army units stationed along the roads. Accordingly, total Seabee KIA numbers for the entire war hovered around the century mark despite the large number of Seabees who rotated through the combat zone. Unfortunately, NMCB-9 was to have the highest number of KIAs in a single deployment while I was with the unit due to the ferocity of the Tet Offensive.

I spent the day with the detachment, watched the bridge construction, and looked across the river trying to see what there was on the other side that was worth the effort of building the bridge and failing. I fired my weapons since it was a free-fire zone and I hadn't had a chance to fire them since joining the battalion. I ate a C-ration lunch out of a box. Talking to the Seabees in the detachment, their biggest complaint was that they did not get to sleep through the night most nights because of VC activity in the area. This enemy movement caused the Seabees to be called out to their defensive positions a great deal. They liked being away from the main body camp because they did not have to put up with the chicken rules the CO and XO imposed in the camp. The food was okay and life was generally good. The young Seabees and Marines I met during this adventure were impressive in their acceptance of the conditions in which they were living with danger all around. They had a job to do and did it without a lot of complaining. I returned to Camp Hoover with the empty trucks before it got dark, with one more lesson under my belt. As we were nearing the end of "Ambush Row," we heard gunfire behind us, indicating that the Marine convoy to our rear had been ambushed. That meant that we had traveled through the kill zone of the ambush without incident because the VC had deemed we were not a high-value target.

Returning to Camp Hoover, I settled into what soon became a boring routine. After all, how much work can be generated in a job making sure the ammunition and weapons are secure and that the radio equipment and phones are maintained and in working order? The men who worked for me were competent in their ratings. There was nothing for me to teach them. Aside from an occasional personnel matter, one day was pretty much like the next, dragging along and culminating in the ordeal of dinner in the wardroom after we moved to a separate facility. The arrival of the CO or the XO generally put a damper on any levity that might be going on, be it a foosball or ping-pong game or just joking around. It was evident that the lieutenant commanders, lieutenants, and warrant officers all avoided the mess as much as possible to not have to deal with the CO/XO combination unless they had to. That left the lieutenants (junior grade) and ensigns to carry on since the CO/XO duo did not want to involve themselves with the "little people" directly. They preferred to counsel their immediately subordinates in the chain of command for their shortcomings in monitoring the conduct of these wayward junior officers. The only breaks in the boredom were joining the officers' basketball team, which played in a battalion league against teams from the companies on a concrete court under lights since the games were held at night after dinner. Games were suspended for the occasional Condition 1 caused by a rocket flying over or when live shows visited the camp. Since there was no shortage of muscular, former high school basketball players in the battalion, the games were quite physical and the officiating "loose." What was hilarious was the center on our team was the doctor, a well-built, former lacrosse player at Swarthmore College, who loved physical contact. He generated business for his clinic by his physical play under the boards that sent many an opponent, and sometimes one of us, spiraling into the concrete deck.

Standing Watch and Collateral Duties

Two other duties took some of my time and provided more learning experiences. One was "standing the watch" as duty officer on a rotating basis, responsible for good order and discipline after working hours as the CO's representative. The second consisted of various collateral duties to which I was assigned as part of the myriad of administrative requirements that burdened the battalion to fulfill one Navy regulation or another. I will relate anecdotes concerning them now serially since their principal effect was upon my understanding of and future dealings with military discipline, leadership, accountability, and military justice.

My first solo "officer of the day" experience, after a practice round in training with one of the other officers, was memorable. I went about my duties according to the instructions, which entailed rounds of the various club facilities, sampling the food in the enlisted mess, inspecting the duty section that carried out various functions after working hours, reading the message traffic that came in after hours and notifying the XO of anything he should see immediately, observing perimeter security, and generally being visible. As I was walking down the main street that separated the security office where the watch section stayed from the enlisted club, I happened to look toward the main gate of the camp just as someone wearing Marine green utility trousers, combat boots, and a tee shirt jumped on our sentry and started pummeling him. I ran into the enlisted club and grabbed the two biggest guys I saw and pulled them outside with the orders, "Stop that fight!" Now this is something that Seabees like to do. They made quick work of the intruder, who had not seriously hurt our sentry but was acting bizarre. I had my deputies drag him to the security office, where I had the master at arms do a pat down looking for weapons and ID. He had neither, but he did have marijuana. I then tried to interrogate him as he became more and more belligerent. When the deputies released his arms, he immediately attacked them—to their delight—and they subdued him again. At this point, I told him if he did not cease this behavior, I would put him in chains (chains and handcuffs were part of the kit for the master at arms, as was the case with the at-sea Navy) until his disposition was settled. His behavior did not improve, and I had my deputies put him in chains and chain him to the wall in the security office. After some consultation with the duty administrative yeoman, we determined he did not belong to our battalion. I called the 1st Marine Division Military Police Battalion since he was wearing part of a Marine uniform. Dutifully, a three-quarter-ton truck with two burly MPs and their gunny arrived. He smiled when he saw the guy trussed up in chains and said he would take custody. His MPs grabbed the guy when we unchained him and literally threw him in the back of the truck and then sat on him as they drove out of the camp. This was the first time I had ever dealt with someone wasted on drugs. It made an impression on me—and no doubt him, when sobered up in the Marine brig. The affair being concluded, I reported to the XO what had happened and what I had done about it. He was glad he did not have to be involved and that it was a "Marine problem."

My other memorable duty officer experience involved a drunken first class cook in the galley. The cook rating existed then, and it described what the individual did. The cook rating was a fleet rating as opposed to a Seabee rating, and in this case, that was the root of the problem. I was sitting in the security office when a mess cook (a nonrate assigned to the scut work in the galley) came running in screaming that the cook had lined the mess cooks up and was threatening to shoot them with his apparently loaded M16 for reasons unknown. "Sir, you have to do something!" I did. I went straight to the chiefs' club, found the Marine gunny, and asked him to come with me. While we headed to the galley, I told him what I knew about what was happening. Should the cook be armed, I expected the gunny to disarm him and turn him over to his company chief. He just laughed and said, "Yes, sir."

Sure enough, the situation was as described when we arrived. The gunny asked the cook what he was doing. When he opened his mouth, it was obvious that he was drunk. The short version was he hated "fucking Seabees" and wanted to be on a ship at sea instead of in Vietnam with a bunch of Seabees and Marines that he did not enlist to be with. The gunny told him to put the weapon down before he hurt himself or someone else. Gunny told him if he didn't put the rifle down, he would have to take it away from him, and he would guarantee the cook would be hurt. The cook looked closely at the gunny and determined he did not want to test this statement. At this point, the mess cooks ran out of the galley. I thanked the gunny as he headed off to find the company chief with the cook in tow to face whatever discipline the chief deemed appropriate. I then related the incident to my boss, Bob Schroeder, and asked him how this should be documented/reported in the logbook. He allowed that it would be best to just indicate there had been a disturbance in the galley, and the cook had been sent to his berthing area while the details were reported to the company chief. He said the cook was a good one, and the battalion did not need him in the brig. The less of the details the XO knew, the better. That is how it was reported, and I heard nothing more about it.

I had two collateral duty experiences that are worth relating. The first was the audit of the chapel fund by the chapel audit board, consisting of the supply officer and me. He told me my job was to run the calculator to make sure the figures came out accurately. As he went down the list of deposits and debits in the ledger, he came to one entry that read, "Missionaries to Stone Elephant [the Navy officers' club in Danang] for dinner," accompanied by an exceptionally large dollar figure. Considering food was dirt cheap and one would think missionaries would not have a large bar bill (if they drank at all), the supply officer asked the chaplain how many missionaries he took to dinner—twenty? There was an exchange that was beyond lame and left the supply officer pissed off; however, that was nothing compared to what happened when we proceeded further down the ledger and found a similar entry for an equally ridiculous amount. After some colorful language, the supply officer took the ledger and told me I was dismissed. He asked the chaplain to accompany him to see the XO and then the CO. I never knew what transpired, but the chaplain was on a plane back to the States in a day or two, and I had witnessed a chaplain, of all people, being fired.

The second lesson involved a court-martial. In those days, military lawyers were involved in only the most serious cases. Offenses that were not of serious enough magnitude to warrant a GCM (things like murder, grand larceny, rape, treason, desertion, etc.) were handled by either a SCM, special or summary court-martial, or captain's mast. Officers of the battalion handled them all without the benefit of lawyers since their intent was to preserve good order and discipline and ensure justice was done. I had gone to the NJS and received training to be part of this process, and I found myself assigned as the assistant defense counsel in a special court-martial of a Seabee accused of taking a swing at his chief during a Condition 1. The operations officer, a lieutenant commander, was president of the court, and the members were other lieutenants that were not in the individual's chain of command. It was open and shut since the Seabee admitted he did it because he was drunk. He was found guilty and sentenced to two months in the Danang Marine brig. What was remarkable was what he told me when he was released, after having served the entire sentence. He said he would never go back to a Marine brig again alive. Not only had the Marine guards punished even the most minor of perceived offenses harshly, but he had also been placed in a cell with two Marines who had been convicted of "fragging" (murdering) an officer. They told him they would kill him if he said or did anything they didn't like. He said, "Sir, I didn't say anything for two months except as a direct answer to a question and generally as a 'Yes' or 'No.'" The purpose of a Marine brig was not to reform the inmate but to make sure they never wanted to come back again. He had learned his lesson, and I had learned mine: military justice is not civilian justice—and it cannot be.

Leadership, Personality, and Consequences

Over the next few months leading up to the Tet Offensive, I lived through several events that reminded me a lot of the things that happened aboard the USS *Caine* in Herman Wouk's famous World War II classic study of leadership, personality, and consequences, *The Caine Mutiny*. They were lessons about what *not* to do when dealing with subordinates in the future. One of the things I came to understand over the years was that the term "pattern of misconduct" meant that an individual act might not be that bad, but the weight of a continuing string of acts usually became extremely detrimental. Accordingly, those that I have chosen may seem trivial, but their cumulative impact was not. The first was taking my first naval message to the XO for him to sign out to higher headquarters, in this case the Department of Ordnance, relating the status of the ammunition

Bill's boot camp graduation, December 30, 1939. Bursting with pride!

USS *Nevada* beached at Pearl Harbor, December 7, 1941.

Max Lee and Bill Shelton, high school classmates, in front of the Royal Hawaiian Hotel on Waikiki, Fall 1941.

Funeral services aboard the USS *Enterprise* following Santa Cruz Islands action where Max Lee was killed. Bill is in the front row of the band, third from left.

Bill and Vicki Shelton wedding photo, May 20, 1944.

Mike, age 4 months, with his parents, Portsmouth, New Hampshire.

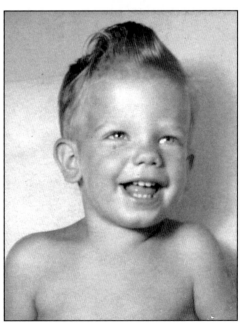

Mike Shelton, age 2, 1947.

New brother Charles, New Hampshire, Spring 1947.

Mike during a visit to Dillier's Farm, 1947.

The Shelton family after arriving in Cuba, February 1948.

Above: Early diversity, Mike's birthday party in July 1948.

Left: Charles and Mike helping Dad fish in Cuba, 1950.

Mike and Charles at Isle of Palms, South Carolina, Spring 1951.

Charles and Mike, May 1951.

Mike's first grade class, 1951-52, Sullivan's Island, South Carolina. Mike is pictured front row number five from right.

Mike and Charles visiting the Illinois farms in 1951.

Shelton family photo at Christmas 1951 before the death of Charles in August 1952.

The last family photo at Dillier's Farm shortly before the death of Charles, August 1952.

Bill's return from Korean War deployment prior to the family moving to Alaska.

Patrol boy, 5th-6th grades, Washington, DC. Mike is in the top row in front of the police woman at far right.

Vicki Shelton pins the Eagle Scout Award on Mike, May 1959.

Mike and Dad after high school graduation, shortly before departure for West Point, June 1963.

H-1 Plebes, 1963

Mike in his full dress gray uniform for a parade during his Plebe Year, 1963.

Plebe Christmas 1963 … lots of snow!

Christmas dinner in Washington Hall with Jim Haas' family, December 1963.

Mike with roommates Jim Haas and Dennis Mikale, Plebe Year, Christmas 1963.

Completing RECONDO at Camp Buckner, Yearling Year, 1964.

Mike with Yearling roommates Joel Matulys and John Kuspa, H-1, 1964.

Room ready for inspection, Fall 1964.

Mike, Yearling picture, Spring 1965

Mom and Mike as he returns to West Point, Christmas 1965.

D-1 First Class, 1967

Mike Shelton and Kenn Harris playing on Trophy Point, Firstie Year, 1967.

Mike and Bob Libutti, full dress white, Fall Firstie Year.

D-1, under Woody Held's coaching Firstie Year, was runner up in brigade intermural basketball out of 36 teams. Mike is second from the left, first row.

Mike, Howitzer First Class

Ready for the graduation parade.

Graduation parade, the day before graduation. The Class of '67 received review from underclassmen.

Mike being commissioned in the Navy Civil Engineer Corps the morning before West Point graduation ceremony.

Dad, Mike, and Mom after commissioning on Graduation Day.

Class Dismissed! Hats thrown in the air. Cadet days are over!

50th Reunion photo, D-1 brothers. Pictured l-r: Bill Cusack, Bob Libutti, Kenn Harris, Woody Held, and Mike Shelton. Still laughing after 50 years!

we were holding. This message contained no verbiage but was a series of columns with batch numbers and inventory numbers of the various types of ammunition we had in our bunkers. As near as I could tell, it was pretty much the same message the battalion had been sending quarterly since it arrived in-country. The only differences in the numbers were the expended ammunition and flares. My senior gunner's mate prepared the message, and I checked it against previous messages and the records of expended ordnance. When I was satisfied that there could not be a mistake, I presented the message to the XO and described what I had done to ensure it was accurate.

The XO could either trust me, or he could do all the research required to prepare the message himself to ensure it was correct. He did neither. He threatened me by saying that if he received any indication that there was an error in the message, my naval career would be over. Apparently, this was his standard threat to everyone and was designed to yield perfection. Even to a lowly ensign, this was a self-defeating methodology. First, it assumed that everything was of equal importance, requiring a high degree of thoroughness and capable of perfection, and second, that an ensign with a few months of service had a naval "career" worthy of torpedoing. I already knew neither was true, so I just said I understood and left the message with him. It was sent with no consequences, as were all the subsequent messages and correspondence that I prepared for signature, except for my understanding that no one was trusted to do their job even though they had done nothing to merit such a lack of faith.

Following this was the infamous "Condition 2" incident. As I have noted, when I checked into the battalion, I was required to read the "Rules of Engagement" sheet and acknowledge my understanding by signing it. One section of this document dealt with the description of readiness conditions. There were only two conditions specified—Condition 1 (under imminent threat of attack or actual attack) and Condition 3 (normal operations). My hut-mates and I were surprised one evening when the loudspeaker blared out "Set Condition 2." We talked amongst ourselves and determined that we did not know what that meant, and it must mean something for the duty section. We went back to whatever we were doing. About fifteen minutes later, one of the duty messengers came to the hut and told me to report to the CO in the command post (CP). The CO asked, "Didn't you hear the announcement that Condition 2 had been set, Shelton?" I replied that I had. "Then why didn't you do it?" My West Point training kicked in, and

I barked, "No excuse, sir!" I then received a royal chewing out, along with several others. This whole episode played out in front of the XO and a handful of others who were in the bunker at the time, including my radioman (who was on watch). I was ordered to report to the XO the following day with a written explanation of my actions, then I was summarily dismissed.

I was in a panic and went to my mentor for guidance. Somewhat to my relief, he said he had no idea what Condition 2 was nor did anyone he had talked with. The plan we came up with was that my written explanation would say that I was at fault because I had not read the instruction that defined condition 2 and would correct this as soon as I could find a copy of the instruction. I would ask the XO where I might find the instruction since no one I had talked with seemed to know where it was—then take the ass chewing for being a stupid, incompetent ensign. I did all this. What I did not expect was that the XO reached into his in-box and pulled the instruction out that he had apparently written and run by the CO but had not distributed to anyone else. The CO had come up with the idea to have a Condition 2 drill, and the XO did not tell him that no one knew what that meant but them. I read it. My only responsibility was to come to the CP to ensure the communications nets were in readiness in case of attack. Condition 2 was just an increase in the level of readiness caused by some indication that there was a possibility of the enemy doing something. What? The enemy always "might" do something, so I was not sure what this meant, but left it unquestioned. The XO said the instruction would be distributed shortly and apparently did not see anything wrong with whole affair. I just hoped that my protective coat of being a stupid ensign and not expected to get anything right would save me at report card or fitness report time. I reported all this back to the lieutenant who told me to forget it.

As I mentioned, the landline telephone system ended with EE-8 field phones that connected to the switchboards where operators routed the calls. During one of the Condition 1 incidents, the CO became upset that he could not talk directly to one of the fighting positions on the battalion perimeter. The system was set up so he could talk directly to the company commanders, who would provide him information and carry out his orders. After months of this working fine, it was no longer acceptable for some unknown reason. The CO decided that he wanted to be able to talk to each fighting position directly. This, of course, was stupid on so many levels as to boggle the mind. To start off with, if he could talk to them, they could also make calls, and that would create chaos—the system would be jammed by this lack of controls or ability to sort out the important calls. The switchboards could not handle the volume, and the entire system would collapse. From a practical standpoint, the battalion allowance of this phone was designed for the system we had in place. There were not enough phones or switchboards to begin to do what the CO wanted. When the CO ordered me to set up what he wanted, rather than pointing out this could not work and risk another ass chewing, I decided that the fact we did not have enough equipment to do this should carry the day. I was wrong. He yelled that he didn't care what the allowance was; I was to get whatever he wanted and have it set up within a week. Since this happened in the early morning hours, I decided to consult my communicators in the morning and discuss the best course of action to carry out the CO's orders, after reporting the unhappy situation to my lieutenant.

The next morning, after talking to the lieutenant, his direction was to make sure there were no EE-8's available through normal supply channels in the foreseeable future and discuss the options my men might come up with later with him. I met with my guys. Of course, they already knew what had happened since one of them was on watch in the CP when the CO gave his order, and they told me they had a plan. They would get the required number of phones and *I did not need to know where or how.* There was some vague mention of cumshawing or trading for them, but they let me know they had the problem to solve and not to worry about it. All they needed from me was to check out a three-quarter-ton truck from the motor pool for their use. Big test for me: would I trust my men and let them handle this or demand details that I might not want to know and end up with no phones *and* pissed off subordinates? One good thing about being so junior was I did not have a career to worry about yet, so I got the truck from the motor pool and gave it to the leading PO. Later that afternoon, he came into my office and asked me to come outside. He pulled back the tarp in the truck bed, and there were the required number of phones. Emblazoned on the side of each were the initials USAF (United States Air Force). "Of course, we'll have to do some maintenance"—by which he meant painting—"before they're ready for installation." I asked how long it would take to set up the system as the CO wanted. "Two days, sir," he replied. "It'll take that long to run commo wires to each fighting position and set up the necessary switchboards."

I reported to the lieutenant that my men had resolved the EE-8 problem; he did not ask how but indicated that two days was fine for setting up the system. He said he would be on hand when the CO tested it.

The two days passed slowly as I knew what the result of all this work was going to be and did not relish being in the CP when it was tested. My men dutifully installed the phones and tested each one to ensure they were installed correctly and functioned as they should. Company commanders were briefed on the new setup and to make sure their men knew to stay off the new system unless under attack or if they were called. A dry run somewhat worked because not all the fighting positions were filled since that would require pulling men from their work sites, which was a nonstarter. The only way a real test would happen would be during an actual Condition 1. This happened within a week and was a disaster, as the lieutenant and I knew it would be. The paranoia of the shadows in the dark led a significant number of the men to believe they were going to be attacked, so they decided they had to report what they saw. The system melted down, and there was now no communication at all. The CO was livid, and I think only the presence of the lieutenant saved me from a terrible fate, whatever that might be. After the CO had vented, the lieutenant asked if he could talk with him alone to offer a suggestion. Nothing more was said.

The next day, the lieutenant told me to put the system back to the way it was without further explanation. Nothing more was said—except by the junior officers, who howled at the CO's folly. I'm sure similar levity at his expense happened among the chiefs and enlisted men, not to mention my communicators, who had been exercised for no good reason. After some time had passed, my leading PO related to me how he had gotten the EE-8 phones. "Was like taking candy from a baby. We just went to the airbase, reconnoitered, found where there were offices with the phones we needed, and walked in and told them we were there to do a PM (preventative maintenance) on one phone at a time and would return it as soon as we were done to do each of the others in the office. Since there was more than one phone in the offices we chose, no one thought anything of it. We got the phones we needed without any real harm to the Air Force." This was the first time I had been saved by the men who worked for me, but it would not be the last over my career. Many of the biographies I have read about highly successful officers in the past (across all the services) contain similar anecdotes from their days as junior officers. Lesson learned: *Take care of your men, and they will take care of you.*

Another lesson from this experience was that no one really knows what a unit in a war zone needs until the unit is in the war zone and the needs become apparent. By that time, the system that is in place to provide equipment is too onerous and nonresponsive to meet the needs in a timely fashion. A perfect example of this was the fact that Seabee battalions were not authorized to have M2 .50-caliber heavy machine guns (affectionately called "Ma Deuce" by the troops) because these machine guns were classified as offensive weapons. Seabees do not participate in offensive combat operations; hence, they have no need for offensive weapons. The reality was that the Marines and Army fitted their trucks with .50-caliber machine guns for protection in convoys while the Seabees had none. Solution? Our problem-solving chiefs talked with the Marine sergeants and a trade ensued. We gave them construction items and help that they needed but could not get—such as plywood, concrete, lumber, electrical wiring, and the like—and they gave us .50-caliber machine guns and ammunition because they could obtain them with little trouble; they wrote them off as combat losses. Our trucks were modified, and everyone was happy except the bean counters and bureaucrats who did not have to live and survive in a war zone. As with the EE-8 phones, I learned that asking too many questions about where things came from was a bad idea if those things improved our ability to perform our mission. Sometimes less knowledge is a good thing.

Death

Within a couple of months after I arrived in the battalion, it suffered its first personnel loss. It was a noncombat death. One of our young Seabees had the day off and went with a group to Red Beach near the brigade head-quarters for an afternoon of swimming and a beach party and somehow managed to drown. The exact details of how this happened were never clear to me since there were lifeguards and markers indicating the safe swimming area, but it happened. His body washed ashore a few days later and was recovered. I always thought these deaths were the most tragic of all for a host of reasons, not the least of which was they were almost always preventable, tended to be the result of carelessness or stupidity on someone's part, and should not have happened. For the family there was not even the solace, such as it might be, of losing their loved one in combat in what they can picture as a heroic death fighting for his country, instead losing him to a stupid accident. We lost one other Seabee in a construction accident when he fell from a piling on Liberty Bridge and broke his neck. As one looks at the statistics from any war, the number of noncombat deaths from accident or disease is much higher than one would suspect because the military population is young (relatively speaking), with better reflexes and overall health than the general population. Luck, timing, circumstances, location, and—most especially—leadership play significant roles. Well-led and disciplined units tend to have fewer accidents because the chain of command is planning and looking out for the root causes of accidents, one of which is bad assumptions.

There was one other noncombat death that had a significant effect on me during this deployment; it occurred after the Seabees' birthday. The relationship between the Marines and Seabees is a close one. On the Marine Corps's birthday, Seabees manned the Marines' defensive positions so they could celebrate. On the Seabees' birthday, the Marines—who happened to be from the 1st Marine Division Band—reciprocated. After the celebrations were over that evening, the Marines were loading up in their trucks to leave. There was suddenly a gunshot, and one of the young Marines fell dead with a bullet through his head. Apparently, he reached up to get help to climb into the truck bed, grabbing a fellow Marine's rifle for a handhold. Unfortunately, that Marine had not only forgotten to unload his weapon, he also did not have the safety on and must have had his finger on the trigger (guns do not fire themselves). You can see where this is going: the rifle discharged, killing the Marine immediately. This experience forever imprinted upon me that there are never enough precautions when handling weapons to ensure they are safe. While the civilian world has its share of needless deaths in automobile and other types of accidents, losing a life overseas in a war zone in this manner is a special kind of tragedy.

Security Officer

A few months later as Christmas approached, I was assigned a new duty in addition to my primary job. Summoned to the CO's office, I found the CO, XO, and my lieutenant waiting. Without explanation, I was told that I was now the commander of the security platoon, replacing the blowhard lieutenant that had the job. It was emphasized how important this job was and that I had better not screw up. Once back in the office, the lieutenant explained what had happened. My predecessor had decided he needed to teach the platoon the correct method of throwing hand grenades and had taken them out to the observation post. It was above the camp overlooking Happy Valley (as we called it)—pretty much contested territory from which rockets were fired at the airbase. Once there, he had gone to the perimeter, explained that to throw the grenade one must pull the pin while holding the safety spoon down, determine where to throw it, release the spoon, and count two seconds before throwing the grenade, in order that the enemy would not be able to have time to pick it up and throw it back. He then demonstrated this technique, all of which was quite correct. Unfortunately, he failed to check out the area where he was going to throw the grenade to make sure there was no one there. As it so happened, there was a crew of Seabees repairing the concertina wire out in front of the bunker. Someone shouted, "Grenade!" and everyone out there dove for cover. Fortunately, only one Seabee received a minor wound from the explosion, but the possibility for much worse, including fatalities, sent the CO and XO into a rage that resulted in the lieutenant being fired and me getting his job.

One would think that security being important in a war zone, the caliber of those assigned to the platoon would be high. One would be wrong. Indeed, it was just the opposite. As I got to know the members of the platoon and its chain of command, I discovered it was filled with individuals who had been fired from the construction or equipment companies for various reasons and were thus available for this nonproductive job. The POs were the weakest leaders in the battalion. Most of the time these men were assigned to man the guard towers and gates to the camp to sound the alarm should they see something suspicious. What I soon discovered was that many of them fell asleep while on watch. This is a serious offense under the UCMJ that is punishable by death during wartime in a war zone. After making the rounds of the perimeter with one of the senior POs on successive nights and not being challenged by the sentries, I got the whole platoon together and read the article of the UCMJ. I described the crime of a sentinel asleep during wartime to them, emphasizing that death was a possible outcome. Most were unimpressed, and I resolved to increase the frequency of the chain of command rounds of the posts in hopes of keeping them awake. Those making the rounds made as much noise as possible, hoping to wake them up if they were asleep. This approach yielded some success when it counted (which will be described later), but the quality of the troops never changed.

The CO and XO continued to provide amazing examples of the worst kind of leadership. Some things were just laughable, such as the way the enlisted men played them to get what they wanted. For example, when the first class and second class POs wanted to have a live girly show in their Acey-Deucy club, they invited the whole wardroom. They made a big deal out of giving the CO and XO the best seats in the front row, so they could provide the proper "leadership and monitoring" of the show to ensure proper standards were maintained. Of course, there was not much the CO or XO was going to do to stop a show in progress, but the play on their egos worked fine. After all, the CO was a "man of the world" (or so he thought), and the XO would not do anything if the CO was there enjoying himself. The show featured popular music and hit songs sung by scantily clad, young Filipina women, in some semblance of English. A striptease dance ended the show, with the most talented performer twirling the pasties on her breasts in opposite directions at the same time. The audience, except for the XO, loved it.

Leadership by Example

Another event illustrates the absurdity of what passed for leadership. One day, every member of the wardroom was summoned to a meeting. This included the detachment officer in charge from Liberty Bridge, who had to travel all the way back to Camp Hoover. When we were all assembled, the CO came in and began working himself into a lather. He had a piece of paper that looked like a letter in his hand and was waving it at us. He said he had been reading the weekly correspondence file that was routed around for the chain of command to see; it contained copies of the correspondence that had been sent out of the battalion. He discovered the letter in his hand contained a "dangling participle"! This was a total disgrace to the battalion and him personally since he was responsible for everything that left the battalion. The WO sitting next to me leaned over and asked me what the hell a dangling participle was and how bad could it be.

The CO said that because of the proven ineptitude of the wardroom, he was withdrawing "by direction" authority from everyone except the XO. This delegation of authority to sign for the CO is given to various individuals to process the voluminous correspondence of any unit. Nothing could be signed by anyone but the CO and the XO. I happened to notice a fleeting smile on the supply officer's face as this was being said. This would not affect me since I did not sign much correspondence that left the battalion. However, the volume of documents that left the supply department in the form of requisitions and orders for supplies and materials, not to mention all the personnel actions of a unit with over a thousand men, was staggering. The next morning the supply officer had his clerks deliver literally box-loads of requisitions to the XO's office, while mounds of paperwork were coming down from the admin office as well. The XO freaked out and ran screaming to his boss. The CO exploded, and we had another hasty meeting in which he explained that he was sure "we knew" what he meant and were deliberately misconstruing it. By direction authority was restored to most of the routine staff areas and eventually back to everyone who had it before. One officer did retain a draft of a letter he had submitted that the CO had marked up in an apparent frenzy. Every single word had been struck through with a red pen except one "the." He was proud of that letter and his "the."

One of the biggest events in every tour of duty in Vietnam was going on R&R for a week out of the war zone. This had been done right, and there were R&R locations all over the Pacific, including Hong Kong, Singapore, Taiwan, Australia, Bangkok, and Kuala Lumpur for personnel to go to rest, get drunk, get laid, and forget about the war for a week. Hawaii was an attractive choice for those who wanted to bring their wives or girlfriends over to meet them. The flights were free to military personnel in-country, and reduced-rate flights, accommodations, and meals were available for dependents coming. Naturally, the most desired and sought-after week for R&R in Hawaii with a wife and perhaps family members was Christmas week, so the allocation of the limited number of seats on the R&R planes was very tight. In fact, the quota for our battalion of more than a thousand men was just one space. In a move that reflected just the kind of leader, officer, and man he was, the CO took that space for himself—much to the disgust of the entire wardroom, not to mention the chiefs' community. *After all, COs can do what they want, and that's what he wanted.*

Two additional memories of that Christmas come to mind. I experienced what many servicemen and women had since World War II—the Bob Hope Christmas Show. Looking back considering today's largely narcissistic entertainers, it is hard to imagine the selflessness of Hope and his troupe entertaining the troops for so many years around the world over the holidays. There are, of course, entertainers, athletes, and others who go overseas to entertain now, but nothing that matches the Hope spectacle in meaning or scope. I was so far back that it took binoculars to see the stage, but we could hear very well. One of the battalion photographers was given access remarkably close to the stage and got some amazing, if tasteless, pictures of the scantily clad women, especially Raquel Welch. Hope's jokes were corny but heartfelt, and the troops loved it all. I cannot guess how many troops were there, but it had to be more than ten thousand—it was like a rock concert. Well behaved and grateful, the dutiful troops enjoyed a bit of home and forgetting what lay in store for them after they left.

The other memory was the battalion receiving its quota of the small Red Cross packages that had been put together by school children back in the States and sent to the troops in the war zone. I do not think this happens anymore, but I remember our grade school doing this during the Korean War. We were all assigned to bring items such as toothbrushes, soap, hard candy, washcloths, instant coffee, and other things that were not perishable and useful in the field. Accompanying these small packages there was usually a handwritten note from the youngster who had assembled the package. These notes were priceless, with their best wishes, commentary, and sometimes admonitions to "Kill lots of Japs!" as there seemed to be confusion as to who the enemy was. We wrote a letter and sent it back to the school expressing our appreciation for their gift.

While my feelings toward the CO had not yet developed into contempt, there were other members of the wardroom who had already crossed that line. One was at the point of leaving the battalion for his next assignment, which was to be in the Pentagon. I remember his comments in the wardroom bar and hoped that the CO or XO did not walk in during one of his commentaries. He had been in the battalion under the previous CO, who had a reputation as a fine leader and had led the battalion through deployment to Vietnam and combat. The previous CO was the antithesis of the current CO, and this fellow junior officer was not shy about pointing this out.

My momentous year of 1967 ended rather quietly, with no hint of what was in store for the U.S. military in Vietnam or more specifically, for me. One of my communicators had regularly come to talk with me whenever something was about to happen that he wanted to be a part of: a road convoy, establishing a new detachment, or just a chance to get out of the battalion area. In later years, the character of "Radar O'Reilly" in the movie and then TV show *MASH* reminded me a lot of my radioman. He always knew what was going to happen before it happened and unselfishly volunteered for dangerous undertakings since he knew he was the best communicator. Invariably, I would go to the lieutenant and ask if some scuttlebutt was true. He would respond in the affirmative and ask how I knew since it was supposed to be on a "need to know" basis. I mumbled something or other and attempted to change the subject. In this case, my radioman had informed me that we were going to send a large detachment north toward Hue to develop a rock quarry that would provide aggregate for the rehab and expansion of Highway 1 going from Danang to the DMZ.

The major roads were being improved with asphalt, making them harder to mine and more weather-resistant—not as susceptible to the monsoon rains that made many of the roads impassable. This would require setting up a secure camp for the Seabees to operate from in Indian Country. I went to several meetings with the Marines where the security of this large detachment was discussed. The Marines agreed to send a platoon of infantry, which seemed like a joke to me since we were sending over a hundred Seabees. The detachment would be established early in the new year with an LDO lieutenant as the officer in charge (OIC) and called "Detail Echo." It would be subjected to the most direct enemy action of the deployment.

Chapter Four

THE ELEPHANT FINDS ME

Ensign SHELTON applied a pressure dressing, suppressing the flow of blood, and remained with the shipmate who was alternately fainting and struggling making it impossible to move him to a mortar hole for protection. Though fully exposed to the enemy attack and with complete disregard for his own safety, Ensign SHELTON remained with the shipmate thus saving his life.

—Navy Commendation Medal
with "V" Device citation

The deadly elephant crept up on us shortly before Detail Echo departed for Phu Loc on the road to Hue that would become a major battleground in the coming Tet Offensive. A Vietcong soldier crept close enough to one of our security posts guarding a helicopter repair facility project near Red Beach to throw a hand grenade into the bunker. EONCN Harry G. Hodges shielded the force of the blast from EON3 Joseph G. Stotko, while attempting to throw the grenade from the bunker. Hodges was killed instantly when the grenade exploded, and Stotko was wounded.

Hodges was our first battle casualty and led to yet another low point in the front office leadership. When the facts of what Hodges had done became known, we all assumed he would be recommended for an award for heroism, but we were wrong. When this issue was brought up with the XO, he reportedly said that this Seabee was only "doing his duty" as we all would have done and, therefore, did not deserve an award. When this was reported to my lieutenant, he immediately went to the CO to protest. The result was the Marines were consulted regarding the appropriateness of an award and replied that Hodges's selfless action should warrant at least a Silver Star, if not a Navy Cross or higher. The CO put Hodges in for a

Bronze Star, but the Navy Awards Board subsequently elevated this recommendation to a Silver Star, and that medal was presented to Hodges's family. The wardroom resented the cavalier manner with which the leadership had disregarded what this Seabee had done. The only good news was the announcement that the CO had received his orders to depart in February.

Tet

Tet arrived with a "bang, not a whimper" on February 2, 1968, with a shower of mortar shells falling near our observation bunker on the line of hills behind our camp. Detail Echo had departed to set up its new camp on January 20. We spent most of the next two weeks in Condition 1 as the rockets rained down on the airbase, and the VC attacked the various outposts guarding Danang and particularly the approaches to the airfield.

Among my most vivid memories were the AC-47 "Spooky" gunships (also called "Puff, the Magic Dragon"), World War II–era cargo planes armed with a trio of 7.62-mm Gatling-style miniguns that fired up to six thousand rounds per minute. This awesome firepower was designed to break up enemy assault forces, and I witnessed Spooky in action circling south of the airfield and firing on the VC who were attacking from that direction. At night we could see the tracers arcing down to the ground in a solid stream, giving the appearance of an invisible giant taking a lethal piss on the enemy. The whirring roar of the miniguns reached us a second or two later. There was every manner of flare in the sky, with the sounds of artillery and small arms fire at varying distances in all directions. It came across as the countrywide operation that we ultimately learned it was. The response was quick and devastating despite the negative reporting the media was feeding the public in the States. The VC units were being destroyed with tremendous casualties. The South Vietnamese were not rising to join them against the government forces and the Americans as the North Vietnamese planners had hoped and counted on. To be sure, U.S. forces were taking their highest casualties of the war, but the ratio of losses was lopsided in our favor. No major unit was overrun or defeated during the entire Tet Offensive. The daily cost in American lives was clear to see as the body bags were transported to the morgue facility on the airfield.

At one point, the VC attempted an all-out attack to get to the airfield from the south. We watched as the prop-driven A-1 Skyraiders took off almost vertically from near the middle of the field to escape enemy fire and then came right back down dropping their ordnance not far off the end of the runway. The combination of the A-1s, helicopter gunships, and Puffs beat back the attacks on the airfield and the LST ramps at the south end of the Danang Bay, not to mention the substantial defensive positions. I went by the LST ramp for some reason the morning after the initial attack and saw how far the VC had gotten, as their bodies were in the concertina wire in front of the last line of defensive positions. Many lay in the fields in front of the positions, burned beyond recognition, probably by napalm, or blown apart by the Gatling guns. Seeing this and then reading the articles in the *Stars and Stripes* newspaper about our defeat by this surprise attack brought the realization that the media reported what it wanted without much regard for the facts. I was struck by two things: a respect for the VC's courage in the face of certain death while carrying out a "forlorn hope" and the awesome power of American armed forces when properly deployed and led. I would never underestimate my enemies or neglect planning to use every asset available to protect my men in a contingency in the future.

The scale of the attack and the around-the-clock Condition 1 even got the attention of my security platoon manning the perimeter guard towers. They were not sleeping on duty now! On the contrary, they kept reporting seeing all manner of the enemy, and that required verification. These often proved to be spurious, but not always. One such report prompted me to visit the guard tower reporting a sighting, where to my great surprise, I saw what appeared to be armed individuals moving around in the rice paddy between our camp and Dogpatch. I hustled back to the CP to report what I had seen to the CO. I recommended that we call the Marine's First Shore Party Battalion located just down the road from us since they were the reaction force for the area and trained to deal with this sort of thing. To my astonishment, he said he did not want to do that but was going to send a patrol of Seabees to investigate what was going on. He called one of the line construction companies and ordered the company commander to send a squad, armed and in battle dress, to the CP for instructions.

All our radios were deployed around the battalion area, so none was available for the patrol. When I pointed this out, the CO said to take one of our commercial radios that we used in the jeeps for local communications and give it to the patrol. The fact that these radios did not mesh with the military frequencies like medevac, the fire direction center for supporting fires and flares, and others did not seem to concern him. Additionally, the squad from a line company would not have a corpsman assigned. I asked the CO if I should get one from the aid station and he said, "Do it." I found my friend, Doc, and explained to him what was happening. He said he would send his best corpsman just in case. I remember feeling bad about the whole thing, as it was being put together in such a slapdash manner. Why were we taking on this mission when the nearby Marines were tasked to do this? The Seabees' combat mission is exclusively defensive in nature. They are not supposed to do combat patrols despite what some John Wayne types might want to say. A reconnaissance patrol is particularly difficult; it is fraught with danger and not something for amateur hour. Despite all this, we were going to do it.

The patrol assembled at the CP, and the CO's instructions to the squad leader were as simple as they were stupid. They were to spread out on a line down the road to Dogpatch and then sweep across the rice paddy in front of our camp, reporting what they might see. This they did. I stood on top of the CP, along with the CO and a couple of others, to watch what was happening. After a few minutes, we saw someone jump up and start running away from our men. The squad leader radioed the CO and asked, "What should we do?" I could not believe my ears when the CO ordered, "Chase him!" It was a well-known VC ploy to do things like this to lead troops into ambushes, and that is exactly what happened. Our Seabees did not get far before an enemy machine gun opened up on them; two of the Seabees were hit by this barrage as the rest of the patrol took whatever cover they could find. We could see the corpsman making his way to the wounded men through the firing and start working on them. While the men were pinned down, it was hard to tell exactly where the enemy was, and firing back was complicated because the airfield was on the other side of the Dogpatch. We would be firing into it if we fired from our perimeter, as the VC well knew. The squad leader called in for direction. He reported that one of the men was seriously wounded. The CO told him to stay put until we could extract them. He turned to me and told me to go get Doc.

I ran to the aid station where I found Doc and some of the corpsman trying to see what was going on as they had listened to the firefight. I told him what had happened, and Doc grabbed his medical bag and ran with me back to the CP. He reported to the CO who promptly ordered him to run out in the rice paddy and "save those men!" The CO was clearly freaked out, but Doc calmly pointed out that he had sent the best corpsman in the battalion with the patrol, that the corpsman had the situation under control, and that he was the only doctor assigned to the battalion and was responsible for all the Seabees in the camp. The CO glared at him and said, "I'm giving you a direct order to go to those men. If you refuse, I will consider court martialing you for insubordination." He then looked at me and said, "Shelton, you're my witness." Doc simply said, "Yes, sir," grabbed his medical bag, and ran down to the main gate of the camp. He sort of crept across the road, and then made a mad dash toward the pinned down patrol. How he made it without being hit I will never know, as the machine gun bullets were kicking up dirt all around him. He radioed in saying that the gravely wounded Seabee needed to be medevaced immediately. As it had been monitoring the radio traffic, the reaction platoon from the Marine Shore Party Battalion was moving toward the sound of the guns and was just arriving on the scene. The Marines quickly deployed and began to outflank the VC. In a short time, the whole affair was over, and the VC attackers retreated leaving no casualties on the field. Due to the volume of enemy action that night, it took a while for a medevac copter to arrive and take the Seabees out of the field. All the while the battalion was a witness to this entire episode.

This needless grandstanding play by the CO, with its tragic results, had a profound effect on me and was always with me throughout the remainder of my career. The idea that a man like this could be given command astonished me. As the years went by, I found that many are given command for a host of reasons that have nothing to do with their competence as leaders. I did not know what I might be able to do about it in the future, but I resolved to try to find a way. I also resolved to be even more diligent in steering clear of the CO while he remained in the battalion and hoped nothing like this happened again before he left. Fortunately, it didn't. The change of command occurred at the appropriate time, and the final irony to this eye-opening experience for me was that the CO not only received an award for his performance of duty as CO but was also selected for promotion to O-6 (captain) in the CEC. What a travesty! It was a good lesson for me to take along about relying on the system to police itself.

New CO

Less than two weeks after this incident, the new CO arrived in a "change of command." We soon found that he was a "Seabee's Seabee." Perhaps the system in its infinite wisdom was trying to make up for what we just had with someone who knew something about Seabees and leadership. We knew very quickly that the new CO was a different animal from what we had been experiencing. The first night after the old CO left our camp, he came into the wardroom bar and asked who oversaw the bar. For propriety reasons, the doctor was the bar officer. The new CO then asked him to make him an Old Granddad and water. The doc took a water glass, put some ice in it, poured in a couple of fingers of bourbon, and started to fill it with water. The CO yelled, "Stop!" He said the doc was ruining his drink. He took it away from him and proceeded to fill the glass with bourbon to within an inch or so from the top, the combination then being about four-fifths bourbon and one-fifth water and ice. He then hoisted the glass and drank it straight down. While we were recovering from our shock, he told the doc that henceforth there should be a bottle of Old Granddad placed in a spot he indicated on the bar and that this bottle was his and his alone. His custom was to drink about half of that bottle before and during dinner and then take the rest with him to his hooch for the evening. While all this was going on, he was chain-smoking unfiltered Camels to the tune of two or three packs a day. I had been introduced to someone out of the mold of my father's hard-drinking, hard-living buddies from World War II.

We went into the dining room where he surveyed the formal table configuration and bluntly pronounced, "This is crap." He wanted the tables broken up into tables for four; he said his officers would be allowed to sit wherever they wanted, with whom they wanted. His only direction was that he wanted a particular table to be designated for himself, but anyone who wanted could sit with him. The look on the XO's face was priceless! The junior officers were won over instantly—they liked his style. I would add that there was never a visible effect resulting from the quantity of bourbon the "Old Man" consumed; he was always "bright-eyed and bushy-tailed" the next morning or if we were called out for a Condition 1. We concluded that he had developed an incredible tolerance for bourbon and Camels, and perhaps that was what fueled his engine, or he did not actually have a liver or lungs!

Shortly after he arrived, we saw the new CO dealt decisively with problems. One night during a Condition 1, our blowhard lieutenant (the one I had relieved as security officer), having been banished from participating in the Condition 1, freaked out for some reason and came running into the CP babbling some nonsense. He was dressed in pajamas with his flak jacket over them. He was wearing his steel pot, but the helmet liner had fallen out, so the pot rode low on his head, blocking his vision. As he hit the top of the bunker stairs leading down into the bunker, he tripped and rolled to the bottom of the stairs in a heap. The CO took one look and told us to get him out of there immediately. The next day, the lieutenant was sent back to our homeport in the States as unsuitable for war zone duty.

The Tet Offensive was still going on, although it was diminishing in intensity, but as February slipped into March, enemy action continued to find our detachments. On the 23rd, VC sappers detonated charges, damaging the south timber abutment and approach to Liberty Bridge, and a stockpile of lumber was set on fire. There was plenty of enemy action in the Arizona Territory. Since 1968 was a leap year, for some reason it was decided to open the Detail Echo quarry on February 29, the extra day that year. I flew up to the airfield at Phu Bai in a C-123, a twin-engine aircraft designed for operating on short runways, to visit my men at the quarry. For those who have not had the experience of riding in one of these airplanes, it is like flying in an aluminum boxcar with engines strapped to the sides; the noise is incredible and the comfort is nil. To make matters worse, the approach pattern into Phu Bai was still under occasional fire from the VC since it was the closest airfield to Hue, where there had been heavy fighting. This led to a thrilling landing as we made an almost vertical descent into the airfield from about three thousand feet, pulling up just in time to manage the landing. I was happy to be on terra firma. I was picked up and driven to the Seabee battalion camp outside Phu Bai, where I would hitch a ride with a road convoy down to the detachment (det).

The trip to the det was uneventful. I was struck by the number of bridges the Marines had to guard to keep the road open. The Combined Action Platoons (CAP) monitored these structures, as well as the hamlets that dotted the road. Each CAP was made up of a thirteen-man Marine rifle squad (augmented by a Navy corpsman) partnered with a platoon of Vietnamese militiamen drawn from the local Regional Forces or Popular Forces (RF/PF, or "Ruff-Puffs"). This was part of the Marine Corps Combined Action Program, which was a remarkably successful counterinsurgency tactic. The Marines trained and equipped the Vietnamese and were quartered in the hamlet, thus gaining their trust. This "hearts and minds" civic action approach paid dividends in denying the VC local support. The evidence of the recent fighting was all around, as the VC had probed for weaknesses, hoping to destroy the bridges and attack the hamlets.

Detail Echo

As I arrived at the det's camp, I noted that it was sited at the bottom of a large hill that was being quarried into. There was some logic to this arrangement as the heavy equipment and trucks needed to haul the aggregate had to be protected inside the wire. Still, locating a camp at the bottom of a hill that we did not control seemed to me to be an invitation for trouble. A short distance away, the Marine security platoon had set up its camp. Both camps were surrounded by concertina wire and dug-in defensive positions with cleared fields of fire. It was mid-afternoon by the time I arrived, and I threw my combat gear, rifle, flak jacket, steel pot, and other equipment in the officers' and chiefs' tent. This was a squad tent that had cots and room for approximately ten men depending upon how it was laid out. I went to find my men.

I carried my pistol on my web belt, along with my canteen, two extra magazines, and the standard combat first aid kit. We had planned to use Conex shipment boxes as the ready-made storage and repair spaces for the ordnance and communications equipment. I saw that they had been dug in, and the ammunition storage locations were appropriately placed in proximity to the defensive positions and the pits that contained the 81-mm mortars that constituted our heaviest defensive firepower. A command bunker that would also serve as a casualty clearing station had been dug in and was where my communications equipment was set up to provide the necessary link to the outside world. My men had done their usual exceptional job of improving on the original plans for camp support and executing them. The feedback I received was the improvements were integral to the operation and much appreciated. My main concern had been that they were the correct men to be in such an environment and were functioning effectively. Subsequent events validated their selection. The men were happy to see me and brought me up to speed on all that had taken place setting up the quarry and camp.

One of the things that sets Seabees apart from other units is that a battalion's equipment allowance contains field galley equipment to provide hot food for the troops in the field if there is a large enough component to justify the setup and there are no other facilities available to feed the troops. While Marine, and later, Army units, with whom we operated in the field, lived for extended periods on boxed C-ration meals one, two, or even three meals a day, our Seabees generally had a hot breakfast and dinner with a C for lunch. Having a galley made the Seabees extremely popular with the Marines and the Army units nearby, who were always looking for handouts to supplement their Cs. Our cooks did a superb job of feeding the Seabees in primitive conditions and tried to support visitors as well as possible. As it was now the evening meal hour, I waited until the men had gone through the line. I got my tray of food and a drink and walked over to my temporary quarters to eat and chat with two of the chiefs who were there. There were two officers assigned to the det—an LDO lieutenant and a warrant officer with a heavy equipment background—to run the quarry operations. They were supported by a few chiefs whose task was to supervise the various functions within the camp, such as equipment maintenance, security, administrative tasks, construction, and so forth. The lieutenant happened to be gone somewhere during my visit. I sat down on the cot I was to sleep on, which was about three feet across from one chief, while the other was sitting diagonally across from me on his cot. We started to talk and it happened.

Two things followed in rapid succession: a sense of something passing between the chief and me like a blur and my body lifted and thrown across the tent like a rag doll. I heard a loud explosion and felt the attendant concussion. Somewhere a disembodied voice yelled, "Incoming!" As is true of many such traumatic incidents, although it happened in an instant, I experienced it in slow motion. My mind raced as it struggled to determine what was happening—I felt surprise, fear, terror, and uncertainty simultaneously. I landed in a heap, unhurt as far as I could tell, and rolled out of the tent as I sought cover. All hell had broken loose with explosions, automatic weapons fire, shouting, screams, and general pandemonium. I looked back at the tent to see the chief who had been sitting diagonally across from me stagger through the opening and stand there in a daze. I jumped up and tackled him to get him down and lessen the possibility of being a target. In addition to a barrage of small arms fire, we were also being targeted by a 57-mm recoilless rifle. It is a direct-fire weapon: the shooter aims directly at the target, as opposed to indirect-fire weapons, such as artillery or mortars, whose shells do not travel in line of sight.

In combat, time is fluid; it is at variance from the physical phenomenon of seconds passing on a watch and is not measured by the participants in that manner. Beyond a swift-ass guess, I could not honestly say how long this action lasted, but the things that happened while it was ongoing replay in my head like a slo-mo video on a loop. I see myself with my knee planted in the chief's chest to hold him down and keep him from struggling as I tried to determine the source of the blood that was rapidly saturating his shirt. It was pulsing through a small hole in his shirt sleeve, which was symptomatic of arterial bleeding. My mind jumped to a first aid lesson from my Boy Scout days concerning arterial bleeding and how fast death occurred by bleeding out. Ripping the sleeve open while I looked around for some help, I saw the other chief whom I had been talking with moments before. He was sheltering in a nearby defensive position in a daze. He did not respond to my yells, and it was obvious he was in shock. The noise from the explosions and gunfire was blotted from my consciousness, as I opened the combat aid pack on my web belt and pulled out the compress dressing, so I could concentrate on stopping the bleeding. While still holding the chief down and telling him to be still and he would be all right, I wrapped the dressing around his arm and made a tourniquet that stopped the blood flow. Just as I thought he was calmed down, he started struggling again, and it took all the strength I could muster to keep him down.

The action continued as I focused on our men and the Marines who were returning fire. I decided we were better off where we were than bringing attention to ourselves by moving. When the noise started to abate I yelled, "Corpsman!" and one responded within minutes. He stabilized the chief and called for a stretcher to haul him to the CP, which now doubled as a casualty clearing station. Once they were gone, I went over to the other chief and walked him to the CP; two F-4s arrived on the scene, having been called for early in the attack by my radioman.

The scene was like watching a wide-screen war movie. The first of our planes made a low pass over the hill trying to determine where the enemy was. The second plane then came down and dropped a couple of napalm bombs that lit up the side of the hill, followed by two more from his wingman. I could feel the heat on my face. This ended the enemy attack completely. I often marveled as I later read that the U.S. military must unilaterally destroy napalm weapons since they were inhumane; those making this claim had likely never been in a situation in which napalm broke the enemy's will to fight. I wonder now what a difference this weapon would have made in the mountains of Afghanistan.

Another war-movie scene was playing out in the clearing station, where the senior corpsman was separating the casualties by the seriousness of their wounds. This is called triage and is performed by medical personnel in circumstances where resources are limited and must be allocated most efficiently. Those who require extensive treatment or those whose wounds will likely be mortal are set aside for evac to a field hospital to allow medical personnel to work on those they can stabilize. My chief was the only seriously wounded casualty, and a medevac chopper (also known as a "dust-off") was already on the way, having been called by my commo man. I helped the corpsman get an IV into the chief, which proved to be difficult as his veins were hard to find. While this was going on, another Seabee, who had been slightly wounded by shell fragments, was screaming that he was dying and needed the corpsman to drop what he was doing and save him. This was still going on when we got the IV in and the chief was stabilized. At that point, the corpsman went over to the screaming Seabee and in a calm voice said: "You are not dying, but if you don't stop scream-ing, I might kill you myself." This, coupled with the no-nonsense look on his face, had the necessary effect and the screaming stopped.

By now it was pitch dark with no lights marking our position, and the medevac chopper called in for landing instructions. The combination of the hill location, the limited landing area surrounded by concertina wire, and the inky-black darkness made a landing extremely hazardous. This information was passed to the pilot. He simply said to have someone stand in the middle of the landing zone with a flashlight, its beam pointed straight up, and others doing the same at the four corners of the area. He said he would land in the spot so marked, relying entirely on us to guide him. The pilot expertly put his bird down on the makeshift landing zone, and I helped carry the chief out and hot-load him into the CH-46, which immediately lifted off. No one who ever witnessed the medevac crews in action, taking amazing risks to save the lives of our troops, will ever forget it. Their skill was matched only by their legendary bravery, and they deserve all the praise they received and more.

The rest of the night passed without incident or sleep as we calmed the men, assessed what we could of the damage in the dark, and reported what had happened to the appropriate commands at Camp Hoover. The next morning I was still being powered by adrenalin as I further surveyed the damage for my report to the CO. The tent where the foodstuffs for the field galley had been stored had been blown apart, and there were canned food and cooking ingredients spread in a comical array from that loca-tion. There had been no damage to the key equipment for the quarrying operations, so all in all, the attack had accomplished little for the enemy (aside from the personnel casualties) and would not hinder our operations at all. I went back into the officers' and chiefs' tent. The full realization of my incredible luck became apparent. There was the tent siding through which the recoilless rifle round had come and the shrapnel had gone. The light from the morning sun passing through the perforated canvas made it possible to see the location of every hole. I sat where I had the night before and marveled at the silhouette where the shell fragments had left the tent unmarked; I realized they had missed me by a matter of inches, and my escape from a body bag had been nothing short of miraculous. In the days to come that experience returned to my mind again and again as I tried to sort out a meaning from this. I was in a bit of a funk; I suppose this might be called PTSD today.

The trip back to Camp Hoover was without incident. I was picked up at the airfield by one of my men and went to my hooch to drop my gear before going to the CO's office. My uniform was covered in the chief's blood, making me a ghoulish sight I'm sure, but I wanted to make my report and then grab some sleep as the adrenalin was beginning to wear off. The CO greeted me with concern and was anxious to hear all that I reported. I made special mention of how the men had performed so well, particularly my radioman and the corpsman. When I had finished, he said he had sent Doc to the Naval Hospital China Beach to check on the chief. He was happy that I was OK and that operations had not been affected. It was short and professional with just the CO, my lieutenant, and me in attendance. I went back to the hooch, took a shower, and collapsed into a deep sleep that lasted most of the day. That night at the wardroom everyone wanted to know what had happened, so I recounted what I had seen. Doc reported that he had seen the chief and talked with the doctors in the hospital. The chief would recover but had been lucky, as he had nearly lost too much blood according to the hospital docs; he was going to be sent back to the States to recover. I had a couple of stiff bourbons (following the CO's recipe) and tried to put it all behind me.

Return North

There was no time to dwell on what had happened at Detail Echo as my boss informed me I would be returning there within the week as part of the first major resupply convoy since the Tet Offensive had started. Highway 1 was reasonably secure, and a large convoy (fifty-five vehicles) with overflight protection from choppers and vehicle assistance, in the form of tactical wreckers capable of towing any disabled vehicles, should not have any trouble. I was to be assistant convoy commander, which landed me the good deal of riding with the rear guard of the convoy and reporting the progress of the end of the convoy to the convoy commander at the head of the column via radio. The next six days were spent preparing for the trip.

This was the first time I had been up Highway 1 over the Hi Vann Pass through the mountains at the northern end of the Danang Bay to Phu Bai.

The road up over the pass was unpaved, relatively narrow, and had many switchback curves. As we drove along, I looked down the steep drop-offs and saw trucks, jeeps, and other vehicles lying in a heap at the bottom. They were the victims of ambushes, and their bullet-ridden and shell-ripped cabs and windows bore that testimony. The view from the pass was spectacular, and we talked about how this part of Vietnam could be a resort area after the war due to the beautiful beaches and lovely scenery. As we rolled north, the rice paddies and fishing villages along the coast looked much like what I had seen coming south from Phu Bai to Detail Echo only the week before. The convoy was well defended; choppers flew back and forth along the route patrolling for any sign of enemy activity. We pulled into the camp in the late afternoon, and the men quickly started off-loading the trucks and storing the supplies and construction materials. The plan was to spend the night and take the empty trucks back to Camp Hoover the following morning.

I talked with my men and tried to get a feel for how they had adjusted to the attack less than a week before. Their bravado was belied by their nervous chattiness and would be further tested by subsequent events. Coming back up the stairs of the CP after a conversation with my radioman, I ran into the chaplain, who had flown up the day before to spend some time with the det. As we stood on the top of the CP surveying our camp and the adjacent Marine camp, we heard *thunk, thunk* sounds from the direction of the hill, and the chaplain said something like, "I didn't know we were firing the mortars tonight." I barked, "We aren't!" As the cries of "Incoming!" echoed throughout the camp, we saw one of the tents in the Marine camp disintegrate from a direct hit by a mortar round. The sound of a mortar firing is very distinct, and they were close enough that we were able to react and most of us found cover; however, there were wounded— two Seabees and a Marine. We once again had to call in a dust-off for one of our Seabees.

There was little damage from the attack on the camp and equipment since these weapons lob their rounds in a high-arching trajectory and require adjustment of fire to bring it "on target." That did not happen. This was apparently more for harassment purposes than anything else, and the initial barrage was not followed by additional fire. Another relatively sleepless night followed with all of us up early the next morning for the trip back to Danang. It proved uneventful except for two things: some firing of indeterminate origin toward the tail end of the column and our passing of a brigade from the 82nd Airborne that was moving north on Highway 1 toward Hue. This brigade had been sent to Vietnam as reinforcements in response to the Tet attack. It contained several of my West Point classmates, who were among the first of our class to arrive in-country. Sadly, within a few weeks, the first of my twenty-nine classmates to die in Vietnam was killed in action while on a patrol. More would quickly follow. Two of my roommates from D-1 were killed in May; they had not been out of the Academy for a year. The awful list would continue to grow, and it included one more of my D-1 roommates.

Perhaps because of these continuing attacks, the Marines moved an 8-inch artillery battery to our location to provide support and conduct fire against the VC. The consequences of this move played out at the end of the month.

Before I left with the convoy, I experienced some good-natured ribbing of the "gallows humor" type that is so prevalent in every war zone. Some of the other junior officers were joking around with me due to my previous experience at Detail Echo. "Can I have your stuff if you don't come back?" and "Where are your keys so we can open your locker and see if you have anything good?" This happens a lot but does not make the highlight reels—it is a "you had to be there" moment. At any rate, when the word got back to Camp Hoover that the det had been hit again and that there were casualties, with no further information about who was wounded or killed, there was some big-time puckering in the junior officer community until I made my timely appearance. Then it was all a joke again. Such is the way it is and always will be when warriors need to relieve their tension.

Sometime around the middle of February, I received notification that I had been accepted at the University of Illinois for graduate study in civil engineering. Before I joined the battalion, the assignment office had asked where I wanted to go to grad school. I had read a book that evaluated graduate programs, and it listed Illinois as the best civil engineering graduate school in the country. It was also located about seventy miles from my grandparents' farms, so I decided to see if I could get in. My second choice was Stanford, which was also very highly rated. I was never sure how I got in since my undergraduate grades were not that great; I figured it must have something to do with the Navy's influence. In any case, I was ordered back to the States shortly before the battalion was due to redeploy to Port Hueneme so I could get to Illinois for the start of summer school.

Tragedy

March 31st was a Sunday, and the CO decided to hold a personnel inspection since the battalion was getting a half-day off anyway. This would add to that time by not making the men travel to the work sites and back. I was the duty officer and, therefore, excused from the inspection. As I was wandering around the camp watching the inspection take place, one of my men came running up and breathlessly reported, "Sir, you're needed at the CP ASAP!" He said it had something to do with Detail Echo, and we double-timed back to the command bunker. I trotted into the bunker, and my radio operator handed me the written message he had just copied down from his conversation with the commo man at Detail Echo. It was a coded message transcribed in the SITREP (situation report) format that was used when reporting enemy action. Of greatest importance was the part of the report that listed casualties. My eyes immediately locked on the lines that reported KIA and WIA (wounded in action). The numbers in those two lines were five and six, respectively. I told the radioman to make commo with the det again, as I wanted to confirm this for myself before I had to relay this terrible news to the CO. As this was happening, I scanned the rest of the SITREP for more details. They were limited, as the format did not permit much latitude. What I managed to glean was there had been at least two mortar attacks during the previous night, with one coming not too long ago. Five men had been killed in the second attack. I talked directly to the radio operator at the det and asked him to confirm each line in the message report, which he did. I then immediately ran out to find the CO.

I ran up to the platoon the CO was inspecting and waited for him to recognize my presence. When he did, I saluted and told him I needed to speak with him privately immediately. I was not about to blurt out the news in front of the troops. He knew this was something bad and walked away some distance with me. I made my report, handing him the written report while giving him the highlights and telling him that I had called the det and confirmed each line of the message. This was the largest number of Seabees that had been killed and wounded in a single action in Vietnam to date, so the magnitude of the occurrence was momentous. He studied the SITREP and then calmly said, "I have to get up to the det now. Order a chopper and let's get this show on the road." I responded in the affirmative, saluted smartly, and took off back to the CP, moving with a purpose. The bird arrived within the hour; the CO and a few others, including the chaplain, climbed aboard and off they went. When the news got out, the battalion was in shock, and the fact that we really had no idea what happened at Detail Echo only compounded the effect.

When the CO returned later that day, he filled us in on the details. There had been some twenty-five mortar rounds fired into the camp in the early morning hours while the men were sleeping, and six Seabees had been wounded, one seriously, and he later died while being medevaced to Danang, bringing the total KIA to six. Our Seabee mortar crews returned fire, along with the Marine 8-inch battery. At approximately 0710, a second attack was launched, with ten mortar rounds and recoilless rifle fire hitting the camp. Two rounds landed in one of our mortar positions instantly killing five crew members, while seriously wounding the sixth. While it would have been more satisfying to believe that our boys courageously repelled this attack, I never believed that. Many of the Seabee casualties in the Vietnam War were the result of attacks on the Marine or Army units in their vicinity. Artillery positions were always a magnet for attacks since they had the greatest effectiveness against the VC and NVA troops thanks to their accuracy and lethality. I always believed our men died because of poor shooting by the VC as they tried to attack the 8-inch guns nearby. Whatever the cause, this tragedy left each of us diminished by the losses. There were four more attacks on Detail Echo and the Marine units before the camp was turned over to the battalion that relieved us. Although there were no Seabee casualties in those actions, it is interesting to note that an 8-inch gun was damaged by a direct hit.

Back to "the World"

For the last month I was with the battalion, I was acting S-2, as my lieutenant had taken the advanced party back to Port Hueneme to prepare for the coming redeployment of the battalion. This did not add much to my other duties and mainly involved going to the 1st Marine Division intelligence briefings and reporting back to the CO anything I thought might be of interest. At these briefings I was struck by two things: first, the small-unit actions launched by concentrated VC forces that occurred almost nightly at the various bridges and hamlets being defended by CAPs; and second, the reports of Marine Force Recon teams operating deep in VC and NVA territory. It seemed to me that the Marines sometimes hazarded their units without a great deal of support, whereas the Army was sometimes almost paralyzed by its buildup of supporting units before it acted. I filed this away for future use.

There was one more bit of unpleasantness before I left that I would carry with me the rest of my career. As I was getting ready to leave, I wanted to make sure my men were recognized appropriately for their efforts during the deployment. This consisted mainly of writing up performance evaluations and, in one case, writing up an award recommendation for performance I considered significantly over and above what could be expected of a third class petty officer. That individual was the radioman I had sent to Detail Echo; he had volunteered for every dangerous assignment—be it road convoys, detachments, and so on—and performed in an exceptional manner. The awards manual stated that awards were to be recommended for actions significantly above what could be expected of an individual at their pay grade, particularly in combat situations. From what I had observed, especially of the XO, there was little expectation of anything from junior enlisted personnel, so what this man had done seemed to really stand out as far as I was concerned. To me, this man qualified for a Bronze Star, and I wrote up a recommendation for same and submitted it to the XO along with my performance evaluations on my men.

The result was the worst ass chewing I received during my entire time with the battalion. The XO was irate that I could recommend any enlisted man for an award since he considered them so inferior, stupid, and generally beneath him. He told me that the only time one of them did something that appeared to be brave was out of "fear for their own necks" and never for their fellow Seabees or the unit. "Discipline," he declared, "is about creating fear in the troops to make them perform. Never forget that, Shelton." The performance recommendations were inflated and what he might expect from a green ensign. He would personally redo them to ensure they were in line with his expectations for enlisted evaluations. It was all I could do to control my temper and get through this sickening episode. I wondered if this was the way the rest of the Navy was. Unfortunately, it was more in line with Navy thinking that I could have ever imagined.

The day before I left the battalion to fly back to California, I met with the CO to receive my fitness report. Given the ass chewing I had received from the XO and the fact that the XO prepared the draft fitness reports for the CO, I had no good expectations. I had received a report from the previous CO when he left that was good but not great, comparing me well with the other ensigns with only one rated above me. Since I was the most junior, it seemed fair to me. This report turned out to be particularly good, and it meant a great deal more to me as the CO praised my actions under fire and my handling of all the assignments I had been given. I was sure that he had written it himself. I could not know then that I would be seeing him again years later in another Seabee battalion when he was the chief of staff for the Pacific Seabees.

Somehow it seemed appropriate that my last night of this tour in Vietnam was interrupted by a Condition 1, with rockets raining down on the airfield. I did not participate; in fact, I slept right through it. There had been a going away party among the junior officers after dinner, and I had exceeded my quota of bourbon. When I got back to my hooch, I passed out in my rack. The next morning my head was pounding as I said my final goodbyes to my men and my fellow officers and was driven to the airfield. Nearly a thousand servicemen were killed in Vietnam on their last day in-country—strange, but true. Airfields were prime targets, so the pucker factor and tension did not dissipate until that big Boeing 707 lifted into the air. The cheering inside the plane was deafening, and there were more than a few teary eyes. To say I had a life-altering experience during that tour of duty is such an understatement it is hard to quantify. Some of the effects were immediate and clear, while others were subtler and became apparent over time. What was truly clear to me was I loved being with Seabees and wanted to serve with them again. The synthesis of the good and bad leadership I had observed at West Point and in the battalion was coming together to shape what I thought an officer should be and how I intended to act in the future.

The postscript to this profound experience occurred several years later. Management and leadership gurus had become the rage in business in the '80s, and one of the widely acclaimed books in this burgeoning field was *In Search of Excellence* by Thomas J. Peters and Robert H. Waterman, Jr. I had been meaning to read it but hadn't gotten around to it. As I was walking through an airport during my first Seabee command tour, I noticed the book—with its tagline, "Lessons from America's Best-Run Companies." I picked up a copy and flipped through it, finally turning to the back cover, where I saw a familiar face: *that's Tom Peters!* He was the junior officer I mentioned earlier, the one who had served under a great first CO in NMCB-9 as well as the one I had served under when I arrived; he was outspoken in his comparisons of the two. Since I had experienced the same phenomenon, only in reverse (having served under the great CO second), I thought it was interesting that we shared the same view of our Vietnam leadership initiation. It was a verification of my observations on leadership, and here was Tom Peters, now a recognized expert on management and leadership. I bought the book and read it. I sent a note to Tom (who I was sure would not remember me) and said tongue-in-cheek, "If I had known that all I had to do was keep a diary of my observations and convert it into a book to become famous, I would have." I never expected to hear back, but I received a nice note from Tom saying there was a lot of truth in my comment about converting his observations of how *not* to do things in leadership into his successful books and consulting career. A seed had been planted.

Chapter Five

JOURNEYMAN YEARS

*We are mere journeymen, planting seeds for someone else
to harvest.*

—Wallace Thurman

The dictionary defines the term "journeyman" in two ways: "a worker who learns a skill and then works for another person," and "a worker, performer, or athlete who is experienced and good but not excellent."[11] Both of these definitions apply to my years of service from my return from Vietnam in 1968 until I was promoted to the rank of commander in 1981. When I was running the CEC Assignment Office years later, I addressed groups of officers who were newly selected for promotion to lieutenant commander and commander. I emphasized that there was a required transition of technical, leadership, and management skills that must be achieved as one moved through a career as an officer if one hoped to continue to be promoted. A junior officer is being trained technically and in leadership and management skills. The successes achieved are generally the result of individual efforts to ensure the tasks are done or micromanaging the efforts of a limited number of subordinates to make sure goals are achieved as directed. Moving up the responsibility levels in any organization forces a transition to jobs where it is impossible for the individual to personally perform the assigned tasks; leaders must manage the efforts of their subordinates to achieve them. Some are weeded out at this stage because they cannot manage the efforts of others and either try to do everything themselves and fail or micromanage others to failure.

The concept that an individual tends to rise to the level of their incompetence was discussed in Dr. Laurence J. Peter's book, *The Peter Principle*. This has been all but forgotten in today's sensitivity-plagued world in which folks are told they can be anything they want, regardless of intelligence, social skill, or management abilities simply because they are "special." My observations confirmed this principle, and I learned to take it into account throughout my career. All the jobs I had during this period were things I had never done before, so I was learning a skill while working for another person. I would say I was experienced and good but not excellent, but this background was essential foundation for what I was going to achieve as a more senior officer, particularly in command.

After an emotional homecoming with my parents and some leave at home, I drove across the country to Illinois to begin my graduate education. I checked in at the University of Illinois's Naval Reserve Officer Training Corps (NROTC) office. I wore my uniform, as this was what I had been taught was required. I did notice the strange looks I received from the students as I passed them. I had been oblivious to the anti-war sentiment since San Diego was a Navy town, and there had not been any manifestation of it there. When I got to the NROTC office, I was told it was not necessary to wear my uniform while I was going to school; indeed, they preferred that I did not. I learned that I had been promoted to lieutenant (junior grade), having completed one year as an ensign—and that meant an all-important pay raise. I was told to check my assigned mailbox at least every couple of weeks, and I was tutored on how to fill out the graduate school tuition and book bills so the Navy could pay for them. Taking the hint about the uniform, I left and changed into civvies before I went over to the civil engineering department to check in and meet my advisor.

I had received a letter from the professor who was to be my advisor and had an appointment with him set up for the day I was reporting in to the NROTC office. He had been a CEC junior officer in World War II and was now one of the heavies in the civil engineering department who advised all CEC officers. He asked me if I knew a certain CEC officer who had completed his program a few weeks before I arrived, and I said that I was not acquainted with the man. He then proceeded to tell me that this officer was one of the most brilliant students he had ever encountered, having graduated at the top of his class at Annapolis, and that he had just completed all the coursework for a PhD in the absolute minimum time possible and received straight As. He asked: "Would you like to take overload courses so that you can repeat this course of action?" When I said I had no interest in a PhD and was sure I could not compete academically with my predecessor, the light faded from his eyes.

Summer school taught me I was not ready to go back to school. Vietnam was still in my head, and I could find little motivation for studying or going to class. I did meet several active duty military officers who were getting advanced degrees, many of whom had also just returned from Vietnam. We were so different from the student body, both undergraduate and graduate, that this fact became readily apparent to me. I also realized that failure or not getting a degree was not an option and that I had to buckle down to accomplish that goal, but that did not make it any easier.

Throughout the summer term I spent a lot of time studying, and more blinding flashes of the obvious came to me. First, the courses I was taking were highly theoretical and probably great for PhD candidates but had little to no practical value that I could see. Second, the population of the graduate program was overwhelmingly foreign males, mainly from the Third World—India, Pakistan, Korea, the Middle East, and so on. I had little in common with them. Many of the American graduate students were active duty military officers, several of whom were Army officers heading back to West Point to teach cadets. There seemed to be a relatively small number of civilian, native-born American graduate students in civil engineering and very few women in the engineering college at all.

There were many brilliant people at the University of Illinois, both professors and students, but I found an alarming number could not carry on a normal conversation with non-academics—they just could not relate to them at all. This reinforced my observation at West Point that the correlation between being "brilliant" and having common sense was a slim one. Far from being a positive endorsement, the terms "brilliant" or even "very intelligent" were a warning sign to reserve judgment pending further analysis.

I had it out with my advisor early in the next semester. The precipitating event was his insistence that I take a graduate course called "Vibration Analysis of Structures." It was about designing multistory buildings that resist motion from earthquakes, wind, snow loading, and other forces of nature. Since the Navy had very few multistory buildings and that was not likely to change, I could not see the point. After one particularly fiery session, my advisor threw in the towel and told me he would approve any courses I wanted from here out if they led to a master's degree in civil engineering. After I mucked my way through that semester, things began to look up. I was on two-year orders that were not tied to my academic endeavors, so after I received my degree at the end of summer school, I spent the next year taking courses I found to be interesting and felt would be of benefit to me.

One of the subtle changes that happened to me in Vietnam that I was not aware of at the time concerned my attitude toward women. Whereas before I went to Vietnam I was not looking for a permanent relationship, when I came back, I seemed to be driven to find one. Perhaps it was the unhappiness with school in general or some subliminal desire to procreate brought on by nearly being killed. It also had to do with the number of unsatisfying dates I had experienced and unsuccessful attempts to find someone to bond with since I had gotten to Illinois. I had nothing in common with the girls in my grandparents' farm town. Nor did I have anything in common with the college girls that I was meeting at Illinois, undergraduate or graduate. I was introduced to the sister-in-law of a fellow CEC officer whose background was totally different from mine. She had a job (as opposed to going to school), and she was attractive, funny, and a good cook. That seemed like enough basis for a marriage to me at the time. We ended up getting married a little over a year after I came back from Vietnam—much to the disappointment of my parents. As I look back on it, this marriage was doomed from the start due to "irreconcilable differences," but we worked at it, had a beautiful daughter together, and finally divorced as the differences were just too great. It was another important learning experience.

Midway through my second year, my assignment officer called to discuss my next assignment; frankly, I had not given it much thought. He said, "Since you did not complete a year in-country with the battalion, that tour didn't count. You are going to receive orders for a one-year tour in 'Nam." I almost got killed, but that didn't count? He said that I could not go back to the Seabees and asked what other type of job would I be interested in. I replied I did not want to be in Saigon for one of those staff puke jobs; I wanted to be doing something in the field. After about a week, he called me back and said, "I have the perfect job for you, but it's highly classified, so I can't tell you much about it." He said he had talked to two officers who had done the job—including the man who had it now—and they both confirmed it was a great assignment. All he knew was it was in the field working with "some Special Forces types." He added that while my orders would indicate that I was stationed in Saigon, that was not in fact where I would be. "So, do you want it?" Without hesitation, I replied, "Absolutely!" and he started processing the paperwork for my top secret clearance.

A final significant event occurred shortly before I left for my second tour in Vietnam. It was the public reaction and demonstrations in the wake of the Kent State shootings by the National Guard. From the study room that all the military engineering students shared atop an old engineering building across from the student union, we watched as the Illinois National Guard was deployed to quell the rioting and damage to property that was taking place nearby. As the crowds started to press in on the guardsmen and it was beginning to look like another Kent State event, a truck with a powered speaker rolled up with an announcement. Under the laws of the state of Illinois, when the governor declared martial law, the National Guard had authority to "shoot to kill" if they suspected crimes might be committed. The voice on the loudspeaker said the governor was declaring martial law in ten minutes. The students did not want to test this edict, and the crowds dispersed. The riot was over, but not the ill will.

The media's coverage of the war had convinced the public that our troops were the bad guys. Whether or not our soldiers' mission in Vietnam was good or bad was not the issue to me. These Americans were only doing what they had been ordered to do, yet they were being condemned for it. Soldiers don't pick their wars, politicians do. When I went to Australia on R&R, I experienced something quite different: older Australians who remembered the Japanese onslaught in World War II came up to me and thanked me for my service with a "Good on ya, Yank!"

Black Ops

My second tour in Vietnam was not as traumatic as the first, but it was a major learning experience nonetheless. My orders to report to the Military Assistance Command Vietnam (MACV) Studies and Observations Group (SOG) in Saigon had come through. I flew from Travis AFB to Saigon with appropriate stops along the way. I was taken to the SOG headquarters compound and spent a few days there being briefed before I left for my real destination—Naval Advisory Detachment (NAD) Danang. In Saigon, I signed all the draconian paperwork stating that the briefings I was getting about the actual classified mission of MACV-SOG were above top secret and talking about them to those without proper clearance would result in unimaginable punishment. They were pretty eye-popping, but the key thing I took away was we had our own budget that was virtually unlimited, and we merited the highest priority for our supply requests. We had our own dedicated air force; our birds were painted black and were bereft of markings. I was assigned to the principal Navy detachment of MACV-SOG; my assignment was to be the public works or facilities officer responsible for all the facilities and automotive equipment associated with these black ops warriors.

Arriving in Danang in a "blackbird,"[12] as we called our special operations airplanes, brought an overwhelming sense of déjà vu. Visually, I did not see a lot of change from when I had left just two years before. The lieutenant that I would be relieving picked me up and took me to Camp Fay, the detachment installation near the Navy base called Camp Tin Shaw below Monkey Mountain and close to the port and logistics facilities. The living facilities were better than those I had experienced at Camp Hoover; they were like the quarters in the SOG compound in Saigon. Given the briefing I had received about no budget limitations, this was hardly a surprise. I was not allowed to wear my Seabee greens; rather, I was issued the standard Army Olive Drab green jungle fatigues with the addition of a Vietnamese military rank insignia pinned to the front for identification to our allies. No unit patches were allowed, though we did wear rank insignia.

After dropping my bags, I was taken to meet my new boss, who was an officer in charge (OIC), as opposed to a CO, for some reason that I never really understood. He was a Navy commander (O-5) with a surface officer background and, as I found out, no experience in clandestine operations. Everyone below him, from his assistant OIC, an LDO O-4 and World War II UDT veteran, through the operations staff, were SEALs, Marine Recon, or Army Special Forces. There was also a "special boat" detachment, with a mobile training team (MTT) from Coronado that maintained the boats that were the centerpiece of our detachment. They were Norwegian-built craft called Nasty–class patrol boats, and they were capable of speeds above fifty knots. They looked a lot like World War II PT boats, complete with plywood construction, although they had no torpedo tubes. Instead they were heavily armed with a Bofors 40-mm gun (later replaced by an M2 .50-caliber machine gun with an 81-mm mortar in piggyback configuration) and two 20-mm cannons, one on each bridge wing, plus smaller-caliber machine guns.

Déjà Vu

Once again, my meeting with a new boss set off alarm bells from what he said, how he said it, and comments the officer I was relieving made. This put me in the defensive mode as I turned over with my predecessor and became acclimatized to the new job. The one positive thing my new boss told me was that while I was en route to Danang, the CEC Lieutenant Board had reported out, and I had been selected for O-3. He promoted me on the spot, and I soon had a nice pay increase together with combat pay and reduced income taxes. I was told to come back later for the detailed briefings on what the detachment really did and was reminded of the papers I had signed about the secrecy of the mission.

The officer I was relieving was going back to the States for a short assignment before he left the Navy for other opportunities. Although he liked the job he had, he was not crazy about some of the people in the command and made sure I knew who and why. He explained that I would have a public works department (PWD) with leadership composed of me, one Seabee chief, and five Filipino contract workers (who were the supervisors of each of the public works functions—carpentry, electrical, plumbing, automotive operations and repair.) The workforce was made up of approximately 180 Vietnamese civilians divided among the Filipino supervisors. A new chief, in fact a senior chief (E-8), was en route, and in the meantime, I had the temporary loan of a Seabee chief from SOG Saigon.

We spent the next several days turning over the various aspects of the job. My predecessor related two important turnover items: we had more vehicles than our authorized allowance; and having an unlimited budget did not mean a lot when there was a scarcity of commodities in-theater that everyone wanted. The SOG guys stole jeeps from anyone they could so each could have their own jeep. Since we had an automotive shop, these purloined vehicles were painted black. My predecessor said I should just look the other way, as that was the nature of SOG operations. The vehicles had been recorded as gained by inventory on our records, which were never going to be audited. My job, in part, was to find commodities that couldn't be obtained through the system—even with an unlimited budget—and get them by hook or crook, no questions asked.

The last thing we did together was to go to the graduation ceremony and party for a class of Vietnamese SEALs who had been trained by our SEALs and were now moving into the operational side of the detachment. It was quite impressive, and I learned some valuable things at the graduation dinner and party that night. First, don't try to drink with any of these guys, American or Vietnamese, as they were crazy and liked chug-a-lug games and toasts. According to my predecessor, the trick was to water down your drinks, so you did not insult them by not drinking their toasts, and to keep your glass full, so they could not top it off for you. More important was the lesson he shared about Vietnamese food. When I asked him what a dish was in the buffet, he said, "There are three rules that will get you through your tour of duty: first, never ask what anything is—it's usually better not to know; second, if you don't like the looks of something, don't put it on your plate; and third, if you take a bite of something and don't like it, just swallow it whole to get it over with as quickly as possible. Oh, and never drink the local water or use the ice; stick with *Ba Moui Ba* ["Thirty-Three," a Vietnamese beer] and you'll be fine." I followed that guidance the rest of my career, and it saved me many times. The next day I took him to the airport and I was on my own.

The next few weeks were spent learning about the people who worked for me. The Filipino supervisors spoke good English and Vietnamese, so they had no problem communicating with the workforce. They were competent, friendly, and anxious to please. For the most part, they knew their functional areas and treated their Vietnamese charges well, and there was rarely any friction. The Filipinos evidenced a strong desire to avoid confrontation. They were sensitive, compared to Americans, and I learned quickly to deal with this while still getting my message across. My parents had numerous Filipino friends from the Navy, so I had already been exposed to the culture and had a head start on this. The Vietnamese tradesmen's skill level was particularly good, and it became apparent that our shops could do just about anything—including manufacturing ersatz parts if we could not get what we needed through the system.

I received the operations briefing from our SOG guys regarding how they trained the Vietnamese recruits and what their missions typically looked like. I was also taken on a familiarization ride on one of the Nasty–class boats and observed the Vietnamese crews interacting with their American advisors.

The officer staff of NAD was small, with just four officers who, apart from the OIC and AOIC, were staff officers as opposed to "mission operators." They included the admin officer, the supply officer, and me (all lieutenants), and a Marine captain served as the security officer. There was also a mobile training team that took care of the boats and trained Vietnamese Navy personnel in these maintenance skills. The OIC for the MTT was also a lieutenant. A smattering of chiefs with some technical expertise backed us up. Several Vietnamese Navy officers were assigned as our counterparts, but they were mostly on the operations side, and none worked directly with me. I attended numerous meetings with them and we socialized together, however, so I came to know them well.

Living conditions in the camp were great; it made me feel guilty when I thought about what the troops in the field were dealing with. We had our own officers' quarters complete with a bar and maid service provided by Vietnamese women, most of whom worked in the club we had in the compound. I observed there were numerous liaisons going on between officers in the BOQ and enlisted personnel in their barracks with these waitresses, and some of the officers talked of their girlfriends outside the camp. This was a new thing for me to see since it did not happen in Camp Hoover. The galley had great food with a wide variety, thanks to the skills of the chief storekeeper. He had numerous contacts throughout the area and employed the barter system to obtain delicacies outside the normal supply channels. There was little to no possibility of enemy attack due to the location of the camp. The camp was bordered on two sides by Camp Tin Shaw and on the others by a Vietnamese village, with a road separating the village from the camp, so the only real possibility of an attack would be through the one and only gate, which was heavily guarded. The gate had signs warning everyone in English and Vietnamese "Deadly Force Authorized," and anyone not obeying the orders of the security personnel would be shot. If I had to be in a war zone, this was the place to be.

Going North

The first eye-opening experience beyond getting used to being in the SOG world was my first road trip out of Danang since I arrived back. There was an outlying support communications location that our detachment was responsible for supporting in a minimal fashion, and this required a visit from me to ascertain any support requirements. It was located just south of Hue up the same Highway 1 that I had traveled in a fifty-five-truck convoy with air cover. My inquiry about the convoy arrangements and what I had to do to join the next one elicited a blank look. "Just take a vehicle and drive up there—the roads are safe." I could not believe it, but I soon found myself riding north in a three-quarter-ton truck loaded with some supplies and one of my Filipino supervisors riding shotgun.

The Seabees had completed the road-building job from Danang to points north, and this beautiful stretch of tarmac was being well used. There were speed limit signs along the route, something that I found unbelievable given the ambushes that had occurred when I was there before. I was stopped for speeding by the military police on this road in the war zone! They told me I had to slow down, and I told them I had nearly been killed on this road two years before and that wasn't going to happen. The compromise we ended up agreeing to was they followed me to Phu Bai as my escort and protection, but more likely to keep me from speeding.

The real lesson learned from this trip was, however, that the Marines had pretty much wiped out the VC and the NVA infiltrators that had gotten into the area during Tet, and now the area was reasonably safe for the Vietnamese who lived there. They could use the roads, farm their rice, and fish in comparative safety—quite a difference from what it had been like when I was there before. Unfortunately, I was to watch this all change as the Marines were withdrawn from Vietnam and replaced by the Army during the "Vietnamization" of the war effort under the disengagement policy of the Nixon administration and Congress. Both north and south of Danang, I saw the results of the last two years of the American pacification efforts with my own eyes. It was nothing like what was being reported in the press. I could drive in relative safety during the day, and that was a significant metric to me at least.

We learned that the OIC had received his orders and would soon be shipping out, but there was one more pet project he wanted completed before his relief arrived: he wanted to put up two fencing barriers with tangle foot wiring between them along the road between the camp and the village, maybe a hundred yards long. The first was the standard concertina wire, and the second would be eight-foot chain-link fencing with posts. The problem was that eight-foot chain link fencing was nearly impossible to find in the supply system because it was in such great demand. Even with an unlimited budget and the highest priority, it was simply not available; it was on backorder in the supply system and would not arrive until after the old OIC was due to leave. When I reported this to him, he looked at me and said he wanted it done and not to bother him with the details.

I went back to the office and shared this with the new senior chief (who had just arrived), and we discussed our options. This was really the first test of his competence since his arrival. We talked for a while and then he said he was going on a scouting mission to see what could be done. He promised to brief me on his findings. The next morning we sat down and he said, "Lieutenant, I have found what appears to be an abandoned supply yard on the airbase that has an eight-foot chain link fence around it with a locked gate. Across the street is a Marine logistics unit, and I have talked with the gunnery sergeant who confirmed that it is an Air Force supply yard that is rarely, if ever, used. He offered to lend us his forklift to load up the fencing if we want to take it. I think we just need to get some cutting tools, some of our guys, and a couple of trucks. We can cut the fencing down and bring it back here in a heartbeat. The zoomies will never miss it." I appreciated his initiative, and I told him, "Let's do it!"

We performed the operation with the chief storekeeper operating the forklift and the senior chief directing the crew while I supervised. Just as we were finishing loading the last roll of fencing, an air police vehicle arrived and asked what we were doing. I said we had permission to remove the fencing, and he could check if he wanted to. Luckily, he did not have a radio in his vehicle for some reason and told me to wait there while he checked it out. Right! As soon as he was out of sight, we hightailed it out of there and got back to camp without further problems. The fence was completed, and the OIC did not even comment on it except to say something in his departing fitness report on me that was grossly inflated about being extremely resourceful. Two things came out of this incident: a solid bonding between the senior chief and me and a smirk every time I drove by the Air Force supply yard with its lonely, locked gate securing a yard with no fencing.

The Vietnamese

Since I had not worked with the Vietnamese military—or, for that matter, the Vietnamese people—during my first tour, this sojourn in-country provided me with insights and understanding of what was going on in their war-torn country and where the war was heading. The first realization was that there really was not a sense of national identity in South Vietnam. It was a kind of confederation of ethnic groups and religious groups, each out for themselves with little concern for the others. The Catholics tended to be the elites and controlled the government, but they were a decided minority that was oppressing the majority Buddhist population. The indigenous tribes, collectively called Montagnard (from the French for "mountain people"), were treated terribly by the other major Vietnamese groups but had reacted well to the good treatment by Americans, especially the Special Forces troops who had lived with them, armed them, trained them, and fought and died with them. There was considerable friction between the Montagnard and the Vietnamese military—indeed, one group had risen in revolt against the government in 1964, and it was their cool-headed

Green Beret advisors who had talked them off the ledge. The Montagnard were fiercely loyal to the Americans. On the other side were the VC and North Vietnamese, who were bound by a singularity of purpose. Failure to do as they said meant immediate punishment or death, and that was well understood. The South Vietnamese government offered assurances of protection that they could not back up except in a specific situational context. The senior officers tended to be far removed from their troops in temperament and care factor for their welfare. This resulted in harsh treatment, yet some of the junior officers were closer to their men and tried to look out for them. This difference between North and South was made particularly vivid to me when observing the crews of the five Nasty–class boats assigned to the detachment.

The boats were manned by Vietnamese Navy crews under a lieutenant, with American advisors assigned. When they were sent on their classified missions, no Americans went with them to preserve "plausible deniability" of U.S. involvement; hence, they provided an instant case study of leadership at the small unit level. Two of the five boats were crewed by descendants of North Vietnamese Catholics who had been ejected from North Vietnam when the country had been divided. Their families were socially elite, and they had lost everything. They carried a personal grudge against North Vietnam but had no great political loyalty for South Vietnam. This war was personal to them; they went looking for fights and generally acquitted themselves well. The other three boats were crewed by sailors from South Vietnam. They were not inclined to seek out combat; they were slack and full of excuses about why they did not make contact with the enemy or complete their missions. They did all right when Americans were there to make sure they did their duty, but left to their own they could not be relied upon.

An incident that happened not long after the new OIC had taken over offers a good example. Our detachment received a "flash" (highest priority) message from the commander in chief, Pacific Fleet (CINCPACFLT) asking if any of our craft were at a particular location the night before at a specified time. I sat in the briefing room listening to the operators talk about this and draft a message back to CINCPACFLT saying we had no craft in that area. Just as the OIC was about to sign it out, one of the lieutenants said, "Where was Dai Uy Hung and his boat last night?" Hung was the leader of the most aggressive of the crews of North Vietnamese descendants and sometimes took his boat out on his own initiative. No one seemed to know, so he was sent for. He was asked if he had been at the location at the time specified. His answer: "For sure!" The next question was obviously, "What happened?" Hung said, "Nothing. We were patrolling, and there was a large contact. We approached at high speed and fired a flare, as we could not see what it was. The flare went off above an American cruiser [USS *Saint Paul*, I believe] and many bells went off. We turned off at high speed. No shots fired. Very disappointing, we could not shoot the ship!" Everyone in the room was silent; we were thinking about the reaction on the ship when a high-speed craft approached the cruiser and fired a flare. There was a flag officer embarked on the ship, so I am sure it was a huge flap that had been reported to CINCPACFLT. The new OIC thought for a few minutes and signed the reply that said we had no boats at that location.

New OIC

The new OIC was an odd duck. Again, he was not a special ops type—just a ship driver assigned to this job for reasons that were not apparent to any of us. After he observed the antics that were going on in the club, barracks, and our bar involving the Vietnamese women, he called a meeting of all the officers. He said he was concerned by what he was seeing, but if an officer could look himself in the mirror in the morning, he did not feel he should have to become involved with this questionable conduct. About two weeks later, he called another meeting and asked, "How are you shaving in the morning without looking in the mirror?" He then put restrictions on what could be done in public but not on women being in rooms.

The OIC's biggest impact on me was his decision to order me to build a house overlooking Danang Bay for the senior Vietnamese Navy officer we were supporting. This was to be from excess material on a "not to interfere" basis with my people's regular duties. Right! It soon became the focus of our efforts, with my senior chief essentially acting as the project manager and procurer of materials. All our routine maintenance work had to be fitted in around this project. Why we were doing this was never explained, other than the Vietnamese officer deserved it for some reason—another example of "the way it was" with the senior officer corps of the Vietnamese military.

One other episode involving the new OIC highlights the reaction within the Navy to Elmo R. Zumwalt Jr.'s ascension to chief of naval operations in the summer of 1970. Zumwalt decided he was going to change the tradition-bound Navy to fix the retention problem by making it a more "sailor-friendly" place. He set up retention teams to make recommendations and then started personnel policy changes designed, in his view, to reduce what he perceived to be chicken regulations and treat sailors like adults. These were promulgated in proclamations known as "Z-grams."

While visiting Navy commands when he was commander naval forces, Vietnam, Zumwalt had made it his practice to essentially bypass senior officers and chiefs and spend his time talking with the junior officers and enlisted personnel, often alienating midgrade and senior officers and the more senior enlisted by ignoring them. It reminded me of the "flower child" generation's mantra, "you can't trust anyone over thirty." A couple of favorite targets were the perks given to sailors as they advanced in seniority and age, which he decided should apply to all regardless of seniority, and his dislike of the traditional Navy enlisted uniform. One of the most controversial Z-grams dealt with personal appearance in uniform in which he allowed beards, mustaches, and longer hair. Zumwalt himself often looked like he needed a haircut and was possibly reacting to his personal preference.

The new OIC reacted very emotionally to this desecration of discipline and appearance, writing his personal views of how stupid and unmilitary this was in red pen and attaching his note to the message boards. He went crazy when someone removed his comments from the message boards and they could not be found. He was sure he was being turned in and would be court martialed for insubordination. That did not happen, but it sure made things interesting for a while.

Probably the kindest thing to say about Zumwalt is that he was ahead of his time in invoking the sensitive management approach to a culture that did not know how to react to it. From my perspective, the results of his policies took sailors from being the smartest in military appearance and best disciplined (next to the Marines) to the worst. They looked and acted poorly on and off duty. This did nothing for retention that I could see, while undermining esprit de corps and the Navy leadership. The leadership vacuum and the ongoing drug and racial problems in all the military services made this worse. The middle and senior levels of officers and enlisted did not know how they were supposed to react to challenges to whatever authority they still had. It took twenty years to recover from this social experiment and get sailors back to looking and acting military again.

Notwithstanding the OIC's attempts to moderate behavior in the BOQ bar, it was always a lively place and never more so than when the SOG operators returned from one of their missions. While they released their tension and stress with copious amounts of alcohol, they almost clinically related accounts of the surreal things that had happened on the missions. One key mission area was participation in the Phoenix program. "CIA veteran Robert Komer ... had been no shrinking violet in his prosecution of the war, overseeing the Phoenix Program, which targeted Viet Cong cadres in South Vietnamese villages."[13] This program involved sundry clandestine missions, including the assassination of specific targets identified by intelligence sources. One major problem was the reliability of the intelligence sources and a suspected tendency to use the program to settle personal grudges instead of targeting the enemy, but that was not our operators' problem as they carried out their assigned missions. Our men were professional killers with exceptional expertise. I was glad we had them and wondered what they would do when there was no war to employ their talents. The difference between the instrument and handler became very apparent to me, as was the amount of micromanagement direct from Washington and Saigon by men who seemed to continuously seek plausible deniability for the decisions they were making.

The Army Takes Over

One of the significant events that occurred during my second tour in I Corps was the withdrawal of the Marines and Seabees and their replacement by the U.S. Army. The Army was tasked with conducting Vietnamization of the war by training and equipping Vietnamese forces so it could hand off to them and withdraw. The withdrawal of the Marines brought the termination of the successful CAP program, which was not favored by the Army, despite the program's success. With just 1.5 percent of all Marines in-country involved, participating units suffered 3.2 percent of the Marines' total casualties while inflicting 8 percent of the enemy's casualties. The removal of the CAP troops opened the countryside to infiltration by the enemy. It was apparent to anyone watching what was happening—that the Vietnamization program was going to fail. It was just a matter of time before the NVA would be pushing south. When Congress cut off air support it sounded the death knell for the South Vietnamese army, which lasted longer than many thought possible.

The effect of the turnover on our detachment—and me in particular—was immediate. All our chief storekeeper's sources for our superb meals disappeared when the Army took over the logistics in I Corps. One day my senior chief came to me and said that he and the storekeeper had done some snooping around and discovered that key senior enlisted in the new

Army logistics units were living in some rough conditions, which translated meant "no air conditioning." Since AC units were like gold, we might be able to solve our food sourcing problems if we could get some AC units for trading. Given our unlimited budget and procurement priority, I decided to order replacement AC units through the system to see what happened. Amazingly, within a relatively short period of time, our supply people got a call that there was a blackbird at the airport with a cargo for us—AC units! When they arrived in camp, the senior chief and storekeeper took charge and shortly we were receiving the excellent meals we had grown accustomed to. In addition to that, the senior chief took a couple over to the Seabees who ran the Seabee warehouses at Red Beach, which were being closed out as the battalions left. That proved to be a key to the warehouses so that we could replenish our building and trades material.

The departure of the Seabees had a direct impact on me. During the farewell party held at the officers' club of the last battalion to leave Red Beach, I was sitting at the bar talking to a CEC officer who was visiting from Hawaii; he was doing something concerning the phase-out of the Seabees. Somehow the subject of assignments came up and the fact that I would shortly be due for orders out of Vietnam. He said pointedly, "Whatever you do, don't let them talk you into being an aide to the flag in Hawaii. He is impossible and has fired one aide after another. They are always looking for fresh meat." I noted his recommendation and was thus forearmed when a few weeks later I returned a call from my assignment officer. He said I had been picked for an especially important job—aide to the flag in Hawaii. It sounded like a cherry assignment, and I am sure he expected me to be ecstatic. I suspect he was surprised when I responded, "Coming out of Vietnam, I'm not interested in being an aide. I'd like to use whatever preference I have to secure a posting in Europe." I think he must have sensed that I had gotten the word about the flag, as his efforts to change my mind were minimal. I ended up with orders to be the assistant public works officer (APWO) for the commander, U.S. Naval Activities United Kingdom (COMNAVACTSUK), located in London. I had been saved by a chance encounter at the bar!

Departure

This tour in Vietnam had been markedly different from my first. In terms of personal combat, there had been none. Our detachment had lost no Americans and only a few Vietnamese. The only dead I had seen were some bodies laid out on a road, after the CAP personnel had repelled an attack the night before, and a thief, who had tried to jump into the back of a supply truck a few hundred yards in front of me. He somehow slipped only to be hit in the head by the tailgate of the truck. His body had just stopped rolling when I drove up to him. His head was smashed, so I just continued.

I learned a great deal about the SOG world, plausible deniability, the Vietnamese military, the Vietnamese people, and Filipinos, and I developed a renewed confirmation of the ingenuity of Seabees and senior enlisted personnel. I also had many opportunities to observe more examples of good and bad leadership. Nothing that happened in Vietnam after my leaving came as a surprise to me, neither the actions of the Vietnamese on both sides of the conflict nor the actions of the U.S. political leadership. The last meaningful event I participated in was when Gen. Creighton Abrams (the new Army commander in Vietnam) visited our detachment for a briefing and a ride on one of our boats. I had last seen him during my final year at West Point, when he told our group that the United States did not have enough troops in Vietnam and could not win without a change in strategy. Now he was responsible for winning with troops being withdrawn and the Congress against the war. He looked much older but seemed to enjoy the day. Every inch a great warrior, he was wasted on an ineptly handled war. Shortly after that, I flew out of Vietnam for the last time; I was on my way to England, more sophisticated in the ways of the world and never to be naive again about the motivations of politicians, senior defense appointees, and senior military officers.

Hail Britannia!

I arrived in the United Kingdom ready to live among the locals (since there was no military housing), experience a deep immersion in the British culture, and use my new home as a launching point for travels in Europe. It would also be my first Navy job outside a war zone in the four years since I had been commissioned. COMNAVACTSUK was housed in the headquarters of the commander in chief (CINC), U.S. Naval Forces, Europe (CINCUS-NAVEUR), at 7 North Audley Street on Grosvenor Square (which had served as Eisenhower's first island headquarters in World War II), just across from the American Embassy. COMNAVACTSUK supported the CINC logistically and administratively with a relatively small staff. The PWD was charged with maintaining the headquarters building, other Navy properties in the area, and the quarters that were provided for the flag officers and a couple of designated senior captains. The tradesmen were all British nationals, about sixty in number, overseen by British supervisors and engineers, with a few Seabees attached for special projects that required security clearances or other training that the British employees did not have. I would be working directly for a CEC lieutenant commander, and our CO was a senior Navy line captain. My education about the real Navy was about to begin.

The headquarters building was full of senior officers, including three admirals and around sixty captains, a significant portion of whom were World War II veterans. My CO was a Naval Academy submariner (1941) who wore the submarine combat patrol badge on his uniform with several gold stars to signify the actions he had participated in during the war. He had been a true diesel boat submariner and had no use at all for the Rickover-inspired nuclear submariners (referring to those officers selected and trained by Admiral Hyman Rickover, "the Father of nuclear propulsion" in the Navy) that he regarded with contempt, saying they were not real submariners. The CINC was an aviator who had been awarded the Navy Cross in the North African landings. Few of these men were Zumwalt converts, and they preferred the Navy the old-fashioned way. Fortunately for them, we were not allowed to wear uniforms because of the antiwar feelings in the UK. The type of civilian clothes to be worn (coat and tie) was prescribed, so the Z-gram rules did not apply to the relatively few junior officers and enlisted in the headquarters. At one point, I calculated that the number of lieutenants assigned to the headquarters was a single-digit number close to the number of flag officers. I liked working for and with these senior officers as I knew where I stood and how to deal with them.

What I discovered after not too much time in my new job was that it was not very taxing. Although it was the largest department in the command with the biggest budget, I needed to find other things to do to fill up my days. The people who worked for me were competent and my relationship with them good, so I did not need or want to micromanage them. My immediate boss handled the interface with the CO and other senior officers. I occasionally dealt with them or their wives on quarters issues and projects they were personally interested in. This gave me some time for professional education in the form of Navy correspondence courses; I found them to be boring and not very enlightening. I decided that I would sign up for graduate school courses at the University of Arkansas overseas campus and take a refresher course in preparation to take the Professional Engineer (PE) test that was a desired professional recognition of competence in the CEC for promotion. I earned a master's degree in management and passed my PE test, which was given overseas by the state of Pennsylvania. I also learned a great deal about the Navy during this period.

The Line Navy

My first truly enlightening lesson about the line Navy was that it was not one Navy but three subgroups with different cultures, issues, and personalities. The line I had worked with before was not really considered part of it by these groups, as they cared less about SEALs and special operations types in general. Each considered itself the "real" Navy. The three navies were the surface navy (or ship drivers); the submarine force, composed at that time by the Rickover-dominated nuclear submarines and a few diesel subs that were still left; and the naval aviation community. The officers in these designations competed for promotion against each other as line officers. To be sure, while there were some quotas to ensure the necessary amount matriculated up the promotion ladder from each group, the control of the Navy at the flag rank would reflect the philosophy and preferences of one group. For years it had mostly been aviators or submariners, with an occasional surface officer thrown in—like Zumwalt—much to the unhappiness of the other groups. The three COs I worked for at COMNAVACTSUK and the three CINCs at CINCUSNAVEUR rotated through these three communities (except for not having an aviator as a CO).

To become a submarine officer, each candidate had to be a volunteer and be personally interviewed by Rickover. Those interviews were the stuff of legend because of his peculiar personality, preconceived ideas and interview techniques, and his own unique history as a maverick and near outcast in the Navy before being proven right (in his opinion, at any rate). Since those chosen for submarines by this process tended to have the highest academic credentials and qualifications (the enlisted submarine personnel were also screened to ensure they were the best), there was a level of arrogance and condescension that was hard to stomach by the other line officers as well as us poorly regarded staff officers. I should point out that the qualifications required in education, academic standing, and other traits to qualify as a nuclear submariner were the same as those required to be a CEC officer. That led to restrictions being put on Naval Academy and NROTC officers, preventing them from placement in the CEC upon graduation unless they were not qualified for a line billet for some physical reason. Those that wanted to fly were also volunteers and had restricted quotas and a lengthy pipeline of training to go through. Candidates who fell out for some reason were made available to the other parts of the Navy, but even that was modified later when they were required to be reassigned in the surface Navy unless physically unqualified, or they could leave the Navy entirely. It seemed that the rocket scientist surface officers in charge at the time thought it was better not to give individuals a choice and impress them into their world.

The surface Navy received what was left after the other communities had their pick of volunteers. This does not mean there were not exceptional officers who wanted "to go down to the sea in ships," but it did mean there were a lot more less-qualified officers in the surface world. That was compounded by the leadership techniques employed by a significant number in this community; they were characterized by many as "eating their young," with the harsh treatment of junior officers, coupled with long deployments on old ships requiring continuous maintenance and unforgiving performance evaluations that affected retention in the Navy. I soon found that it was necessary to adjust my logic and the manner that I used depending upon whom I was talking to, their background, and attendant prejudices. Pilots tended to be the easiest to work with because most realized they knew how to fly planes and not much else, although there were exceptions to this. Nuclear submariners tended to think they were smarter than everyone else and acted accordingly. Surface officers ran the gamut between the two and were generally harder to figure out, at least initially.

The rub between the submariners and the surface types was illustrated to me in the support of the Polaris submarine squadron located at Holy Loch, Scotland. This was the responsibility of COMNAVACTSUK through a detachment established there for that purpose. The commodore of the squadron (COMSUBRON14) was located on a submarine tender in the middle of the loch where the Polaris submarines came in from their transits and patrols to provision and be maintained. There was an extraordinary logistics pipeline set up to provide the most rapid logistics support possible to the submarines by flying parts and provisions in on chartered or military aircraft. That was fine given the priority of the submarine ballistic missile program as a key component of the strategic defense triad in the Cold War. What was *not* fine were the constant demands for priority on other support requirements that had little or nothing to do with getting the subs to sea. I visited Holy Loch many times to try to help the PWO assigned to the detachment and evaluate the situation for my boss. Nothing was ever good enough for the nukes.

Holy Loch was extremely isolated, remote from any large city. There was no available military housing, and the local Scottish housing—when it was available—was austere to say the least. There was a small commissary with limited stock due to the long supply line and a small club facility with few frills and little choice in food. This was the subject of constant complaints by those stationed on the tender (who could bring their families). The commodore and CO of the tender continually complained about the quarters that were provided by the Navy through leases with locals because they were considered to be below their standards.

The solution to these facilities problems was not within the realm of the U.S. Navy as it required negotiations with the host nation British government and faced thorny problems like local resistance, environmental concerns, and political considerations. The nuclear folks could not care less about all these real problems, and to use their term, COMNAVACTSUK support was UNSAT (unsatisfactory). Considering the senior detachment officer was the OIC and a lieutenant commander, while the PWO was a lieutenant (junior grade), it was a recipe for abuse of power and friction. That is exactly what happened, and it reached its height during the period when the CINC was a submariner and dumped on COMNAVACTSUK (then a surface officer) constantly in response to the whining from the commodore, without suggesting any solutions to the problems at his level. This was further aggravated by the fact that virtually every captain assigned to be the commodore was selected for flag rank while they were in the job. The worm only turned when a surface CINC replaced the submariner CINC.

The fact that I was involved in the negotiations with the British Ministry of Defence (MOD) to procure land and build housing through a UK contractor placed me in the middle of the Holy Loch support issue. The Navy guaranteed to rent this housing at negotiated rates for a specific period with termination conditions should the housing no longer be needed. Not only did I participate in the intergovernmental discussions and strategy, but I was also heavily involved in the selection and negotiations with the designer and construction contractor that the British chose to build the housing. This proved extremely educational and prepared me for future issues I would face when dealing with foreign countries and militaries. In the end, an agreement was reached and the housing completed while I was still on duty in London, and the new quarters lessened some of the complaints. The "what have you done for me today" attitude of the nuclear sub community did not go away and was still a problem when I left.

Beating Boredom

My tour of duty as APWO was to be three years, and after a year I was really bored. The PWO I worked for was due to leave after two years, and I started lobbying the assignment officer to move me up to the PWO job when he left, though it was an O-4 position, and I would still be an O-3. I was getting excellent fitness reports, and I got along well with the senior CEC officer on the CINC's staff (a captain), who I am sure put in a good word for me, as I received orders to "fleet up" (move up and take his place when my boss left). I also had a set of additional duty orders to the officer in charge of construction, Spain (OICC Spain), since all construction, maintenance, and repair contracting came through the Naval Facilities Engineering Command (NAVFACENGCOM, or more commonly, NAV-FAC) chain of command as opposed to the CINCUSNAVEUR chain. I needed these orders to execute contracts. I had gotten to know that CEC captain well, and he had pushed me to get my PE certification. This helped with my fleet up since I had a PE and not many lieutenants did.

While I traveled extensively throughout Western Europe, the most interesting trip was when I accompanied the supply officer to the Soviet Union at the height of the Cold War. Here is how the junket came about: we got to talking during a happy hour about the fact he had taken Russian at the Naval Academy, and I had taken it at USMA. We decided it would be interesting to visit the Soviet Union and see how we got along. The British are well-organized travelers, and there are many relatively inexpensive tours from London to just about everywhere, so we booked ourselves on a ten-day excursion to Leningrad, Moscow, and Kiev. The primitive nature of our enemy startled me. The shops were poorly stocked, the equipment we saw was old and generally poor in design, and the people looked unhappy or just apathetic—resigned to their lot. They might have a strong military, but I questioned how strong the public support really was. One other thing that I found to be interesting was a hint of what was to happen in the future. Our guide in the Ukraine was quite vocal about how the Ukrainian people had supported the White or Czarist army versus the Red or Bolshevik army during the Revolution and had to be forcibly put into the Soviet Union. Again, during World War II, numerous Ukrainians had initially joined the Nazis to rid the country of Communists. Stalin's murderous actions against the land-owning peasant farmers had guaranteed this. Only when the Nazis treated them more brutally than the Communists did they switch sides. The later collapse of the Soviet Union and the continuing internal problems in Russia attest to the accuracy of these lingering resentments.

Another event that reinforced my love of Seabees came in the form of a story from World War II that I was told by the commander of the 24th Air Force, a major general, during a Founder's Day dinner in London. Founder's Day is the annual West Point alumni get together where the oldest and youngest graduate present make remarks, and old grads reminisce about what they remember of the way it was back in the day. I had gotten a call from a retired colonel, who informed me I was the youngest graduate in the London area and was expected to attend and make remarks.

I showed up in my Navy uniform, causing the usual stir. There was a size-able turnout, but mostly of older, retired grads who had chosen for whatever reason to live in the UK. During my remarks, I talked about my experiences with the Seabees in Vietnam and afterward. When I had finished my remarks, the general came over and said: "The Seabees were life savers for me in World War II, and I have always thought they were great. Let me tell you why." He related that as a young B-29 pilot, he was on Tinian flying bombing runs over Japan. He and his crew had a problem—no way to wash their uniforms except by hand, and that was difficult due to the flight scheduling and lack of laundry facilities. His crew chief came to him and said he had been talking to a chief in the Seabees on the island and that they had washing machines they had built. The two of them came up with a solution to problems both groups had. While the bomber crew had uniforms that stunk, the Seabees had warm beer since there was no way to cool it. The chief said if they delivered beer to the crew just before they took off, the crew could strap it to the bomb racks on the bomber, and when they returned the beer would be cold. In the meantime, the Seabees would do the crew's laundry. The general then pinpointed the fly in the ointment: "It worked great, and we only had a few problems during particularly long and stressful missions. We would decide to help ourselves to some of the beer to take the edge off. Do you know how hard it is to find a little island like Tinian when you're drunk?" he chortled. The resourcefulness of the senior enlisted in all the services is what makes the military work, and officers of all ranks who interfere with this equipoise do so at their own peril.

Line Mentor

My interactions with the last CO I had at NAVACTSUK served as great lessons about how to deal with line officers, particularly surface officers.

He was one of the most senior captains in the Navy and had come from ten straight years at sea, moving through destroyer positions from CO of a destroyer to a destroyer squadron staff to be the commodore of a destroyer squadron. He had zero patience for anyone telling him he was wrong about anything or questioning what he said or who had no understanding of the shore establishment and the rules that applied to it, and he had a real dislike for submariners. He was an "old Navy" guy. He came a couple of months before I fleeted up, so I got some free lessons watching my then boss deal with him unsuccessfully. I had an early indication of how he viewed his command, his subordinates, and those who impinged upon them from outside, together with an excellent lesson in understanding "you don't know what you don't know."

A new CINC had taken over CINCUSNAVEUR, and with him came his new executive assistant (EA), an officer who had been selected early for captain and was quite self-important. Most amazingly, he had somehow gotten the approval for Navy-leased quarters for himself in London, even though he was the most junior O-6 in the headquarters. Good on him, but what happened next was not. He laid out a set of unrealistic demands for the location of his new quarters and what amenities must be included. Nothing that came up to snuff was available at the authorized lease price. To make matters worse, the Air Force served as the leasing agent for quarters in the UK for some strange reason (Congress authorized the AF to act as the "leasing agent" in the UK, while the Army and Navy shared this role for the rest of the world). I was the point of contact with the Air Force, and my staff and I worked with our AF counterparts to try to find something. One day, I received a phone call directly from a major general in Germany who oversaw the Air Force leasing program asking me what the hell was going on; his boss, a four-star, had received a personal message from our CINC saying the Air Force leasing efforts were UNSAT. He asked me to make sure that did not happen again and told me what he thought of this high-handed action. His leasing people and our staff managed to find an apartment that came close to what was desired, and the captain reluctantly agreed to it. His move was scheduled the Monday after the lease was to be signed on Friday. On Thursday, I got a call from the leasing office saying the deal was off because the landlord would not agree to the boilerplate clauses regarding auditing that had be in the lease. There was nothing that could be done about it. This was going to be ugly since I was told I must tell the captain what had happened and incur his wrath.

Since I was sure this captain was going to be calling the new CO to tell him how UNSAT I was, I decided to go by the CO's office on my way to give him a heads-up. I explained what had happened, including his EA's apparent use of a CINC's personal message; I elaborated on what my staff and others in his command, like supply and admin, had done to try to appease this guy without success. I let him know that I felt sure he would be receiving a complaint about this from the EA. The CO listened and then said he did not have anything on his schedule right then, so he would accompany me while I broke the news to the captain.

We walked in the EA's office and my new CO introduced himself and said I had some bad news to relay about his quarters situation. Before I could say anything, the EA looked up and said: "That's UNSAT and I don't want to hear it." Again, before I could say anything, my CO leaned over the EA's desk, put a finger in his chest, and said, "All this bullshit about your quarters, harassing my staff, and sending messages to the Air Force is because the CINC personally told you to do this, right? It better not be because you are just being an asshole because I am going to ask the CINC right now!" He then turned and walked across the hall to the CINC's office and told the aide to tell the CINC that he, by name, needed to see the CINC immediately. All the color drained from the EA's face and about five minutes later, I heard a buzzer that was evidently used by the CINC to summon his EA. The EA got up and went in to his boss's office, closing the door behind him. A few minutes later, my CO walked out with a huge smile on his face. He said to me, "Lieutenant, I don't think there will be any more problems with the EA. Proceed in an orderly fashion to find appropriate quarters for him. The CINC is going to send his personal apology to the Air Force and tell them there is no urgency for this lease. Do not get me wrong, the CINC's EA is a good man who just needed some counseling about expectations and using his boss's name. He thought he knew it all, but he did not. One of the things he didn't know was who the CINC's roommate was at the Naval Academy," he said with a hearty laugh. My own reflection on this encounter and lesson for future dealings with individuals placed in powerful positions was Lord John Dalberg-Acton's admonition that "Power tends to corrupt and absolute power corrupts absolutely."[14]

When I became the PWO not long after this and was working directly with the CO almost daily, it became clear that he liked to make decisions quickly (as on the bridge of a ship) and did not see the need for staff work on facilities-related matters since they were really only common sense. Unfortunately, as I had discovered, they were not common sense in many cases, as the Congress had passed laws that were extremely specific about what money could be spent and what levels of approvals were required to spend money on the various categories of facilities-related contracts. In the United States this spending was called "pork," since where and how it was spent equated to jobs—and that is the stuff of political favor, something Congress likes to control. I had seen my predecessor chewed out on several occasions for telling the CO, "You can't do that!" in response to some direction or order. Unfortunately, these dressing-downs often took place in front of his staff colleagues. When I took over, the CO told me that I better not pull any of that "negative BS."

I hit upon the plan of always agreeing with whatever the CO directed with a "Yes, sir." Then I drafted a message for the CO to sign out to whatever level in the chain of command authorized to give a waiver to the CO's limits of authority on that matter. I attached the instruction that set the CO's limits on the issue to my draft. Finally, I went see the CO and tell him that in trying to execute his wishes I had found this instruction. All he had to do was send the message, as I was sure it would be approved since it made common sense. He would rail about politicians, the civilian appointees, and various and sundry other bureaucrats and tell me to leave it with him to work on. They were never sent, and he never regarded me as being "negative." One time, however, he was about send one, and I was afraid he would actually do it. I convinced him he should talk to the senior CEC officer on the CINCUSNAVEUR staff about the issue since I knew the man happened to also be a classmate of his. At the appointed time, the CEC captain and I met with the CO in his office, and the CO started to rail about the issue. After some unsuccessful attempts to dissuade him, the CEC captain said, "George, I want to show you something about facilities, and we need to go outside for me to do it."

The CO agreed and we all went out into the park in Grosvenor Square that was right out front of the headquarters. The classmate then declared: "Order left full rudder and see what the building does!" The CO started to blow up, but his classmate interrupted, saying, "The rules at sea don't apply here, and you need to get over it. The lieutenant's job is to keep you out of trouble and from looking foolish. Trust him until he gives you reason not to, and your life will be easier." The longer he thought about it, the more this wisdom sank in, and the CO and I developed a very professional relationship. He kept track of my career over the years and came to my retirement ceremony as a flag officer, where we laughed over some of these episodes. The CEC captain had verbalized what I had learned at West Point: that as an officer, my job was to protect both my superiors and subordinates from making mistakes if it was in my power to do so. I used the same approach several times over my military and civilian careers when faced with bosses who wanted to act arbitrarily.

Esprit de Corps

One other comment on my time in England (and up to that point, my time in the Navy) is appropriate. Although I had to deal with some tough days and unreasonable leaders, the jobs, people, and social interaction within the commands had made it seem fun. The pay was not much, but the esprit de corps was high. The happy hours every Friday afternoon in the headquarters building were a source of camaraderie and a place where a surprising amount of real work and information exchange was accomplished in an informal atmosphere. The change from the "old guard"—World War II officers—to the new generation was most apparent in the CINCs. The World War II pilot went to the happy hours and mingled with everyone; in fact, he would come out of his office and say, "Happy hour!" and expect everyone to shut down and go, which they did. After he left, I rarely saw a CINC there, but the happy hours continued as there were still many senior officers who were World War II vets and "old Navy." After happy hour, the staff officers and their wives or girlfriends usually went out to dinner in one of the many superb restaurants in downtown London. We had great parties at each other's homes and went to formal military balls. These affairs included British military officers and their wives or British neighbors. Many of these friendships lasted a lifetime and became valuable later as we all became more senior in our fields and knew we could rely on old "shipmates" for help. Everyone was responsible and accountable for their own conduct, and there was no need for the "Big Brother" approach later adopted by the Department of Defense (DOD). This decried the "glamorization" of alcohol and, along with all the rules regulating even speech between the sexes in the military, has essentially killed any concept that there is fun involved with being in uniform.

A final career-changing event occurred that year I became PWO. The chief of civil engineers, Rear Adm. Albert R. (Mike) Marschall, came to London accompanied by his aide, a classmate of mine from CECOS.

Admiral Marschall was an "old-school" officer who had graduated from the Naval Academy in '43 and served on a destroyer in World War II before transferring to the CEC. He told me once that his destroyer had been shelled, bombed, and hit a mine at the Leyte landings in the Philippines during World War II, while he observed the Seabees living in a nice camp ashore, so he decided that was a better option! He had a photographic memory and never forgot anyone. While he was visiting the senior officers at the headquarters, I entertained my CECOS classmate. He asked me a lot of questions about my job, London, and so on. It was a good visit, and I was extremely impressed by the chief. Several weeks later, I received a call from the CEC captain on the CINC's staff who asked me to drop by for a chat. We made some small talk, and he asked me about a couple of ongoing issues. He then said: "If you could have any job in the CEC now, what would it be?" Without hesitation I responded, "operations officer in a Seabee battalion," adding that I was not senior enough since that is a lieutenant commander job, and I would not be up for promotion until late that summer. He said that was a great choice, and he hoped I would get it someday. Another week went by and out of the blue I received a call from my assignment officer. He said, "There is an immediate opening in one of the Seabee battalions for an operations officer that would require you to leave in about three months to catch the battalion on deployment. Are you interested?" When I asked about the rank issue, he said, "The CO of the battalion wants you, so that won't be a problem." I asked about a relief for me, and he said it was being worked out and he would let me know when I called him back with my decision. I did wait a couple of days and talked to the CEC captain about my good fortune. He said that was really "good luck." When I called back to accept, I was told that my relief would be my classmate from CECOS, who was the chief's aide, and that's when everything suddenly became crystal clear. I did not care how it happened, I was going to the job I wanted most and could not wait to leave.

A crucial leadership lesson I learned after my Vietnam tours was that "brilliance" did not guarantee good leadership, though it could sometimes impede it. Empathy can be difficult when personal superiority gets in the way. Good leaders understand not only their limitations but also those of their superiors, peers, and subordinates, and they chart a path to success in spite of them.

Chapter Six

ONWARD AND UPWARD

*I may not have gone where I intended to go, but I think I
have ended up where I needed to be.*
—Douglas Adams, *The Long Dark Tea-Time of the Soul*

For the first but certainly not the last time, Rear Adm. Mike Marschall—
my first real mentor—had intervened in my life in a big way. NMCB-4
deployed to Guam where I was to join them. I left London in early April
1975 to travel halfway around the world. It had been almost four years since
my last tour in Vietnam and working with troops. A great deal had changed.
At the top of the list was the draft had gone away, and we now had the All-
Volunteer Force (AVF). I had not given much thought to what that really
meant because in London the junior officers and enlisted personnel had
been carefully screened, and there were few manifestations of this change.
Although Zumwalt had retired as the CNO, the previous four years had
stamped the Navy with his imprint. This, coupled with the high-profile
racial incidents and publicized drug problems within the Navy, made the
Navy and the Seabees far different from what I had previously experienced.

The first inkling came as I waited for my military charter flight to Guam
at Travis Air Force Base. All the passengers for the plane were waiting in
a large holding area. There were many dependent wives and children, in
addition to the full range of military personnel from mostly the Navy and
Air Force since Andersen Air Force Base was located on Guam. There were
all pay grades represented, from junior enlisted to O-6—all in uniform. As
I was sitting there, I became aware of a disturbance several rows behind me.
There were three or four junior Navy enlisted men sitting next to a chief
who were being loud, obnoxious, and drawing stares from all those within
earshot, including several officers more senior than I. The chief seemed
to be with them but said nothing to them and was oblivious to the stares

he was getting. I waited for someone more senior to deal with this, but none did. Finally, I walked over to the chief and said: "Chief, these men are disturbing the passengers, and I want it stopped now. Take care of it!" The men looked at the chief to see what he was going to do. No doubt he noticed that I had three rows of ribbons from what had to be at least two Vietnam tours and decided he was not going to take me on. He simply said: "Yes, sir," and told the enlisted men to "Stifle it." As I returned to my seat, I noticed all the military personnel looking at me, some with a look of amazement. I felt I had done nothing more than was expected of an officer in this situation but was troubled by the fact that the chief had not taken care of it without being told, and no one else had stepped up.

Guam Deployment

I landed at Andersen AFB on a Saturday afternoon and was met by the officer I was relieving as operations officer (S-3). As we drove from the northern end of the island to Camp Covington near the center, he said the battalion's five-and-a-half-day workweek had ended at noon, so he thought I should rest up from the trip until Monday morning and then we would start turning over. I took his advice, though I did meet the CO and XO, along with a few of the other officers first. Early Monday morning, I was awakened and told there was an emergency officers' meeting in the wardroom. It seemed the battalion had received a flash message from CINCPACFLT directing it to cease normal operations, close ongoing projects, and mobilize the battalion for an immediate contingency construction operation. While I had seen the reporting on the fall of Saigon and the South Vietnamese government the week before, I had pushed it from my consciousness, as I did with all things concerning Vietnam, never thinking it could possibly affect me. Our contingency construction orders were to move out to the abandoned Japanese airfield on Orote Point and construct a temporary camp to house fifty thousand Vietnamese evacuees, the first arriving in a week. It was called "Operation New Life."

The officer I was relieving said that since this was going to be my job, not his, he would help close the ongoing jobs, provide whatever insights he could, and be on his way. The CO and XO agreed this was the logical plan, so I pulled all the company commanders and senior enlisted together, and we laid out a plan and started executing it. Chief among the priorities was producing a list of construction and other materials to be flown into Guam since the existing stocks were going to be depleted quickly as we constructed the same SEA huts that the Seabees had become experts on erecting during the recent war. Many additional items would have to be brought in to accommodate the women and children who would occupy the camp. We reconnoitered the abandoned field and determined where we would put up the camp, while the engineering department drew up the camp layout, continued determining the material required, and pulled out the plans for the facilities to be constructed. We moved all the bulldozers we had, plus those we could borrow, to the site and started clearing the jungle that had overgrown much of the field. I have often thought of these good old days before the necessity of Environmental Impact Statements that would have caused needless delay until the proper level of waiver was obtained.

I jumped into what I loved to do, and the Seabees did what they do best—contingency construction. The battalion worked 24/7 for months and had the first SEA huts and supporting facilities such as showers, toilets, dining facilities, and laundries completed as the first Vietnamese began to arrive. The flow of Vietnamese was set by the speed we completed the camp, which was in turn dictated in a large measure by the personnel available, including more Seabees to be flown in from another battalion located on Okinawa. Another limiting factor was the time involved in procuring the massive amount of lumber, cement, plumbing fixtures and piping, electrical materials, washing machines and dryers, and the like. The importance of adequate logistics planning was a major lesson for me from this operation—having the *capability* to do something was meaningless without having the materials to do it.

The CO and XO were incredibly supportive and outstanding individuals—much to my relief considering my previous battalion and Naval Advisory Detachment Danang experience. I ran the show. The officers and men responded in an amazing fashion with few exceptions. Initially, the CO of the Seabee battalion on Okinawa was brought in to be the refugee camp commander, but after it reached critical mass, an Army battalion was flown in from Hawaii to take over the administration of the camp. One tasking we received required us to build a temporary bank that would support a large safe to hold the gold and diamonds that some of the refugees had brought out with them. *Gold and diamonds?* These were clearly not the Vietnamese I had worked with; I wondered what their fate would be. I also wondered what criteria were applied in deciding which Vietnamese were to be saved and which would be left to their own devices. I could not think about that now—I had a camp to build. After months of 24/7 operations, we completed the camp and largest contingency construction operation in recent memory and turned it over to the Army. We started working on our previous projects, while continuing to support the Army running the camp.

Shades of some of my experiences with the Army in Vietnam came back to visit me as we supported the refugee camp. When we had coordination meetings with the Army leadership, especially the camp commander and his operations staff, they did not seem to be content with providing us the tasking they wanted completed by specific dates but also wanted to micromanage how we were going to do it. The first time this happened, I respectfully said that how we did the work was our business, but it would be done on time and completely. Since I was a lowly O-3, the more senior Army officers informed me that I would provide them a complete plan of the work for their approval. I answered that I would report that request to my CO and get back to them. When I briefed the CO, he observed that the Army colonel who had given this order outranked him as an O-5, and we needed to brief the commodore (an O-6) of the 30th Naval Construction Regiment from whom we received tasking and get his guidance. This we did, and he told us to set up a meeting with the Army colonel and his staff. At the meeting, the colonel repeated his demands somewhat arrogantly and condescendingly. The commodore replied, "Lieutenant Shelton will complete the work as requested without submitting anything to you for approval. If he does not complete it in a satisfactory manner, let me know; otherwise, I do not want to be bothered again like this. Any questions?" There were no questions, and there was nothing the colonel could do about it. The importance of the support of the chain of command and the tendency of the Army to micromanage were logged away for future days.

During this operation, I got to know the CO and the XO as well as the other officers and senior enlisted personnel in the battalion. They were a cut above those I had worked with in Vietnam for the most part, and the performance of the battalion reflected it. Both the CO and XO were Naval Academy graduates from before the "flower child" days, and their approach to discipline reflected it. There were regular personnel and barracks inspections, and disciplinary problems were handled evenhandedly. I had an old-school master chief Seabee as my operations chief who seemed to have done everything and knew everything about construction with Seabees. We hit it off and formed a credible team. Two old acquaintances showed up to survey the work the battalion had done—my last CO in NMCB-9, who was now the chief of staff for all the Pacific Seabee battalions out of

Hawaii; and Rear Admiral Marschall, who had been instrumental in me getting orders to NMCB-4. Both were obviously impressed and told the battalion so at quarters (morning formation).

My old skipper had upped his bourbon intake to over a bottle a day, so we had to put one in his room in addition to the one that was placed on the wardroom bar for him. Unfortunately, but not unexpectedly, it would not be long before this finally took its toll, but then he was still the "Seabee's Seabee" and loved getting out with the men. Admiral Marschall also loved being in the field and the camaraderie of the wardroom. I was astonished when he said to me, "I didn't finish that story I was telling you in London at that reception when I was jerked away." He then started up almost exactly where he had left off. That he would even remember talking with me was incredible and impressive. Notwithstanding my impression of the wardroom, the senior enlisted, and our important visitors, I soon saw more of the effects of the new Navy within the battalion.

All-Volunteer Force

About three weeks into Operation New Life, the ensign who was my engineering officer came to me and said he needed to report something to me concerning a couple of the junior enlisted men in the operations department. As operations officer, I had no chain of command function, and disciplinary matters concerning these men were generally not of concern to me and I said so. The ensign persisted, saying that what had happened concerned me, and he thought I should know about it. It seemed that both men had missed the morning formation as a protest of the change in the working conditions since I had become the S-3. Specifically, they did not like the long hours and more "military atmosphere" I had brought with me, whatever that meant. For the first time, I was being told some of my troops did not like working for me. While I saw the causal actions as necessary for mission accomplishment, this marked my first awareness that my leadership role had changed from advocate for my men as a junior officer to "organization man" for the commanding officer, ensuring the proper use of resources to accomplish the mission. The ensign was caught in the crossfire of cultural change and troop advocacy versus the organizational needs I embodied. For me, it brought home that while I did not need to be liked by my subordinates, I did need to be respected. I told him to get these two individuals, two forms for placing them on report for a military offense, a copy of the UCMJ manual, and the master chief and be in my office in thirty minutes.

He did as I asked, and these men were standing in front of me in a half-hour's time. With the UCMJ manual open in front of me and the report forms laid out where they could see them, I asked them if it was true that they had missed quarters as a protest. They answered "Yes, sir" in unison and started to explain themselves. I interrupted and told them I did not want to hear it and that I wanted to read them something—it was the UCMJ article on the offense of mutiny. At the end of the article, it said the penalty for mutiny was death. I then looked squarely at them and pronounced, "I am placing you both on report for mutiny and intend to have the penalty carried out. Dismissed!" All the color drained from their faces as they tried to stammer something, but I cut them off and told them to get out.

I could see the master chief in the back of the office suppressing a belly laugh, but the ensign was as white as a sheet. He said, "You're going to have them killed?" I replied that these two would be running down to the JAG's office to tell him what had happened. They would be told that technically they were guilty of mutiny. They had better change their story before the case got to the XO for disposition. By the time that happened, they would say it was all a misunderstanding and that they had overslept and were willing to take whatever punishment the XO thought appropriate. This is exactly what happened; I gave the XO a heads-up, and that got him laughing also. I told the ensign that the point was the word would quickly spread throughout the battalion that the new S-3 was not to be tested as the results would not be pretty—and so it was. What troubled me most was that this could even happen, and they could think they could get away with it. Things had indeed changed in the Seabees and the Navy.

Not long after this I found that the new Navy extended to the wardroom. Every morning, I had a meeting with the company commanders and senior enlisted involved in the operation to review where we were and what the priorities were for the day. The battalion did not have a full allowance of lieutenants, and my predecessor had placed some junior officers in positions of authority. Among them was an ensign who had been quite a standout at the Naval Academy. He had been a five- or six-striper, meaning he was high in the midshipman chain of command, in the top of his class academically, and captain of a sports team. I had not formed an opinion of him yet and took him at face value. One morning, I told him that I wanted him to close the project he was working on, secure the project materials and tools, and move his men to another higher priority tasking. As was my custom, I asked everyone if there were any questions at the end of the meeting and received none. That afternoon, the master chief and I toured all the worksites. When we arrived at this one there was no one around, tools and material were lying everywhere and easily pilferable, and the site was a mess. The master chief and I picked up the most expensive tools and put them in our jeep. Then I sent him off to find the ensign and his senior enlisted man and have them report to me.

I asked the ensign what I had told him to do that morning to ensure he understood me. He repeated my instructions almost verbatim. I then asked why he had not carried them out. He said, "We have been working this 24/7 routine [as had the whole battalion, but I guess he had not noticed], and I decided my men were tired, so I told them to take the day off and we would move tomorrow." I said, "I gave you an order and I am not accustomed to having anyone disobey my orders, especially an ensign on his own authority. I want them carried out immediately, and I do not care if that means you do it by yourself or you and your senior chief do it together or you find your men and they do it. When you are finished, you report back to me that it has been done. The master chief will be available if you need further help understanding my orders." He started to explain, but I cut him off.

Later he came into my office to report that he had accomplished what I had directed, but some expensive tools were missing and could not be located. I asked him if he understood they would have to be paid for if not recovered, and he was on the hook for them. He said he did. Then I had a little "come to Jesus" talk with him about what was appropriate behavior for an ensign or any officer receiving an order from a superior officer, particularly in a leadership position, which he should have learned at the Naval Academy. He remained visibly defiant but simply said "Yes, sir." The master chief and I let him and his senior chief swing in the wind for a few days before the master chief returned the tools to the senior chief with an ass chewing that I wish I could have seen. I related all this to the CO and the XO, who told me they had also been disturbed by what they were seeing in some of the junior officers. I was more concerned that the senior chief had failed to professionally train this ensign as that is the job of a chief. My master chief agreed.

The CO went on a trip to visit detachments of the battalion that had not been recalled to Guam for Operation New Life and asked me to chat about his trip when he returned. He said he was concerned about the detachment in Japan at Atsugi and wanted me to visit it before the site was turned over to the Okinawa battalion as part of the realignment of projects caused by New Life. He wanted my observations and recommendations and said he would not prejudice me with his concerns so I could give him my unfiltered views. There was a lieutenant (junior grade) assigned as the OIC at Atsugi, with a senior chief as his assistant, and they picked me up at the airport in Tokyo. During the drive back to Atsugi that night, I asked them about the CO's visit and could not believe what they told me; I guess they thought the CO had already related the story. When the CO's plane had arrived in Tokyo, they had missed the announcement because they were drinking in a bar and only realized it when the CO found them some time later. He was already upset; then they started driving back to the base when the CO stopped the vehicle and took over driving because he was concerned about the amount of liquor they had consumed. They assured me that the CO had overreacted but did understand that they had let him down. The turnover to the other battalion was in two days, so I said I would inspect the det the next morning. I would look over their barracks spaces and then check the status of the project they were working on. To use a baseball analogy, the det went 0 for 3.

They showed up at the quarters formation in cutoffs and shower shoes since they were packing out, and they all unlooked unkempt. The barracks was a mess, with only a few rooms satisfactory and beer cans and liquor bottles lying on the floors of some of the rooms. Worse still, the project was a mess. They had known I was coming before the turnover, and this was how they prepared for me. Once again, it was apparent the OIC and his assistant were more worried about being buddies with the men than doing their jobs. I told them I wanted everyone in his uniform and in ranks for an inspection in one hour. After that, I wanted the barracks and project site squared away even if it meant they stayed up all night, as we were not turning over a disgrace. It took most of the available time to get things reasonably into shape, which included haircuts and trimmed beards. I called the CO and reported my findings, along with a recommendation that this officer and his chief be removed from any leadership position. He concurred and said they would be dealt with when they returned to Guam with the det that week. This experience ratcheted up the importance in my mind of selecting the right men to be OICs of detachments away from the main battalion camp and my respect for the CO, who let me handle the turnover personally rather than responding as a knee-jerk reaction during his previous visit to the det.

The Wardroom

Despite the missteps related above, the wardroom was sound and the camaraderie good. Among the things I liked in the wardroom was a dubious award called the DSMS (Don't show me shit), which was awarded every week during the formal dining night to the officer who had been observed pulling the most infamous feat of the week, without regard to rank. Candidates were voted upon and the winner received a figurine of carved wood depicting a man bent over with his head inserted into his anus. While such a thing could not be imagined in today's PC-sensitive world, it provided a means to humble the mighty with some laughter, and everyone—including the CO, XO, and I—won it at least once during the deployment. The junior officers loved nominating the leadership, and it was done with respect. The wardroom had great parties when we got time off and went down (minus the CO and XO) to the clubs with exotic dancers for laughs. *Work hard, play hard* was the order of the day. With this backdrop and the superb job done by the men during Operation New Life, the battalion was awarded the "Battle Efficiency 'E'" as the best Seabee battalion in the Pacific Fleet for that fiscal year. Not long after that, the Society of American Military Engineers (SAME) awarded us the Peltier Award as the best Seabee battalion in the Navy in a competition with the Atlantic Fleet Battle Efficiency "E" winner. My first deployment was all I could have hoped for, and we headed back for a six-month homeport period prior to deploying to Rota, Spain, as the European Alert Battalion.

The purpose of a homeport period between deployments is to refit the unit by rotating personnel in and out, training the unit, exercising the unit, and preparing/planning for the upcoming deployment. It is always a very demanding time on the battalion leadership, both officer and enlisted, with a lot to do and never enough time to do it in. One of the major leadership problems is there can be too many opportunities for the more junior personnel to get into trouble; their supervision suffers because they live in barracks, and the chain of command generally lives in residential housing. The inspections, military training, parades, and other events were generally not greeted with glee, and most Seabees wanted to be on deployment working to get away from these things. With the new officers and chiefs who were reporting to replace those who had rotated out, assignments for the next deployment needed to be made quickly and accurately. The process we used was that I, as S-3, prepared a draft with my recommendations for all the positions in the battalion for the upcoming deployment and then sat down with the CO and the XO to discuss these recommendations and my reasoning for them. This was done before we left Guam and made assumptions relative to the incoming officers and chiefs based upon what the assignment people had told us, as well as any personal knowledge we might have. Since we agreed on the most important assignments and our evaluations of the personnel we knew, the three of us reached a quick agreement.

We received some exceptional officers and chiefs who had strengthened the best battalion in the Navy further, but there were also a few problem children to deal with. We were going to Rota, Spain, with detachments posted in Sicily, Greece, Italy, Crete, Diego Garcia, and Scotland. This strained the available leadership resources to the maximum and required some unique solutions. The preference was always to send officers who had completed at least one deployment and proven themselves to be OICs for the larger dets. The same was true for senior enlisted personnel for the smaller dets. A couple of the lieutenants waiting for us bore some significant watching, as they appeared to have issues, so I assigned them jobs in the main body that would be based in Rota. My assessment was we would have a good deployment and continue to build on our reputation.

Deployment Issues

The one issue that we could not control and had the potential to cause a great deal of trouble during the deployment was that the logistics system used by the Atlantic Fleet Seabees to support Europe was 180 degrees different from what was used by the Pacific Seabees, for reasons that made no sense except to perhaps some bean counter. I am sure it was justified by some defective cost analysis. In the Pacific, all the construction and project material was sent to Port Hueneme, where it was all checked against the list of required materials for accuracy, packed and stored together as a project, and then finally loaded on the same vessel and shipped to its destination in the Pacific. This generally worked well with few material deficiencies when a battalion started the project.

In the Atlantic, the project materials were individually ordered from the suppliers and shipped by the suppliers directly to Rota or the det sites, where they were to be stored together by project until needed. The problem was the material was not adequately checked because the battalion personnel in Rota and on the dets were not going to be working the project, did not generally have the material lists or manpower to do it, and really were not concerned about it. It was a ridiculous system that continuously led to finding out the wrong material had been ordered and shipped or that the right material had been lost in the mail or, more likely, been used by the battalion before us to make up for their shortages. This required time consuming reordering and expensive air shipment of material if the items were small enough or project delay if they had to be moved by ship. All of this made it exceedingly difficult to plan the work schedule for all the European sites since we were guessing whether there was a critical mass of material to keep the projects going. I belabor this because, like the logistics observations during Operation New Life, logistics support of forward forces is the Achilles' heel of all operations, and the "for want of a nail" analogy applies. The old saw is true: "Amateurs talk tactics; professionals talk logistics." Unfortunately, the amateurs in the White House, the Department of Defense, and the Navy continue to fail to understand the importance of logistics, ignore it, or just wave it away, much to the detriment of the operating forces.

My pre-deployment trip to Rota and all the det sites gave me concerns, and my worst fears about the state of the project materials waiting for us was confirmed. Turnovers between battalions tend to be stressful events as the outgoing battalion tries to justify what it has accomplished (or not) and claim a greater completion percentage on turnover projects. The incoming battalion wants to show it inherited a mess that will require a great deal of rework to get the projects back on track. This is exacerbated by the normal personality issues between individuals of different units that add to the competitive atmosphere, especially in this case when an Atlantic battalion was being relieved by a Pacific battalion in the Atlantic theater of operations. I could hardly wait for the two months to go by when I would bring the advanced party to Rota to begin the official turnover. The day I returned from the trip, the promotion list to lieutenant commander came out and my name was on it, so I was immediately "frocked" (promoted without pay) since I was occupying an O-4 billet. It would be many months until I was finally officially promoted for pay purposes, but wearing the rank did make a lot of difference, particularly outside the battalion.

Rota, Spain Deployment

In February 1976, I took the advanced party of the battalion to Rota in a DC-8, with the CO, the XO, and the rest of the battalion to follow in a few weeks. Some of the personnel taking over the dets went directly to the det sites, while the large dets' personnel came with me to Rota so the logistics/administrative support arrangements would be locked in. I told my people to be as nonconfrontational as possible and accept the turnover figures of the other battalion. We would correct the record later. There were representatives of our operational boss (commander, Construction Battalions, Atlantic Fleet or COMCBLANT) there to oversee the turnover, and we wanted to ensure they saw any issue we would be bringing up later. The turnover was capped by the outgoing battalion's wardroom throwing a party for those they had befriended and worked with in Rota, including the nurses at the hospital. I was told that our officers were not invited. This did not break my heart but spoke volumes on how petty personality issues can sometimes overwhelm professional relationships and leave a lasting bad taste.

The battalion performed in an exceptional fashion during this deployment, completing nearly 100 percent of its tasking, including several high-priority additions in support of the nuclear submarine dry-dock facility in Rota and establishing a new det in La Maddalena, Sardinia on short notice, which supported the submariners and tender there. The battalion received a personal message from the four-star at CINCUSNAVEUR when we departed, confirming it was an outstanding deployment. Once again, the Seabees performed brilliantly under the junior officers and senior enlisted, overcoming a host of logistics and chain of command leadership problems.

Leadership Change

What is not supposed to happen in officer personnel management did happen on this deployment. The CO and XO are supposed to be on a rotation schedule that ensures they do not leave the battalion during the same deployment or homeport so there will be continuity of command philosophy and operations. Our superstar CO and XO left within two months of each other before the middle of the deployment. The charitable thing to say is their replacements were not in the same league. Of course, the key officer is the CO, whose personality is reflected in the battalion almost immediately. On paper, the new CO had all the right stuff, having been an apparently highly regarded battalion S-3 in Vietnam and already having had a command as an O-5. The reality was, however, he had read his own press clippings and thought he knew it all, not needing or wanting advice from anyone. And he was happy to let this be known to one and all. This put us on a collision course within days of his taking command since

I was responsible for battalion operations that were running well, and he decided he needed to put his stamp on them by directing changes without any knowledge of what was going on or why.

The conflict started innocently enough with him calling me to his office the day after the change of command and telling me that he and I would be leaving on a trip to visit all the detachments in two days. This was a bad idea for several reasons, not the least of which was that there was a briefing schedule that had been put together to familiarize him with what was going on in the battalion. He would be meeting the key officers and senior enlisted, touring and inspecting the main body site, and making calls on the senior Navy commanders in the area. It was starting that day and would continue for at least a week. Additionally, it was not a good idea for the CO and S-3 to travel together, as one of them should generally be in the main body in case an unexpected operation dropped, such as Operation New Life, occurring with no notice. It had always worked well to send the operations senior enlisted chief with the CO to brief him on what was happening on the dets and the personnel he was meeting. Finally, I had just returned from a det swing a week earlier and had significant catching up to do preparing for the coming homeport and next deployment.

He tried to blow off all these points by telling me he had been an S-3 and knew what the job entailed. I finally convinced him to wait and be briefed by asking him how he was going the answer all the questions he would get regarding homeport personnel policies, such as who would be required to live in the barracks and who could live off base; what would be the weekly routine; and a host of other things the men expected the CO to tell them. He grudgingly agreed to go with the senior chief from operations, who would act as his guide, but told me if he did not like the experience, I would go with him in the future. We gave him a detailed operations briefing that included my assessment of the personalities of the senior officers in command of the various bases he would be meeting, paying attention to their hot button issues. After a week or so, the new CO departed for his trip. It was a disaster of major proportions for him personally and the battalion by extension.

The first place he went was Holy Loch, Scotland, where the top-rated lieutenant (junior grade) in the battalion was doing a masterful job completing projects in support of the submarine commodore. He was well liked and exceptionally competent; his father owned a construction company, and he had grown up in the construction trades. He not only understood the engineering of the plans but also had considerable trade skills that helped in training the more junior men. The living conditions for the det were not the best. They were berthed on the submarine tender, and this cramped their work schedule because meals and other ship's functions conflicted with the ten-hour days dets normally worked. All of this had been discussed at length at the beginning of the deployment.

The decision had been made by COMNAVACTSUK, who was responsible for the support of the det; there were simply not enough funds or available accommodations off the ship to support them living elsewhere. This had been approved by CINUSNAVEUR and reluctantly by our operational boss, COMCBLANT. This had all been briefed to the new CO. He did not like this arrangement, and when he went back through London, he unfortunately ran into the current COMNAVACTSUK at a happy hour in the headquarters building and told him so. This precipitated some heated words between the two, and COMNAVACTSUK told our CO he was not welcome in the UK ever again and to get out on the next plane. He also sent a personal message through our chain of command reiterating this message. I learned of all this from my CECOS classmate who had relieved me as PWO in London via a phone call the following Monday. He had been CO for less than two weeks and was already behind the eight ball.

About this time, I received a call from my assignment officer asking me if I was interested in being placed on a list of candidates to be the aide and administrative assistant to the deputy chief of naval operations for logistics (DCNO Logistics), a three-star submariner. He mentioned that Rear Admiral Marschall himself would make the choice and talk with the three-star about it. Getting out of the battalion at the end of this deployment was the top thing on my mind, and this sounded like a good educational job. I said, "You bet!"

Things did not improve in my relationship with the CO as he continued to want to do my job with no real feel for what was going on with the projects or, more importantly, the officers and chiefs in the battalion. I knew them all very well and had worked with them over the course of two deployments and a homeport. He had a passing acquaintance with them and had not really had an opportunity to observe their performance. Nonetheless, he kept insisting that individuals be moved because he did not like the rank of the person in a key job. He felt it was too junior, but the more senior individual he wanted did not have the skill sets to accomplish that job. This came to a head when I came to him with my recommendations for the officer and chief assignments for the next deployment to the Caribbean, also a COMCBLANT domain, with a large det going to Diego Garcia to construct a pier. He told me that he had already made the decision of who would be assigned to each job and did not need my recommendations. That certainly was his prerogative, even though it made no sense since I had the most knowledge of everyone as the longest serving officer in the battalion. I asked him if I might be permitted to ask him some questions about who was going to be assigned to a couple of key jobs.

I said the most important upcoming assignment with the highest visibility, would be the OIC of the Diego Garcia det, particularly after the firing of the senior chief OIC we had sent on a similar detachment on this deployment. He told me his choice, and I was incredulous. He had picked the weakest lieutenant in the battalion because he was the most senior. I had kept this guy with the main body in Rota in a staff job because he was weak in leadership and particularly in presence. I related this to the CO, and he asked who my choice would be. I told him the strongest officer for the det was the OIC we had in Sicily. Unfortunately, he was needed to run the largest and toughest company job in the main body site, the equipment company, because of the multiple det sites around the Caribbean. He also needed to be a presence in the wardroom that would be filled with new, unknown officers. The only other lieutenant who could do the job was the current equipment company commander, but I felt he would be reluctant to do it because he would be on his own far from the battalion. He knew the OIC on the current det had been relieved for unsatisfactory performance and would not want to ruin his career on what he would view as a risky job. He was right. It was a high-risk job, but I felt comfortable that once he got over being assigned, he would do an excellent job.

After discussing this position for quite a while, he said he would talk to this lieutenant about the job and look at my other recommendations. I think he was realizing that there was risk for him also if the OIC failed. At any rate, I recommended that he tell this officer he was going to be assigned to the job and not ask him if he wanted it because if he said no, I did not believe there was another choice. Despite this advice, he did ask, and the lieutenant flatly responded, "No." In the end, the CO finally called the lieutenant back in and told him he was going and that was it. He did go and did a fine job despite his reservations.

As this was happening, I received my orders to the aide job and knew I was leaving as soon as we got back to homeport. The CO had seen the orders and knew Rear Admiral Marschall had picked me for this assignment. The bottom line was we had more discussions concerning yet more changes he wanted, and I told him there could only be one S-3. If he let me do my job for the rest of the deployment without interfering, I would guarantee him a successful deployment and a personal message of commendation for our performance from the four-star. If he made the changes he was asking for, all bets were off, and I would not guarantee anything. I further suggested he work with the assignment office to find a suitable officer, whom he would be happy with, to take my place. He told me what I promised had better happen or else, but he said he would leave me alone and he did. We got the four-star message.

Out of nowhere and with little warning, the battalion received tasking to establish a det in La Maddalena, Sardinia, to support the submarine tender personnel there by completing a club facility and a sports field. This came after we had already deployed all our other dets with the pick of the litter officers and senior enlisted personnel, leaving only a few quality personnel in the main body to ensure the tasking there was completed. The "nukes" were, of course, demanding the best officer and senior enlisted for the det because nuclear tasking was most important. After looking at the situation and remembering what I had seen in Holy Loch with the submarine squadron commodore's demands, I met with the CO and XO (the previous good ones) and discussed my plan. To meet the submarine commodore's demands would end up screwing up several other dets and jeopardize completing our other tasking, which the nukes did not care about.

A workable alternative involved taking the construction master chief who had worked for me in Guam and was then the AOIC in Sigonella and make him the OIC, even though the commodore had requested a list of junior officers that he could chose the OIC from. My reasoning was that a junior officer would be eaten alive by the commodore and his minions, while they would not faze the master chief. We would need to go to our Seabee boss who was also a commodore and have him tell the submariners that was the way it was going to be, so get over it. That is what happened, and it worked like a charm. Although initially pissed off, the commodore was soon eating out of the master chief's hand. They became "new best friends" because of the master chief's skill and ability to meet any demand of the commodore. The Seabee det became celebrities at La Maddalena and earned great praise when they finished and left. This would have never happened with a junior officer in charge.

Two final comments on the deployment are important. First, knowing that the XO was leaving the battalion to take the advanced party back to homeport, the CO decided to leave early also to visit det sites and other things. This made me acting CO for the turnover of the deployment sites to the next battalion, a situation I had never seen before. I was happy to be acting CO and things went well, despite the fact the incoming battalion commander was extremely unhappy that a lieutenant commander was his counterpart in the turnover. The second, and in my mind most important, was I met a cute Navy nurse stationed at the hospital during the deployment, with whom I would get back together when she left Rota later that year and I was in the Washington, DC, aide job. We became soul mates and were married toward the end of my aide job in late 1977. Marrying Mary was the best decision I ever made, and she has been my best friend and confidant for a lifetime, while completing twenty years as a Navy nurse, retiring as an O-5. She raised our two children and my daughter from my first marriage, who came to live with us when she was ten.

My relief as S-3 was waiting for me when the battalion returned to homeport and impressed me as someone who could work with the CO; that is, someone who would do exactly as the CO directed with no questions asked or comments given. My unceremonious departure from the battalion included my fitness report debriefing, during which I received a much better than expected report, considering the relationship we had, but tempered by the CO's comment that he did not care for my attitude but could not fault me for the success of the deployment. He also mentioned he knew I would not be going to the job I was unless I was a favorite of the chief and let that hang in the air. Seeing his office in my rear-view mirror was the best thing I had experienced in the last six months. One postscript on the futures of the officers I served with in NMCB-4 should be mentioned. Both the CO and the XO who departed in Rota were promoted to O-6, and the CO was on the fast track to flag when a family issue caused him to retire before that could happen. Of the CEC officers in the wardroom, three went on to be promoted to two stars and two others to O-6. Those five went on to command battalions and higher, and all had a major impact on future Seabee operations for the next thirty years, including the Grenada invasion, Lebanon operations, Desert Shield/Desert Storm, and the 2003 invasion of Iraq. Neither the incoming CO or XO made O-6, nor did the incoming S-3 make O-5.

Falling Off the Turnip Truck

One of my favorite expressions is "I didn't just fall off the turnip truck," yet when I arrived in the Pentagon, it felt like it. There is a traffic bypass that surrounds the city of Washington, DC, called "the Beltway." I came to believe, after four tours of duty inside it, it had unearthly powers akin to those seen in science fiction movies. Normal individuals, who have been good at their jobs in the field, reasonable to work with, and generally possessing the qualities desired to be productive contributors at a higher level, crossed the Beltway and became different creatures. They suddenly saw themselves as all-knowing and adopted a control-freak mentality. They were desperate to survive the experience without being embarrassed or shown up, while being recognized for their brilliance. This is not peculiar to people in the military but extends to politicians, the bureaucracy, the Congress, and even the White House. I did not understand this when I arrived on the E-ring, the outer perimeter hallway, of the Pentagon's sixth floor, where the Navy leadership resides in offices with views. I have said many times over the years that I learned more about how decisions were made in the Navy, and by extension in Washington, DC, in general, during my Pentagon aide tour than anywhere else.

Crossing the Beltway was for me, and I am sure many others, like Caesar crossing the Rubicon. Once crossed, there was no going back to those naive days of yore when I took it as a cardinal belief that those in the Pentagon and Washington, DC, knew what they were doing.

Permit me to describe the position of aide and administrative assistant to a three-star on the E-ring as a frame of reference. All aides wear an aiguillette or colored loops around the left sleeve of their uniform to designate their status; the number of loops corresponds to the number of stars their boss sports, in my case three. The term "loafer loopers" describes how many view the position of aide being one of much leisure and little work (with generous perks to boot). There is truth in this, and I always classified it as a high-visibility, low-risk job.

At any rate, while the job generally entails making sure the admiral is where he is supposed to be on time, in the correct dress, and understanding what it is he is supposed to be participating in, it was really the administrative assistant part of the job that took the most time. I was lucky as my first admiral did not live in government quarters, so I did not have to deal with a quarters' steward, the gent who takes care of the quarters and prepares the flag's uniforms and cooks the meals. The anti-military feelings caused by the Vietnam War were still present enough in late 1976 that those stationed in the building did not wear uniforms to work and changed in the building if something arose requiring it. Almost all my duties were completed in the Pentagon, and I spent a great deal of my time in mufti.

The front office staff was composed of an executive assistant (a line captain), an executive secretary, and me. Between the three of us, we answered the telephone and dealt with the voluminous correspondence that cycled through the office. The division of responsibilities between us belied the seeming overkill of positions. The secretary prepared correspondence for the admiral's signature from drafts and other input and kept track of the packages of correspondence that were routed through our office for "chop" (reading by the admiral and concurrence or nonconcurrence signified by his initials or note on the package). I did the first read of everything that was headed for the admiral's desk, to ensure it was complete, grammatically correct, and devoid of spelling errors, and answered any questions asked by incoming correspondence. It was surprising how many times the proposed response to be chopped did not answer the questions in the incoming correspondence. I did not comment on the quality of the content for brilliance or making sense for the Navy. That was the job of the executive assistant, who would read the stuff to give it a professional line officer analysis and alert the admiral if he saw any problems.

The breadth of the span of control of the DCNO for logistics was enormous, covering not only providing supplies to the fleet and shore installations but also being the sponsor for ship and aircraft maintenance, shore facilities, military construction, maintenance and repair programs, Navy environmental policy and issues, ordnance, and a host of less important items that made the Navy ready to conduct sustained operations at sea. Each of the principal divisions under the three-star responsible for one of these areas was overseen by a one- or two-star with a specialty in that area, for example, a supply corps flag running the logistics division, an engineering duty officer flag running the ships maintenance division, and a CEC flag running the facilities division. As the environmental area had not quite exploded yet, there was a CEC captain running that. The logistics planning division was run by a line two-star. The captain and I got to work around 6 a.m. to read all the message traffic that had come in and determine the importance to prepare the admiral's message board. We generally were there until between 6 and 8 p.m., depending upon the admiral's schedule. One of us worked a half-day on Saturday when the admiral came in to do paperwork.

A word about the three-star for whom I worked. I have always thought of him as a prototypical nuclear submarine flag officer, with the exception that he did have more of a sense of humor than most, although he worked on keeping that hidden to fit the profile. He was one of the original officers for the nuclear program who were personally selected by Admiral Rickover and was very loyal to the man. He was intelligent, dedicated, and no doubt a superb handler of submarines, or he would not have been selected for three stars in an extremely competitive group of officers. Of course, he was a Naval Academy graduate in June 1945, making him the last World War II veteran that I personally worked for. He carried the Rickover mania for perfection in all things that was bred into nukes by Rickover since failure was not an option. Perfection is not possible in the world of logistics; it is a world of tradeoffs and budgeting compromises. This led the admiral to have three boxes on his desk: in, out, and too hard. The too hard box was reserved for thorny issues with no clear choice evident and downsides to all that obviously did not fit the perfection formula. Sometimes packages languished in this box for weeks before some forcing function made the admiral make a choice.

How It Worked

What I came to understand during the eighteen months I had this job molded my thinking for the rest of my Navy career and professional life. It ranged from forming an intense dislike for the pettiness I observed in individuals treating subordinates callously because they could to national defense policies being made to garner votes for an election without regard for the effect on the readiness or war fighting capabilities of the armed forces. Since I reported to the job just after the 1976 presidential election that brought Jimmy Carter (a Naval Academy graduate) to the White House, I was able to observe the change in administrations with all the new players in the Defense Department and Navy Department. This involved setting up meetings for the admiral with the appointees that were involved or interested in logistics issues under his purview. The sheer number of positions that had been created in the DOD and the Navy Department was staggering, but I was more overwhelmed by who was chosen to fill them. First, there were the long-time "experts" who were loyal to the winning party and were selected for positions when that party's administration took power after doing something or other in academia or business while they were out of power—the so-called "revolving door." They tended to move up with each new administration. The next group comprised newcomers to the more significant jobs from industry or academia who might have some previous military experience but had not been part of an administration before. Last, there were the newcomers who had worked to secure the party's victory and were being paid back with jobs and titles they hoped would put them into the first group at some time in the future.

I came to see the last group as the most dangerous because it tended to contain smart people who had no real experience; some worked for think tanks like the RAND Corporation, where they were paid to think deeply about a variety of current issues. One of these folks called upon the admiral and pissed him off so much that he called me in and told me, "I am never available to talk to that SOB again. Make sure I don't!" The magnitude of the micromanagement of the armed forces that was going on under the guise of civilian control of the military, which had exploded under McNamara, started to dawn on me. I became aware of a new term for a sizeable number of the people parading through the office to meet the admiral and permeating the staffs in the Pentagon. They were called "wonks." While the dictionary definition of the colloquial term "wonk" is a pundit or functionary who delves deeply into the arcane technical details of a political policy, I like my definition better: "WONK is an acronym for Without Necessary Knowledge" (or as I saw it, *experience*). It was during this time that I first encountered an up-and-coming political appointee named Everett Pyatt, who had been appointed principal deputy assistant secretary of the Navy (logistics). Our paths would cross again during my first Seabee command with interesting consequences.

Another fascinating phenomenon that I was exposed to but did not fully appreciate until much later was the relationships and friendships I developed during my time on the E-ring as a lieutenant commander. Within perhaps a hundred yards of my office were the offices of the secretary of the Navy, the CNO, the VCNO, and several key three-star positions. I became friends with—or at least an acquaintance of—the aides to most of the key players, and I ran into them off and on as we progressed through our respective careers. There were two commanders, one lieutenant commander, and one lieutenant I knew from that time who became four-stars and one, Vern Clark, became the CNO I ended up working for in my last job. Vern was the officer who promoted me to one-star rank while he was the deputy at the Atlantic Fleet command. I had lunch and played golf with him several times over the years as he moved up, and we compared notes.

One revelation that answered questions I had wondered about while I was in the field was how policies were developed and promulgated in the Navy. There were two groups that molded policy and shepherded it through the approval process. The first were action officers, who were usually lieutenant commanders or commanders. They created the answers to questions, direction to fix a problem, or came up with their own ideas to deal with issues in their assigned functional areas. Once a policy was formulated, it was their job to sell it and take it through the chops, obtaining sign-off from the appropriate staff element necessary to obtain its ultimate approval. This could require coordination and chops from many other staff components, and it could take some time, but more importantly, it called for skill in working the bureaucracy. Strategies to get around those that did not agree were especially important. Sometimes they were as simple as waiting until that person was away from their desk and finding someone else in that function that either did not know or care. This kind of action had potentially serious ramifications.

When the system worked properly, ideas were vetted and massaged and resulted in the best solution (within certain constraints). Generally, they were not liked by everyone, which I thought was a good sign. The flaw that I saw was when there was no interest in the issue by other staff groups or the knowledge of the issue was scant or nonexistent in the superiors in the chain of command; alternatively, when the approval chops were gamed, some dumb or even terribly bad things could come out as CNO policy. This is what led to the questions I had when I was in the field and saw something come down from the CNO that made no sense to me or that I thought was stupid. Issues regarding the Seabees fell into this pattern, as the other staff codes knew little about the Seabees and tended to view them as wasters of resources that would be better spent on the fleet, or worse, giving resources to the Marines for which the Marines did not pay. I stored this away and used it to my and the Seabees' benefit in my next job, where I was the principal action officer for enlisted Seabee personnel matters.

The second group of players was composed of analysts, a creature that came into its own during the McNamara years of the adoption of business practices by the DOD. Most were, at least in my mind, wonks. Analysts analyze, at least after a fashion. These people multiplied seemingly without limits in the Pentagon, particularly in the budgetary and auditing areas. Over my four tours of duty in Washington, DC, this was the group I developed the largest disdain for because it was predominantly composed of smart people with little to no practical experience in anything but number crunching. Since they rarely had any field experience at all, they tended to discount it as not important. A career analyst who had been promoted to a top senior executive service (SES) flag-equivalent rank once told me that all that was needed to make any decision was intelligence and data. When I pointed out that without experience, there could be no understanding of data and its validity, I was lectured on how ridiculous that argument was since that was inherently obvious to smart people. My experience had shown me that relying on intelligence and data in a void resulted in the stupid decisions to save money at the cost of necessary capabilities. The adage "Good judgment comes from experience, and a lot of that comes from bad judgment" has been attributed to many people, Will Rogers, Mark Twain, Bob Packard, and Rita Mae Brown among them. Regardless of its source, the truth of the statement is self-evident; still, those who lack experience disputed it—wonks, analysts, and many SES government employees.

One other group that was especially important was the executive secretaries to the key staff officers. They could make sure a package was placed on top of the pile and seen relatively quickly or buried or even more drastically "lost," if it suited them, with impunity. Treating them well, complimenting them, and generally making them feel important (because they were) was another valuable lesson I took with me. Along this same line, I was amazed at the senior to subordinate treatment I witnessed while I was in the aide job. When I came to the job, having never really been exposed to the inner workings between officers with stars on their shoulders, I thought that once a person was elevated to flag rank, they were joining a collegial club of gentlemen who offered each other mutual respect. Nothing was further from the truth. There were several wonderful exceptions, but as I saw not long after I arrived, there were many more egregious examples. I can recall two distinct examples. The first was being present when a two-star was chewed out in a manner that was worse than any I had seen dished out by chiefs in the battalion to junior enlisted personnel. It was profane, very personal, and certainly not an inducement to spend a career trying to make flag. The second was watching my boss, a three-star with over thirty years of service, being ordered about in a demeaning manner like a common seaman by some of the four-stars. Even worse was the condescending treatment by some political appointees of senior military officers. After that, nothing surprised me in what I observed of the inner workings on the "flag deck." For some of these individuals, each promotion just confirmed the superiority they felt over everyone else. They displayed this to their subordinates while shielding it from their superiors.

There is an old saw to the effect that if one wants to enjoy eating sausage, he should not watch it being made. The same is true of the formulation of defense policy. Since I read all the packages that came through for the admiral's chop, I saw what the Navy's uniformed staff felt about key issues and what it recommended. When packages were signed out by the CNO or VCNO, copies were generally sent to the key staff officers, so they knew what the result of the process was. At the top of the list of issues that drew the biggest controversy was the creation of pork to feed the political election system through procurement of weapons systems, facilities, ship maintenance, and a host of other items that could create jobs, not to mention decisions on base closures. It was eye-opening to see the number of times the Navy and Marine Corps made a recommendation to the secretary of the Navy or the secretary of defense that was completely reversed. That reversed position then became the Navy's position with the expectation that it would be strongly supported by Navy leadership to those in Congress known to oppose it. This could take the form of adding to the procurement account types of aircraft the Navy had no use for and did not want, keeping Navy bases open for which there was no use, cutting the end strength of the Navy when there were already personnel shortages, directing personnel policies that were counter to military readiness, and a host of other things that were done for political reasons by one or both major political parties when they were in power. Two major flip-flop issues depending upon the party in power were "strategic homeporting" (the building of additional homeports along the East Coast and the Gulf Coast so strategic assets would not be easily targeted) and the requirement for a six hundred-ship ship Navy. These competed with social programs for funding. I learned a new meaning of civilian control of the military. This had been going on since the founding of the United States and could be argued to have been a significant factor in the repeated lack of preparedness of the armed forces at the outset of major conflicts.

After more than a year in the job, the admiral called me in one day and told me he was retiring from the Navy and was not going to have a big retirement ceremony. He just wanted to be retired in the CNO's office with a small, invited group in attendance. The front office staff made all the arrangements, and the admiral retired quietly and without fanfare, just as he desired. His relief was also a nuclear submariner but a much different personality. First, he wanted to live in Navy flag quarters in the Washington

Navy Yard and have a quarters steward to help his wife with entertaining. The process of getting the quarters he wanted was interesting because of the jealousies that the status of certain houses and their locations engendered, particularly among the flag wives. Shortly after he assumed the position, he called me into the office and pointed at the desk saying: "Let me guess: in, out, too hard?" When I said yes, he said something that I always remembered and tried to practice from then on. "Nothing is too hard. I read the package with the supporting material and either sign it, disapprove it, or return it with a note asking for clarification or more information. Get rid of that third box—I don't sit on things." The other thing he told me was he had a sailboat that he was berthing near Annapolis and liked to sail, so he did not plan on coming into the office every Saturday to do paperwork unless there was a crisis. I liked this guy and was not surprised that about six months after I left the job, he was promoted to four-star status.

Ghosts of Christmas Past

While I was in this assignment, I became involved with two things from my Seabee past. The first involved the fate of the awards I had recommended to the CO for my personnel after Operation New Life, especially the enlisted types below chief who had been so instrumental in achieving our success. There were not a large number, and together with a couple for deserving junior officers and chiefs, the recommendations were well written and fully justified in accordance with the awards manual. When I checked on them, I found that almost all the enlisted awards had been downgraded to letters of commendation, while awards for the officers and the chiefs had been approved. I was incensed to the point that I decided I would do something to attempt to get recognition for all the enlisted folks in the form of a ribbon to wear on their uniforms for their hard work. I wrote a recommendation for a Meritorious Unit Citation for NMCB-4 with full justification, including copies of all the commendatory messages and letters that the battalion had received from the chain of command up to and including the commander in chief, Pacific. I then sent it up the chain of command above the battalion, to commander, Construction Battalions, Pacific (COMCBPAC); CINCPACFLT; CNO; and finally to the secretary of the Navy. Amazingly, all of them favorably endorsed my letter, and the battalion received the award. Mary and I flew out to Port Hueneme and were present on the parade field when the award was presented to the battalion at a special parade.

This experience with the Navy awards system, coupled with my experience with the XO's chewing out in NMCB-9, led me to write an article for United States Naval Institute *Proceedings,* which I will digress momentarily to review. The fundamental prejudices inherent in the Navy award system caused me heartburn throughout my career; they are the antithesis to good leadership.

What I discovered in researching the piece, "Who Are the Heroes?" was summarized in the lead in to the article: "There is, however, ample evidence that the initiation fee one pays to join the fraternity of heroes is higher for the enlisted man than for the officer."[15] After both World War I and World War II, there was an outcry about the Navy awards that focused on the high number of awards made to senior officers versus junior officers and enlisted personnel. After World War I, there was a congressional investigation during which Secretary of the Navy Josephus Daniels joined in the criticism of the awards that had been proposed. These criticisms were as follows: (1) the large number of officers recommended who had either served on ships that remained in home waters throughout the war or who had been on shore duty in the United States, (2) the small number of enlisted men who had been recommended for awards (119 out of 500,000), (3) the small number of Navy Reservists recommended, and (4) the small number of awards allocated to those serving as armed guards on board merchant ships. Congress was particularly incensed that awards were recommended for every commanding officer who lost a ship or had one damaged in enemy action. After World War II, controversies again arose over the way awards were made during the conflict. The secretary of the Navy appointed a board of review for decorations and medals under Admiral F. J. Horne.

The criticisms and the board's findings bear examination. The major criticisms were like the World War I criticisms: (1) inconsistency among the various delegated authorities in awarding medals (the board agreed with this without comment), (2) a disproportionate number of awards to regular Navy officers (the board found no discrimination against reservists even though the clear majority of serving officers were reservists by saying, "After considering all factors involved some of which cannot be reduced to a mathematical figure," and that virtually all senior command positions were regular officers), (3) not enough awards to enlisted men, (4) the depreciation of higher awards, and (5) questionable practices in awarding automatic awards. The board's comments on awards to enlisted personnel were outrageous, particularly since neither the Army nor the Marines had any problem awarding most awards for valor to enlisted men. The board stated, "Enlisted men were not frequently in a position of responsibility nor were their courageous and heroic acts always witnessed by someone who could make a recommendation.... . Only in serious emergencies, catastrophes or battle actions do such opportunities occur for them and then it is often difficult to 'distinguish' one's self. Heroism is commonplace, i.e., there is too much competition."[16]

My conclusions in the article were that (1) defending the larger proportions of awards to officers seemed to be a primary concern of the naval establishment in any situation; (2) the predominant theory with regard to enlisted personnel was as expressed in the Horne report, that is, "it being natural to give him (the officer) more credit than individuals in lower echelons ... much of whose combat is performed as a matter of necessity"[17]; and (3) there is profound belief that the commanding officer is deserving of recognition as a matter of course when awards are being considered for any action. My active duty experience (and observations since that time) have seen little change in these basic tenants of the Navy award philosophy with one exception, which is the proliferation of awards to females and minority groups, who were also given preference in promotion and assignments as part of the drive to establish "role models/diversity." One only has to look at the pictures displayed on the various Navy bulletin boards proclaiming Sailors of the Month (Quarter, Year) to see the disproportionate number of female and minority group members who are chosen against a larger number of white males eligible.

The other blast from my Seabee past was being asked to come over to a senior CEC captain's house for dinner only to find one of the superstar CEC O-5s there. I was told he was relieving the second CO I had worked for in NMCB-4. I was asked to give him my observations on my deployment to Rota and offer any recommendations I might have for things to do when he took command. One did not have to be a rocket scientist to figure out there must have been some more issues after I left. Never being shy, I gave him my opinions and wished him luck. This was more reinforcement of the value of personal reputation. The fact is that much that is important to know is not written in fitness reports; rather, it is learned by keeping one's ear to the ground and knowing who can be relied upon for help.

Shortly after my new admiral arrived, I received a call from the assignment officer saying it was time for me to move on. He had a job in Washington he knew I would like: running the Seabee assignment branch in the Bureau of Naval Personnel (BUPERS). He was right. The plan was to move me early for a temporary assignment in NAVFACENGCOM inspecting the Construction Battalion Unit (CBU) Program. This program was composed of small Seabee units, under junior officers on major Navy bases, that took on construction and maintenance projects, while giving Seabees additional shore duty opportunities. Additionally, I was to be on the Chief Petty Officer Selection Board for six weeks to understand that process and review the records of those eligible in order to get a feel for the state of the force. This all sounded wonderful to me, plus the guy I would be relieving was a friend who I knew to be very competent, so I would not be inheriting any problems. I had just gotten married, and this would get me out of the long hours of the aide job. Mary had been assigned to the U.S. Naval Hospital, Quantico, Virginia.

A final humorous story of the changing times in the Navy involved a female yeoman who worked in an office close to ours. She was extremely attractive and had quite a figure, so she drew the requisite stares as she walked up and down the E-ring. She had the reputation of not being a rocket scientist, but still competent in her job. Sticking her head into the offices on Friday afternoons where there were single aides, she asked if anyone wanted to go to happy hour at the club at Fort Myers with her. This looked like trouble to me, so I was always too busy, but others were not. One day one of the chiefs came into the office with a copy of *Playboy* magazine that had a feature on "Women in Uniform," and there was the yeoman in all her glory! She was kicked out of the Navy for this but left a fond memory with those who knew her.

Back to the Seabees

The temporary duty at NAVFACENGCOM was uneventful, but I gained an appreciation of two things. The first had to do with the CBU Program. I visited a number of these units and noted how well they were doing; they validated the decision to establish them by illustrating the talent and skills of the junior officers and senior enlisted personnel who ran them.

The second was the incredibly talented senior officers who were assigned to the key positions in NAVFACENGCOM as O-6s and who essentially ran the headquarters for the chief. In those days, senior executive service (SES) civilians worked for them and not the other way around. The results showed because they had the experience that most of the SES lacked, while they were markedly devoid of focused self-interest that an unfortunate number of SES types displayed. Later, I observed that when the roles were reversed—when some civilian politico decided that an SES civilian was a flag equivalent and an O-6 could not be his boss—the quality of the officers assigned to the headquarters declined because the type of quality officer I had seen did not want to work for an SES civilian.

Chiefs Selection Board

I found the Chief Petty Officer (CPO) Selection Board to be a superb leadership experience. The board was composed of an equal number (about thirteen) of commissioned officers (mostly commanders and lieutenant commanders), with a few of the senior warrant officers for flavor, and master chief petty officers under an O-6 president of the board. An officer and a master chief from a specialty area were paired up to review enlisted rating groups—in my case the seven Seabee ratings—and make recommendations to the board on the best qualified personnel for selection to fill the quotas. The quotas reflected the number of vacant authorized end-strength positions approved by Congress at the E-7 level. Each officer/NCO pairing determined what they thought were the most important criteria for selection to CPO in a rating. This would then be briefed to the full board before the slate of selectees and non-selectees was voted on. No names were shown to the board, the candidates being labeled Selectee (or Non-Selectee) 1, 2, 3, and so forth.

Disciplinary issues, such as NJP and courts-martial convictions, had to be briefed on any selectee, along with an explanation of the reason selection was recommended despite this issue. The process took all of six weeks, although we finished the Seabees faster. We were then assigned some other small fleet ratings that had not been assigned, so those finishing early could do them. In the case of the Seabee ratings, our criteria were simple: superior performance in Seabees battalions, demonstrated leadership skills, no significant disciplinary breeches or behavioral problems in the record, and completion of the required military education courses. Some allowances were made for individual ratings owing to the smaller number of billets in battalions for them as opposed to other ratings. Selection for special duty such as the State Department or Camp David added plus marks. I came away being impressed by how talented this group was and how difficult that made the selection process.

After going through this process, I was left with an even deeper appreciation for the Navy enlisted community, and I had learned some fundamental truths as well. Regarding discipline, it seemed that getting in trouble when young was a kind of rite of passage, especially in some ratings, such as boatswain's mate, engineman, and other deck ratings in the fleet. The same was true in the Seabees, but to a lesser extent. It seemed that many of the selectees recommended in these ratings had disciplinary scrapes during their first enlistment, including nonjudicial punishment and even courts-martial, but had straightened themselves out and had stellar careers since. The common factors seemed to be related to key maturity markers after the age of about twenty-five: they had reenlisted, married, and settled into adulthood. This is another major change with today's Navy—drive for perfect, sensitive sailors whose value seems to be more determined by political correctness than rating skill. The fact that young people do stupid things when they are young is seemingly lost on many of the civilian politicos driving new standards that tend to be inflexible and unforgiving. The difference can best be illustrated by one of the records that the board voted on.

The number one selectee in the boatswain's mate rating had a conviction by a special court martial on his record. The officer briefing his record explained that this man had been convicted of striking a recruit while he was a recruit training (boot camp) company commander. He then read from the performance evaluation signed by the O-6 in command of recruit training that rated this man the number one recruit company commander and stated that no man alive could have withstood the provocation in this case (being spat on in the face) and noting that the special court martial gave the man the lightest possible sentence due to the mitigating circumstances. Other than this incident, the man's record was spotless, and the recommendation was in favor of promotion.

As the briefing officer was nearing the end of the report, a female commander (the only woman on the board, as there were not many in the Navy then) asked to comment. She said, "There is no place for any violence for any reason in the Navy. This man cannot be promoted!" As I was reflecting on this amazing statement in a service whose mission was to bring violence and death to the enemies of the United States, a CWO4 (the most senior warrant officer grade) spoke. He was a boatswain and simply stated, "I have been on deck all my career and have learned that it is necessary to get some people's attention when they don't listen or fail to follow orders. To do this, I whack them upside the head and continue to do so until they understand. That's the way it is in the deck force." The whole room exploded in laughter, and the female commander went red-faced. There were no more comments, and the board voted 25 to 1 for selection. I would say the chances of this sailor making chief today would be zero, and he would probably be thrown out of the Navy.

The other lesson that came across loud and clear was the arduous nature of the life of an enlisted Sailor or Seabee—especially in ratings where the rotation between sea and shore duty was six years at sea for two years ashore because the bulk of the billets were on ships. In the Seabees, the rotation was forty-eight months of sea duty for twenty-four months of shore duty. This meant these men were away from their families a great deal, and the high number of divorces reflected the marital strain in the records we reviewed.

While much has been said about the pay issue and comparability with civilian pay, I would say that for those who chose this life, pay was not a major factor. It takes a certain motivation that is hard to quantify and difficult to understand from the outside. My coming tour running the Seabee assignment office reinforced what I had already seen in my battalion tours, in my days in the Army while at West Point, and in the records I read on the CPO Selection Board concerning enlisted personnel. The good ones understood the needs of the service and that sometimes they would trump personal preference. The job required executing orders that were not desirable, but that is what they signed up for. They "sucked it up," explained it to their families, and went off to do the best job they could despite their personal feelings.

Our office bent over backward for Seabees with special problems, such as children with disabilities or family illness, while being consistent with policy for those who tried to game the system to get out of work they did not want to do. Word travels fast around any community, and unmerited special treatment can cause major morale issues, so we worked hard to ensure that this did not happen and were successful a remarkably high percentage of the time. All these experiences served to increase my desire to return to a Seabee battalion as soon as I could because working with these men was what I wanted to do.

Seabee Assignment Branch

When I took it over, the Seabee Assignment Branch was manned by a lieutenant commander, with a lieutenant serving as the rating assignment officer (RAO), a master chief who assigned E-7s, E-8s, and E-9s, and three senior chiefs, each with a petty officer assistant, who assigned their rating groups. The groups consisted of builders, steelworkers, and engineering aides; construction electricians and utilitiesmen; and equipment operators and construction mechanics.

The system was straightforward and simple. There was a rating system that evaluated each empty billet in the Navy and prioritized it on three lists—the Atlantic Fleet, the Pacific Fleet, and the shore component. The empty billets were in priority order by rating/pay grade vacancy, and there was a separate determination of which fleets or shore billets were to be filled first. Against this there was the list of all personnel eligible to move each month because they had completed their assigned sea or shore tour. The detailer would then match the assets available against the requirements in priority order considering the qualifications for the billet such as training, past performance evaluation levels, and so on. The problem was there were never enough of the right individuals to fill the billets, so billets were gapped or filled with lower quality personnel.

Issues with assignments were first brought to the lieutenant for resolution and then to me before going up the chain. This gave me more opportunities to work with officers who felt they were special and the rules should not apply to them or their need for enlisted personnel. Occasionally the rules did not apply, but not often. I was never reversed by the chain of command when I presented our reasoning for an assignment, but we were required to make some special selections for key billets like Camp David or the State Department detachment that required additional screening and took priority over other assignments. The one area that caused the greatest heartburn with our good people was recruiting duty. In the AVF, there was tremendous pressure on recruiters to feed the system with strict quotas; if the quotas were not met, the recruiter was fired. Additionally, the locations for many recruiting billets were not popular. The reward for doing a great job on deployment was an evaluation that had a Seabee automatically screened for recruiting duty despite his aversion to it. It was a major lose-lose scenario the enlisted detailers were powerless to change.

While the assignment of Seabees was the function of my office, I was more involved in personnel policy issues than the actual detailing of individuals—that was done by my staff. I used what I had learned in the Pentagon from watching action officers who were effective in creating policy. I was in a somewhat unique position in that I wore three hats in three different commands because of additional duty orders attached to my primary orders as the head of the assignment branch. That billet was under the chief of Naval Personnel (CNP), but I also had a position on the

CNO's Manpower Policy staff (OP-01), as the Seabee enlisted community manager (ECM) responsible for advising the CNO on Seabee personnel policy, and on the NAVFACENGCOM staff, as the technical advisor to the commander on Seabee personnel policy.

I spent time talking with the senior enlisted Seabees in both fleets and my own master chief looking at personnel issues that were affecting the Seabees from recruiting to training to retention. Together we came up with changes that needed to be made to current policy that would make the career of a Seabee better and increase retention and readiness. This was reduced to a briefing for the approval of the commander of NAVFACENGCOM as the technical advisor to the CNO. If he approved the change, I would draft a letter for him to sign to the CNO that went to the DCNO for manpower requesting the change. Since I was the ECM on the DCNO manpower staff, that letter would come to me to answer. I would recommend it be approved, and that is what happened since no one much cared about Seabee stuff as it did not affect the fleet. Once approved, I would be directed to draft a letter to the chief of Naval Personnel directing he implement the policy change. That letter would come to me as the assignment branch head, and I would write the implementing instruction. For example, this process was used successfully to change Seabee rotation policy to make sure that Seabees received their fair share of shore duty in the United States instead of constantly being assigned to overseas shore duty, as was then the practice. There were two ratings in which Seabees might get one shore assignment in the United States in twenty years of service, and that had a predictable negative effect on retention.

The biggest issue on my plate was the integration of women into the Seabees and all the emotion that entailed. Just as in several areas in the armed forces, while the actual number of women that were interested in being integrated into this field was (and remains) relatively small, the changes required to make it possible were large. One issue that continues to be a challenge in the integration of women in the armed forces is the physical requirements. Construction electricians are required to climb telephone poles using leg strength that many women do not possess. This was the first time I ran into the argument that because most women could not do this, it should be removed as a requirement for the rating. The requirement to string wire and cables from poles was not going away. Someone had to do it and then maintain the cabling or wire, but somehow that did not matter. It took more time and effort than it should have to get this issue back in the box, but it provided useful insights about women's issues that I would be involved with later in my career.

A bigger issue was integrating women into Seabee battalions, a change that I knew was eventually going to happen. I tried to put together a reasonable plan. The Achilles' heel of this prospective program was that there were not enough senior enlisted women Seabees or women CEC officers to put into battalions as role models, mentors, and counselors for the women that might be assigned. The idea of assigning fleet rating women and female line officers (also in short supply) was a bad one. It was bad because they had nothing in common with the Seabees, knew nothing about them, and would not likely volunteer to serve in the field, having joined the Navy precisely to prevent that possibility. Additionally, there were few ships in those days to which women were assigned, and there were other places the Navy would rather place the women it had.

The most detrimental effect of the initiative to increase the number of women in the Navy was the mandatory recruiting quotas placed on the recruiters to find women that wanted to be Seabees. The problem was not that they could not fill the quotas; rather, it was that there were only so many seats available in the Seabee schools that trained new recruits for the Seabee ratings. Every seat was tied to a recruiting quota. The Seabees ratings were so popular that we had added an extra year to the initial obligation to be a Seabee from four to five years, and there were waiting lists for males to join. Hence, it created a real problem when directives required recruiters to hold quotas open for women. After several discussions with Seabee players, I was able to brief the commander of NAVFACENGOM about a plan that did away with quotas for women and instead stipulated that the Seabees would accept and train every woman that was recruited. Since this seemed like a victory for women in the Navy by those who did not understand what was going on, it was approved and implemented. Even though women were introduced into amphibious construction battalions within five years, it would be almost twenty years before they would be put into regular Seabee battalions—and I also found myself in the middle of that brouhaha.

Faster than I thought possible, I received a call from my assignment officer telling me I had been selected to attend the Naval War College (NWC) in Newport, Rhode Island, for the Command and Staff course. He had also talked with the Nurse Corps assignment people, and they were willing to send Mary to the hospital there for a year and then move her with me from there. That was a surprise, as we thought she would have to leave the Navy. Being selected was a big deal since there was only one slot per year for a CEC lieutenant commander. I felt incredibly lucky.

Naval War College

The 1980–81 class year at the NWC was a great one for several reasons. It was an election year, and control of the White House changed from Jimmy Carter to Ronald Reagan. Against that background, there was much discussion of the Cold War, the Soviet Union, and how U.S. military policy would be affected. Several of the key Republican thinkers on defense themes were instructors at the NWC.

The composition of my class was interesting because among the thirty-odd Marines in the class were Oliver North (of future Iran-Contra fame, but then an unknown major), a future four-star Marine general, and some very bright future leaders in the USMC. The quality of officers from the Army and the Air Force (about thirty each) was also top drawer. All the other services viewed the NWC as the premier service war college, and the selection criteria for attendance was stricter than for promotion to O-5.

The speakers included not only the members of the Joint Chiefs of Staff (JCS) but a host of other thought-provoking individuals that included one of the few German Navy officers to survive the sinking of the German battleship *Bismarck* in 1941.

During my tenure at the NWC, Mary and I were able to experience what would be the last win of the America's Cup in Newport that fall with its carnival atmosphere. With its history, magnificent mansions, proximity to the Kennedy compound, and its magical aura, Newport was an exciting place to be.

Having commented on the quality of the members of the other services in my class, I should also mention who the line of the Navy chose to select and send, which are two different things from the line perspective. It was important to be selected to go because that was a quality indicator that was good to be in one's record, but for fast-track, high-flying line officers, this year of education was viewed as a waste of time that should be better spent in career-enhancing jobs at sea. What I learned was while the other services had career paths for their officers designed to produce general officers if all the proper wickets were passed, the Navy's career path was primarily about getting enough officers to command at sea at all levels by completing the various tours required satisfactorily to be selected by the command screening board. This did not leave time for much besides technical education and key fleet staff jobs and certainly no time for graduate school and service colleges. This was a dramatic change from the interwar years, during which the NWC was a strategic think tank for the battles against the Japanese that were sure to come. There is a quote in the war-gaming center to the effect that nothing that happened in the conduct of the war by the Japanese was a surprise (except kamikazes) because all their moves had been gamed at the NWC.

The result of this thinking was there were no submariners (the group then running the Navy and holding many key flag billets); few cruiser / destroyer officers; and few combat fliers, who would be running the Navy in the future. Instead, there were mostly surface officers from the amphibious and auxiliary ships, specialty staff officers, and pilots of reconnaissance and logistics planes plus helicopters. Few of these would make flag rank, and fewer still would ever be in positions running the Navy. This problem was later partially corrected by the Goldwater-Nichols law that forced joint duty for selection to flag rank—which included service school attendance—but my observation was the Navy line never cared much for professional military education or civilian graduate school other than for an anointed cadre of line officers that rotated through Pentagon and fleet jobs where their credentials could be shown off. The running of the fleet was too serious a business to waste time on anything beyond competent ship driving.

The Command and Staff course at the NWC was divided into three parts: a study of warfare history and strategy, a study of nonquantitative (subjective) decision making, and a naval operations course that was essentially war-gaming with assigned roles in exercises. My previous studies at West Point (in military history and strategy), my field exercise experience in the Seabees plus combat experiences in Vietnam, and my tour on the E-ring (where nonquantitative decision making was the order of the day) made the courses relatively easy for me. That the courses were not difficult does not mean they were a waste of time. They concentrated on some areas I had little experience in. The role-playing aspect of the naval operations section was eye-opening for the lessons that were intended to be taught versus the lessons learned.

The reactions of the many combat veterans in the class from the other services to the war-gaming problems were far different than the Navy officers because few of the Navy types had any combat experience. This was most apparent on the rules of engagement issue, where too many who had been in combat had suffered from ambiguous rules that got people killed and were far less worried about breaking the rules if they perceived an eminent threat. The teaching point was that the ROE were sacrosanct; they had to be obeyed because of the potential for unintended consequences. Easy for someone to say who had never had their life on the line!

Courses I found particularly useful were the electives I could choose. The first was a course on the origins of the Arab-Israeli conflict, and the second was a course on ethics training and the military officer. For the Middle East course, the voluminous reading assignments on the perspectives of both sides was supplemented by presentations by an officer from the Israeli Navy and one from the Egyptian Navy (they spoke on separate occasions). They had fought against each other in the Yom Kippur War in 1973, but I found the Egyptian officer's stories about being advised by the Soviet Navy more fascinating, as he spoke of how poorly he and his people had been treated. He said it was evident that not only did the Soviets not trust them, but they did not want to be living in the same camp with them. The logistics support provided by the Soviets was terrible, resulting in inadequate fuel or spare parts to keep their boats operational. Good information to know about our biggest potential adversary.

The ethics course was superb. The prime mover for the course was Vice Adm. Jim Stockdale, the Medal of Honor recipient and senior POW in Vietnam; the course was his brainchild. He believed that his liberal arts education—mostly self-taught because he enjoyed studying philosophy and ethics—was a key factor in his ability to deal with his terrible experiences as a prisoner and essential to defeating the enemy's attempts to brainwash him and get him to collaborate. It was his firm belief that his ability to endure the years of solitary confinement would not have been possible without this preparation. A professor emeritus in philosophy at Columbia, Joseph G. Brennan, essentially ran the course from day to day. Shortly after the class started (and when the admiral was not present), Professor Brennan told us that the effects of Stockdale's punishment resulted in the admiral sometimes retreating inside himself right in the middle of a discussion, with his mind returning to his cell for some unspecified time. We were to ignore this and continue to carry on with the class, and sooner or later he would come out of it. I witnessed this several times, and it was something I will never forget. The class members talked about how we were all measuring ourselves against the admiral and wondering if we could do what he had done.

One of the most illuminating chats the admiral had with us involved the appropriate punishment for a Marine deserter who had lived in Vietnam since the war was over but had recently asked to come back to the United States. When asked, Stockdale looked at us and said, "Nothing." He could see we were shocked by his answer, so he followed up with this comment: "This man was a junior enlisted man probably with nothing more than a high school education if that. How smart he was or fit for military service, we do not know, but just like most of the turncoats in the Korean War, he came to see he was wrong and asked for forgiveness." Contrast this situation to an O-5 prisoner I charged with treason, collaboration with the enemy, and everything I could think of for his traitorous activities that harmed his fellow POWs. I told the secretary of defense that I wanted this traitor publicly executed. He was an educated officer who had volunteered to be a pilot yet sold out his fellow prisoners for perks and special treatment. I was told the country did not want to hear this, and there would be no punishment for this man other than he would receive no medals for his time spent in captivity. To me, this was such a travesty that I have never gotten over it. How could we punish this Marine corporal when we let that SOB off with a slap on the wrist?

Apart from the association with the top-quality officers in my class and the courses I have mentioned, I was impressed by reading Thucydides's account of the Peloponnesian War; it brought home the timelessness of the lessons of war and how little has changed regarding men in positions of power—put another way, "Power tends to corrupt and absolute power corrupts absolutely."[18] Why should I expect leaders to be different now if they had not changed since Thucydides's time?

It was once again time for the assignment officer to send me to a new job coming out of the NWC. The O-5 promotion list had come out and I was on it, so I was moving out of the journeyman level and into the leadership sphere of the CEC, albeit at a most junior level. The complicating factors were two: one was how Mary's assignment in the Nurse Corps played into the equation, and the other was that it had been determined that I needed a contracts job running a construction contracting office to round out my career profile. The Nurse Corps had selected Mary for graduate school, and they had a list of schools she could attend. Fortunately, one was the University of California, San Francisco's medical school, where she could receive the master of nursing administration she wanted. There was also a position that would open within a year as the resident officer in charge of construction, San Francisco Bay area, that appeared to be a good fit for me, as I could have a longer turnover with the incumbent, owing to my not having had a previous assignment in construction contracting. Going to graduate school worked out well for Mary as she had given birth to our daughter, Jessica, and this would allow her more time with the new baby than a regular job. It all came together with the added benefit that my parents were located on the West Coast. I graduated from the NWC with "distinction" by ranking in the top ten percent of the class academically, but the subjective lessons I learned were more important in my career.

These journeyman years marked my transition from doing things myself or managing a limited number of subordinates to leading larger organizations with less direct supervision. The leadership lessons learned in interaction with flag officers and senior captains, particularly in Washington, DC, were crucial to my further development and career success.

Chapter Seven

TAKING COMMAND

Command—the highest of highs and the lowest of lows, sometimes separated by milliseconds.

—Anonymous

The change in professional status between the ranks of lieutenant commander and commander can be viewed as subtle depending on perspective, but I always felt it was a significant break point in responsibility, accountability, and expectations. I was not going to command immediately, but the responsibilities of running a large construction contracting office were significant. There was a difference between this and being an S-3 because I was essentially independent in running the office, with only occasional inspections from higher headquarters. *I would choose what to inform my bosses about and when to do it.* The staff was not that large, but being responsible for the execution of over $100 million in construction contracts was a large amount at that time. The San Francisco Bay area was a major fleet concentration of the Pacific Fleet. There was a large installation between Sunnyvale and Mountainview called Moffett Field and a smaller one called Alameda Naval Air Station (NAS) on Alameda Island near Oakland. Moffett Field served as the home base for P-3 reconnaissance squadrons and a NASA facility that flew SR-71 Blackbird spy planes. (These bases—along with many others—were later closed as part of the Base Realignment and Closure program or BRAC.) Our office was also responsible for all the military construction on Travis AFB and the highly classified Sunnyvale Air Force satellite downlink facility. In short, not only was there a large workload, but there were also important mission-related concerns tied to the successful and timely completion of many of these projects. This placed great responsibility on the small number of CEC junior officers assigned to me who were in their first construction oversight positions.

Being the known heir apparent and assigned as deputy is tough on the incumbent principal and the deputy since every decision that is made has the potential to be reversed when the incumbent leaves. But we worked it out and there were few difficulties. The junior officers assigned to us were high quality, and those who remained in the Navy had successful careers. The civilian staff was not as good, with a few exceptions. The clerical staff was particularly poor and made getting the required paperwork out correctly and on time a full-time problem. The administrative assistant job had spoiled me with quality admin staff, so the poor level of grammar, typing, spelling, and so forth in the clerical staff really irritated me. Even answering the phone correctly was not a routine occurrence. The technical staff, which comprised the supervisory engineers and construction project inspectors, was a mixed bag with the spectrum of skills from outstanding to unsatisfactory. Since they were all government employees, and this was the first time I had U.S. government service (GS) civilians to supervise, it marked the beginning of a career-long bout with the world of human resources (HR) and its Byzantine rules governing the hiring, evaluation, promotion, and firing of employees, in and out of the government.

Over my career I was fortunate to work with many superb GS employees who worked awfully hard and did more than was asked of them. I was frustrated that I could not recognize this with the pay or promotions they deserved. I also encountered quite a few useless GS employees that gamed the system, which seemed to be designed to protect unproductive workers from being fired without extraordinary paperwork and counseling requirements. This placed a huge burden on the supervisor who had real work to do. The laws that were enacted to protect classes of people from discrimination seem to assume that no one is incompetent and deserves to be fired. Any problem is the problem of a callous supervisor discriminating against a righteous employee, regardless of gender or ethnicity on either side of the issue. The HR professionals frowned upon having an opinion like this, so I would just go to them with whatever the employee issues were and tell them to put together a plan of action that would either result in the individual becoming satisfactory in performance or being fired. We would follow the plan, and if it did not work, it became an HR performance issue. The rotation of military officers through supervisory jobs was a factor in this problem because by the time the problems with an employee were recognized and the routine counseling had occurred, the officer was usually approaching the end of his assignment, and the poor performer could wait him out. It became my methodology to begin documentation as early as it was warranted so that the process was initiated, and a file could be turned over to my successor that would preclude the wait-it-out out syndrome.

One additional new phenomenon was working in a chain of command where, although my direct bosses were CEC officers, officers were in the minority, with many senior GS civilians holding key positions in the hierarchy. Just as there was a spectrum of competence at the junior levels of the GS, it also existed at the senior levels. I was lucky because my ultimate boss was a CEC O-6 with whom I had worked on Guam during Operation New Life, when he was the camp commander until the Army took over that function. He was an old-time Seabee officer, and we had hit it off then and continued to do so. This gave me an advantage when problems arose with his civilian staff. They recognized our relationship and did not want to take me on with him.

Lessons Learned

The principal lesson I learned during this job was, contrary to the media's continuous vilification, most of the contractors that won government contracts and executed the work were good Americans who generally gave the government more than it deserved as a product. Why? The contract specifications and plans were poor; the military customers were continually changing what they wanted; the funding for the projects was usually not adequate, making changes difficult; and the timelines imposed were often unrealistic. Many contractors would point out mistakes in the plans and offsets that would not increase the cost. They would negotiate fairly expecting a reasonable profit, but not an unfair one. The adage, "you get what you pay for" was never truer. Were there bad and unscrupulous contractors? Yes, and I dealt with them myself to free up the junior officers from these kinds of difficult situations. My guess is over ninety percent of our contracts were completed without any major issues because the contractors and our staff just worked out the issues. For the contractors that were a problem, I worked closely with the Navy lawyers and higher headquarters to put together plans of action to minimize poor results, although sometimes things were so screwed up with the contracts that was impossible. All these lessons served me well when I was the higher headquarters trying to anticipate where programs might run into trouble.

The two years passed quickly, with Mary not only earning her masters but also giving birth to our second child, a son, Tom. My daughter from my first marriage, Michelle, had also come to live with us, so we had a busy home life. I received a call that I had been selected to command a Seabee battalion, and after some ridiculous demands placed on Mary and me by the Pacific CEC flag to live on base at Port Hueneme when the closest hospital Mary could be stationed at was in Long Beach, I was assigned to command Amphibious Construction Battalion Two (ACB-2) in Norfolk, Virginia. Mary was assigned to the clinic at the NAS Oceana in nearby Virginia Beach.

Amphibious Seabees

There are important differences between an amphibious construction battalion (ACB) and a naval mobile construction battalion (NMCB). The most important is an ACB's primary function is to support amphibious landings by the Marines by offloading logistics support across the beach when there were no port facilities. This meant working in the surf zone in conditions up to sea state 3 (SS 3), or one foot, eight-inch to four feet, one-inch wave height, which is an inherently dangerous business. Rather than constructing facilities, the battalion constructed steel pontoon sections (90 feet long) and then put them together into pontoon causeways (four sections, or 360 feet) that could be run up into a beach to offload vehicles and supplies. They assembled floating hose lines that filled bladders that held petroleum products that were offloaded from ships to support the fight ashore. The unit was composed of roughly half Seabee ratings and half fleet ratings since the causeway sections were pushed around by converted LCM-6 landing craft operated by boatswain's mates and enginemen with seamen as crew members. The wardroom was divided between CEC officers and line officers, with some seasoned boatswains for good measure.

The ACB was in the fleet chain of command, working for a naval beach group (NBG) that in turn worked for the amphibious group (PHIBGRU) that worked for the surface force commander, who worked for the fleet commander. Whereas there were several levels of CEC commanded staffs above a NMCB such as a regiment and what was called a "type commander," such as CBLANT and CBPAC, charged with the oversight of the NMCB and the planning for its requirements, support, and operations, none of these existed in the fleet chain of command to support the ACB. No one above the amphibious construction battalion—including its immediate superior in the chain of command, the beach group—really understood what an ACB did or how. That meant the ACBs essentially acted as their own staff element to plan virtually anything they were tasked to do. There was no cover from higher-ranking CEC officers in this chain of command.

Not long after my orders were announced, I received a call requesting that I visit Port Hueneme for indoctrination on ACB-2 Seabee equipment status. This sounded like a good idea since I was on the West Coast and could travel there easily. The indoctrination I received was not what I expected. This was really a heads up that there were some major problems in ACB-2, and I should look things over thoroughly when I got there. Of concern was the state of the equipment used to support beach operations, of which bulldozers and tactical vehicles such as trucks and jeeps were critical. This equipment was the responsibility of NAVFACENGCOM to procure and inspect. I was also told that the pusher boats that maneuvered the causeway sections were all World War II vintage and had constant maintenance problems. This equipment was the responsibility of the Navy Sea Systems Command (NAVSEA) to procure and inspect through the fleet chain. There was more, but they thought I should make my own assessment.

Mary and I drove across the country to arrive in time for a weeklong turnover with my predecessor at ACB-2 and then a change of command ceremony on a hot July morning in 1983. My predecessor was four years senior to me and had, in fact, been selected for and frocked to O-6. This made our turnover awkward. He was now the same rank as his boss in the NBG and the CO of the base of which our unit was a tenant. He knew it and they knew it, and that made for some interesting fallout. The difference in ranks and time in the service between him and me was made painfully plain to me. While I had two battalion tours under my belt, there was a lecture quality to the discussions we had. That would have been OK had it not been for the observations that I was making of the state of the unit from discipline to equipment readiness to reputation in the NBG and on the base.

"It's fucked up and you better fix it!"

We made a call on the CO of Naval Amphibious Base (NAB) Little Creek, arriving appropriately early, and were directed to sit in the outer office. We waited for over half an hour, all the while seeing the base CO in his office having been told we were waiting. My predecessor announced he would wait no longer, and I should come meet the base CO after the change of command. I had never been treated like this in my Navy experience and looked forward to finding out why later. Later, at the weekly staff meeting that my soon to be boss at the NBG held, I was introduced to him and the other COs in the command and listened to the discussions. When it came time for my predecessor to talk, the commodore asked him when he was planning to set up a meeting for me to call on him since he noted none had been set up. He said I could set it up after the change of command. The commodore became visibly angry and said, "He can stay after this meeting and talk with me." I did this and after some small talk he said to me, "Have you made any observations about ACB-2?" I knew this was a loaded question and where it was going but did not want to throw my predecessor under the bus. My answer was, "I haven't seen everything yet, but I have seen some areas that need to be worked on." He looked at me and said, bluntly, "It's fucked up and you better fix it." I replied simply, "Yes sir."

As is the usual custom, the change of command was held on a Friday morning. What seemed strange to me was the guest speaker (invited by my predecessor) was a CEC flag from the local NAVFAC command, Atlantic Division NAVFAC (LANTDIV), and not someone from the fleet chain of command. This was funny since ACB-2 had nothing whatsoever to do with LANTDIV. It was hot and humid that morning, and everyone was grateful when it was over. The real business of command would start on Monday. I will preface my comments on this command tour by stating one of my favorite observations: "You can't make this stuff up!" As bizarre as some of these things sound, they all happened and are a mere fraction of the things that happened. I would also say they were the reasons that I loved being with the Seabees since no two days were ever the same nor were the leadership challenges in any other thing that I ever did. Truly, there were the highest of highs and lowest of lows, sometimes separated by what seemed like seconds. Those that have experienced military command will know exactly what I mean, while those that have run civilian organizations will think they do but really do not, as I can testify from my experiences in that world.

Monday morning started with the military formation known as quarters, where the battalion was assembled for roll call before starting the day's work schedule. When the report was given to me, a double-digit number of personnel were reported absent. This was something that I noticed during the turnover week for two reasons. One was the apparent lackadaisical attitude about the requirement to be at this formation. The other was when I had asked the XO how many individuals had been put on report for disciplinary purposes for failing to come to quarters, the numbers were always zero or one, as they seemed to be excused by the chain of command for some reason. This was gross to me since the simplest thing to do in the military was to show up on time in the correct uniform for a formation. After the formation was over, I called the XO in and told him that no one in the chain of command from the squad leaders to the CPOs to the junior officers to the company commanders could excuse anyone for being absent. I expected everyone who was absent or late to be placed on report and go to executive officer's investigation (XOI), where he could excuse anyone he felt had a valid excuse. The rest would go to captain's mast (an Article 15 of the UCMJ Nonjudicial Punishment Hearing) with me, and I would determine whether and how much to punish them. As I knew would happen, he excused none, and they all went to captain's mast that week. A couple were excused because they could prove valid car trouble or family emergency, but I heavily fined the rest, with the more senior getting higher fines. I had learned in previous tours that taking money was the fastest way to get someone's attention for this kind of thing. The word spread quickly, and suddenly absentees from quarters were a rarity.

The next thing I did was have a talk with the command master chief (CMC), a Seabee E-9, and asked his opinion of the state of the battalion. He was blunt. "It is lax, has poor discipline, bad equipment status, poor morale, drug problems, and I doubt we can do our mission effectively. There are good troops, but they need leadership and support." I asked why the morale was poor if things were lax. He said that the lack of discipline and inconsistencies with the treatment of various groups within the battalion had caused a lot of uncertainty in the chain of command. There were "gangs" of individuals who it was perceived were immune from the rules or punishment. He said one problem was the fact that the women assigned to the battalion seemed to be immune from disciplinary punishment, while their male counterparts were not. They also received preferential treatment on standing watches and other duty, especially if they had children. There had been problems in the barracks that had made the base CO unhappy, and little had been done about. He went on and vented for a while but was just confirming what I had observed. Additionally, sitting in my inbox were more than a dozen cases for captain's mast, which my predecessor had chosen not to take care of before he left. This was a very unusual thing as traditionally no disciplinary cases were left for the new CO that could be resolved by the outgoing CO. A number of these were serious offenses, including one for "assault on a CPO" by an individual with three previous captain's masts for not insignificant offenses.

The battalion had around four hundred pieces of civil engineering support equipment (CESE) assigned for beach operations, supporting the camp facility that would be erected during operations on the beach, and the manufacturing process for building the pontoon causeway barges. I looked out on the equipment yard from my office window, and visually it was apparent a great deal of the equipment was nonoperational and in poor shape, as the CMC had reported. When I looked at the watercraft, they were not in much better shape. I could see where both the commodore and CMC were coming from with their comments. Since every unit in the Navy must report its state of readiness up the chain of command every month, I asked to see what ACB-2 was reporting and was disappointed to see it was reporting it was mission capable when it did not look like it to me. I directed the equipment company commander and the waterfront company commander to put together requests for Management Assistance Visits (MAV) to the appropriate chain of command for an outside evaluation of the equipment status. I then inspected the barracks where my unit's personnel were assigned and found our rooms to be not ready to be inspected. The last thing I had time for that day was to have my yeoman call the base CO's office and get me an appointment for a call on the CO.

My first day in command crystalized my thoughts of the previous week. As I saw it, my predecessor was inconsistent, preferential, credulous, and overly concerned with being liked. In this next stage of my leadership evolution, I would not worry about being liked. Rather, I would focus on creating as safe an environment as possible given the inherently dangerous nature of the mission. Further, I would ensure everyone was treated as fairly and appropriately as possible within the constraints of regulations and direction from higher headquarters.

I disposed of the captain's mast cases the next day. The legal officer in the battalion was a former enlisted female ensign who had this job as a collateral duty with her assignment as administrative officer. When she came in before the mast started to discuss the cases, I asked her why some of these bad actors were still in the Navy given their records of offenses. I was told they were good workers and that counted for a lot. Since I expected all my people to be good workers, that logic did not go far with me. The individual who had assaulted a CPO was a big man with an attitude that was very apparent. He was surly in his responses to my questions from the outset. After hearing the witnesses, I told him that based upon his record I was going to have him processed out of the Navy for "a pattern of misconduct" under conditions other than honorable. If he caused the slightest problem while this was happening, I would have him sent to the Navy brig in chains if necessary until he was kicked out of the Navy. I did this with three other individuals from the pile of cases I was left. The word got around. I told the XO to set up captain's call with all the personnel in the battalion by groups: nonrated E-3 and below, petty officers E-4 to E-6, CPOs, and officers. Captain's call was a direct meeting between the CO and either the whole unit or some part of it, so the troops could hear something important "direct."

At these meetings, I told them it was amazingly easy to work for me as I only had two rules: "One, you obey all the rules all the time, and two, if you don't, I will take whatever action I feel appropriate to ensure you don't do that again." They were told that in determining what was appropriate, gender or marital status preference would not happen. The more seniority the offender had, the more severe the punishment. I further told them I expected that when faced with a situation where it looked to them that they could not obey the rules, they should go up the chain of command for help in resolving the situation. The chain of command was instructed in a similar way and told it would be given flexibility in resolving issues when it demonstrated to me it was worthy of that privilege. My final comment was that I realized there would be those who would test me, and that was fine since they would find me true to my word.

There was further guidance to the two groups responsible for the day-to-day operations in the battalion, the officers and the chiefs. I told the chiefs that my father was a chief and of the immense respect I had for that community, but there was a way a chief could piss me off. It was to sandbag his junior officer. Their job was to train the junior officers (JO), and they did not have to like them to do that. They had to give them their best advice when asked. I told them I would be telling the JOs I expected them to ask their chief's opinion before they launched off on tasking. That did not mean they had to do what the chief offered, but it did mean they needed to consider it; therefore, they could not be sandbagged. When I told the JOs this, I added that I would hold them accountable for their decisions, but they needed the input from the chiefs to make a proper decision, and the sure way to piss me off was not to ask for it. Now everyone understood "the rules of the road."

My call on the CO of the base was a good meeting. He met me as I walked into the outer office and ushered me into his office right away. He started by apologizing that I had to be a part to his lesson for my predecessor, whom he regarded as an ineffective CO running a poorly disciplined problem unit. While he could not comment on operational issues, he could on the barracks problems and disciplinary cases that he became involved with. I told him I knew what he meant and was acting to correct the problems he saw. It would be my hope that he would see a significant change in the battalion over a short period. As it turned out, after the testers tried me out and found out that was not a good idea and the chain of command was reinvigorated, ACB-2 dropped from the cross hairs and became a disciplined, smart military unit that was operationally outstanding. I always believed that people join the military for a structured environment, and many who get into trouble do so because they have not been given the structure and rules they were looking for and the enforcement they expected to make them obey or face the consequences. When this was in place, the mast cases dropped from 40-plus a month to a handful that were mostly drug related.

Throughout my command tour, the drug problem was perhaps the most significantly disappointing issue I faced. Unlike the standard of one positive drug test being cause for dismissal from the Navy that currently exists, I commanded when it was "three strikes and you're out." This reflected how widespread the drug problem was in the armed forces and the serious consequences to the manning levels of kicking out everyone who failed one drug test. While there could be the possibility that there had been unknowing drug use, I found most of the attempted excuses laughable: "My girlfriend must have baked it in the brownies she gave me." When I asked why she would do this, I was told it made the sex better! My published policy was that drug offenses would automatically draw the maximum punishment I could give without sending the individual to a court martial. On the bright side, a number of those who were caught (which was going to happen since we conducted full unit urinalysis testing on an unscheduled but frequent basis) told me to just kick them out after one incident because they were not going to stop using drugs. I was happy to oblige, and I would estimate that in two years I probably out-processed nearly a hundred drug users.

Some Are More Equal Than Others

Given my comments on the widespread drug use problems in the Navy and the state of discipline I found when I took command, I will make one other observation concerning personnel distribution in the Navy. At the top of the pecking order for quality personnel (officer and enlisted) was the nuclear submarine force that received extra pay and many perks as inducements for volunteering. The education and intelligence requirements were high and had to be met to man the submarines, so whatever it took happened. The quality of the enlisted force in submarines spoiled the submarine officers, who generally lacked an appreciation of the personnel problems of the rest of the Navy. The next group of volunteers was flight crews (officers and enlisted). There were other groups that required volunteers like SEALs and explosive ordnance disposal (EOD) that sought more skilled and highly qualified personnel. When all the special pay volunteer personnel were eliminated from the available pool, what was left had to be distributed to the remainder of the Navy. Some, like the Seabees, enlisted specifically for that training and specialty. I found most were not interested in doing anything else in the Navy. This further reduced the available general assignment assets.

When it came to manning the ships, the remaining enlisted personnel were spread by the enlisted distribution system that I had worked with while assigning the Seabees, so quality was spread somewhat fairly despite attempts for special cases and manipulating the system. On the officer side, it looked to me that there was a caste system in the surface Navy, with the top officers being assigned and moving up through the cruiser/destroyer force (and carriers) unless they were weeded out along the way and assigned elsewhere. Lesser officers went to the logistics and amphibious ships, and the lowest quality officers went to the NBG. Harsh words, I know, but based upon facts.

One fact I dealt with concerning the line officers assigned to ACB-2 was all except one seemed to have been fired from some shipboard assignment and sent to the battalion to complete their obligation before being released from the Navy. The one that had not been fired had not been selected for Department Head School, which was essential for a further career in the line, because of his gross appearance from being overweight. As I interviewed each of them, they told me what had happened, which was invariably something like they could not qualify to drive the ship as officer of the deck (OOD) or achieve their surface warfare qualification (SWO) in the allowed time or had some personality issue with the CO. This did not change throughout my tour.

The overweight officer told me he loved the Navy and was willing to do anything to stay in for a career. I looked at his record with a BUPERS eye and then talked with his assignment officer. This officer had a particularly good record except for the negative marks in appearance. He would have been selected for Department Head School, but for that. I told him this and said I was willing to send him to the Navy program for overweight individuals (called the "fat farm" by the insensitive). He could work on his weight while deployed. If he could get within Navy standards, I would do everything I could to get him selected. He agreed, and he did all that was asked, losing over a hundred pounds in the next seven months and returning from his cruise almost unrecognizable—and within standards. I asked the flag who commanded our amphibious force to write a personal letter to the Department Head School selection board recommending his selection and it happened. He was the only one in the NBG out of forty-eight eligible in all commands, I believe. This really irritated the flag, and he complained to the Surface Line Assignment Branch in BUPERS about the quality of officers being assigned to the NBG.

The flag complaint led to the second fact. The Surface Line Assignment Branch sent a senior captain down to discuss this problem with our commodore and the COs. I was included in the group even though I was not a line officer, probably because I had line officers working for me. After some pleasantries, he said, "BUPERS does not want to hear anymore complaining about the quality of officers assigned to the beach group. If a line officer is assigned to the beach group at any grade, his career is over, and he will not be promoted further in the Navy. Do you all understand?" Considering every other officer in the room was a line officer assigned to the NBG in command, I found it amazing. He was telling them their careers were over too. All of this made the quality of the boatswain WOs assigned to ACB-2 critical. Fortunately, all of them were exceptional and, together with some outstanding boatswain's mate CPOs, carried the day for the craft handling, sling rigging, and hoisting of causeways on to the LSTs that carried them. All of this reinforced my belief that the Navy's bacon was saved by its enlisted personnel and their ingenuity.

Given the reality of changing jobs every two or three years during my military career, one of the things I came to look forward to was going through the in-basket that was left for me by my predecessor looking for surprises. The fact that the disciplinary cases had been left for me in this case did not bode well for whatever else might not have been done and left for me. When I was going through the in-basket that first week in command, I found a copy of a memorandum signed by the CNO and the commandant of the Marine Corps agreeing that the Maritime Prepositioned Ships (MPS) squadron would be offloaded in forty hours across a beach in up to sea state 3. The Initial Operation Capability (IOC) of this MPS concept was scheduled in two years. Since this had not been mentioned during the turnover, I called a meeting of my executive officer, operations officer, and the company commanders to find out what this meant and where the battalion was in planning for all this. At this point, I should explain what an ACB was assigned to do.

Required Operational Capabilities

The primary peacetime mission of ACB-2 was to support an amphibious ready group (ARG) that deployed to the Mediterranean on six-month deployments with a Marine expeditionary unit (MEU) embarked for contingency response by providing a detachment led by a junior officer or boatswain. They handled causeway sections for the barge ferry that were loaded on the LST and the fuel reel and LCM-6 pusher boats loaded on the dock landing ship (LSD). Additionally, dets were provided for exercises for training at Camp Lejeune, in the Caribbean, and as far north as the North Sea for NATO exercises. ACB-2 was supposed to be able to deploy five teams simultaneously, but personnel and equipment shortages made this problematic. Loading and offloading causeways at sea was unheralded but dangerous work crucial to the support of the Marines, with equipment that was generally older than the sailors using it. All this would have kept the battalion busy going through the cycle of training, deploying, and recovering, but life was changing in a big way as a fallout of the British experiences in the 1982 Falkland Islands combat operations, which generated a question that no one wanted to answer. Can the U.S. Navy handle that type of operation with the current container and tanker ships being used to support it? The simple answer had been "no," because the systems in place were for break bulk cargo ships and the small fleet tankers of World War II and could not unload container ships or supertankers.

The work that had been done to correct the deficiencies in over-the-beach offloading of logistics support for the Marines and other forces was impressive and imaginative but also defective in one key aspect—planning for the manpower to execute this new system. A new concept for offload had been developed with a new generation of equipment to enable the ACBs to handle containers and supertanker offloads. I will not describe the system in detail other than to say theoretically it was great and would meet the requirement. The problems were in the details of procurement of the equipment, the establishment of the doctrine for its use, development of the preventive maintenance procedures, and the development of the training and qualification standards for the personnel needed to accomplish the mission, together with the provision of the proper mix and number of officers and enlisted ratings to accomplish the mission. As I found repeatedly over my career, a lot of attention had been paid to the acquisition of equipment, while a lot of assumptions were made concerning the personnel requirements to operate this equipment and where they would come from. These assumptions were generally wrong and made by those with no real knowledge or experience with the units involved. The briefing my staff gave me convinced me that not only they but also our superiors in the chain of command did not understand this or its implications. "Showtime" was around the corner with the first Joint Logistics Over the Shore (JLOTS) exercise the coming spring at Fort Story, located close to Little Creek, to test the concept of offloading containers across a beach with some of the new equipment.

In addition to the revolution in offload technology to match the changes in how the fuel and cargo were being carried on commercial shipping, a new readiness concept had been developed called the MPS squadron (mentioned earlier). This concept called for a squadron of four or five ships, which included roll-on/roll-off (RORO) ships, to be loaded with all the equipment and supplies necessary for a Marine amphibious brigade (MAB). It would be positioned at a strategic spot close to a likely contingency, say in Diego Garcia, where it could be sailed quickly to the trouble spot, with the troops being flown in to marry up with the equipment. While the desire was to offload in a port, the squadron had to be able to offload across a beach, so once again the ACBs were the enablers to accomplish this. Doctrine and training were required since the same next generation equipment would soon be used. Until then, the old equipment would have to do. This brought me back to my question to the staff. What had been done to prepare to meet this CNO/CMC-driven requirement? The answer was *zero,* other than being aware it was coming, because day-to-day operations had been considered more important.

I asked for a follow-on briefing on the new generation of equipment that had been and was being developed. This occurred within a few days, and I learned that one key system was called the elevated causeway (ELCAS). This consisted of a barge ferry that would be run into a beach, then piles with a jacking system attached were driven in, and finally, that system pulled the causeway ferry out off the beach to serve as a pier with a turntable at the end so trucks loaded with containers could be turned around. A mobile crane lifted the containers that were to shuttle between the ELCAS and the container ship. ELCAS had been delivered, and the JLOTS exercise would test this concept as a new type of crane ship would also be involved in offloading the containers from the container ship to the barge ferries.

The other key critical component of the new equipment to replace the LCM-6 pusher boats—a side-loadable warping tug (SLWT)—would soon be delivered to the Navy and had to be tested and accepted as meeting the specifications. ACB-2 was designated to do this. This craft used water jets for propulsion and maneuvering, as opposed to propellers, and was therefore a radical new concept that required new operating procedures. The same was true of the complicated fuel offloading system for the supertankers, called the Offshore Petroleum Discharge System (OPDS), that once again needed to be tested by ACB-2. All the above was to be done without any augmentation other than from ACB-1, the Pacific Fleet ACB, and while meeting all the other tasking assigned to the battalion. There was no additional manning in the plan for these additional missions. No one in ACB-2 had thought much about any of this since getting the next deploying ARG detachment ready to go was the gator closest to the boat.

The mission creep and the tasking that had been laid on ACB-2 was extraordinary, and it was accomplished over the next two years on the backs of the officers and the men and women of the battalion with little outside help besides ACB-1. The Management Assistance Visits determined the lousy shape of the equipment, and the subsequent readiness reports indicating the inability to do our mission led to funding to fix a number, but not all, of the problems and we were ultimately able to report essentially the lowest state of readiness. Long hours of planning and training enabled the JLOTS exercise to be carried out successfully while ARG teams continued to deploy. The new generation of equipment with the new side-loadable warping tugs (SLWT) and the OPDS was received, tested, and accepted, along with the development of the maintenance programs (called the Navy Maintenance and Material Management System, abbreviated as 3 M Program in the fleet) and Personnel Qualification Standards (PQS), together with doctrine and operating procedures for use in MPS and other beach operations.

This is not meant to be a treatise on ACB operations. I will not dwell on how all this happened with the assets available. The battalion was rewarded by being presented the first Joint Meritorious Unit Award ever given to a Seabee battalion by the secretary of defense and a Navy Meritorious Unit Award by the secretary of the Navy as a testament to what was accomplished. I think what was going on at the same time this was being carried out serves as a better illustration of keeping focused amid leadership challenges of the first order. I used to frequently come home and tell my wife, "You remember what I told you happened yesterday? It's nothing compared to what happened today!"

As an operational unit supporting the Marines, the ACB-2 det supporting the deploying MEU was critical and the training intense to make sure it did not fail. The first det to deploy after I took command was tested with the real thing as it participated in the Grenada invasion on October 25, 1983, and performed very well under the boatswain assigned as officer in charge. A Marine expeditionary unit was en route to relieve the MEU that was ashore in Beirut, Lebanon, with the peacekeeping force that was also being supported by another ACB-2 det. Two days before the Grenada operation, the barracks housing the MEU in Beirut had been bombed, killing the most Marines to die in a single day since Iwo Jima. Fortunately, our det did not live in that barracks but on the beach and were not harmed. They were very involved in the subsequent rescue operations and praised for their actions.

Reality set in quickly: our mission could and did put the unit in harm's way, and the personnel looked differently at the training that had seemed a pain only a few days before. I subsequently visited the det in Lebanon and shared time with them. This required getting the personal approval of the flag commanding the amphibious group, but he understood the importance of the CO sharing, however briefly, the dangers his personnel were being subjected to, and he was supportive. These experiences were the backdrop of everything else ACB-2 did and were never far from my thoughts or concern. Along with the MEUs, our dets were awarded the Navy Unit Commendation, Combat Action Ribbon, and Navy Expeditionary Medal.

Personnel Problems

Personnel issues are a constant distraction for any commander. I have already mentioned the disciplinary issues that were dealt with and the actions taken to provide structure and discipline to ACB-2, but these could not prevent the actions of individuals whose personal failings and lack of judgment caused the most serious offenses. These were not limited to the enlisted personnel but found their way into the wardroom and chiefs' mess. The first of these occurred within months of my taking command and involved my supply officer. The short story: I was forced to relieve him of his duties and process him out of the Navy as a flasher. He readily admitted this to me after he was arrested by Naval Investigative Service (NIS) and said he did not think he would be caught, that he drove around naked from the waist down to relax. I also had to relieve the next supply officer some months later after taking him to captain's mast for submitting a false official report up the chain of command regarding correcting audit findings that he had not, in fact, corrected.

This paled in comparison to the theft ring that was uncovered in the supply department. I had asked NIS to place an undercover agent there because of a nagging feeling something was not right. This was even though the supply department had just received the "Blue E" for excellence from the three-star Surface Force Atlantic Supply Inspection Team after a sup- posedly thorough review. One of the members of the ring cracked during interrogation and revealed a complicated operation that involved ordering and then selling military equipment after falsifying reports to state the equipment never had arrived. The senior chief petty officer (second most senior person in the department) in supply and several of his subordinates were sent to general courts-martial for this, and it became a major flap up the chain of command to the three- and four-star level.

Cases involving death are naturally massive attention getters. I had to deal with two, and they were both tragic. The first involved a young sailor who had never been in trouble and just returned from a deployment having done a fine job. Unfortunately, he went to the enlisted club at Fort Story when he was off duty, got drunk, and then tried to drive back to the base. He hit an Army MP standing in the middle of an intersection, killing him instantly, and then sped away at high speed back to Little Creek, with wit- nesses who had seen the incident in hot pursuit. He was caught at the gate and arrested. Since the crime occurred on military property, I sent him to a general court-martial for vehicular homicide. There were no winners in this case: a soldier died needlessly, and my man had to live with his remorse for the rest of his life. He was given a dishonorable discharge and sentenced to serve prison time at the U.S. Disciplinary Barracks located on Fort Leavenworth.

I used the other death in my talks to all the units I commanded for the remainder of my career; it was a perfect storm of the failure of the chain of command and a can-do attitude resulting in another needless death. This one happened not three hundred yards from my office when a young Seabee and his petty officer supervisor violated strict safety rules designed to prevent something like this from happening. They had received every training course in safety and vehicle operations required and then some, so they were completely aware of what the rules were. They were trying to jump-start a military cargo truck and decided to pull it with a short chain they had that was only to be used for emergencies during causeway offloads in beach operations, which this clearly was not. With the petty officer behind the wheel of the truck that had been jumped, the Seabee crawled between the trucks to unhook the chain. Just as he did, the petty officer's foot slipped off the clutch causing the truck to jolt forward catching the back of the Seabee's head between the bumpers. I happened to be leaving my office when I heard the cry, "Corpsman!" and saw our chief corpsman take off at a run from the dispensary across from my office. I ran after him and I arrived at most two minutes after the accident, where the chief worked desperately to save this young man. From my Vietnam experiences, one look told me he was dead. The duty of notifying the victim's wife fell upon me, and it was just about as bad a scenario as could be imagined. She lived in a trailer park near the Naval Weapons Station Yorktown, about an hour away. I dressed in my service dress blues, picked up his company commander, the command master chief, and a chaplain and drove up to the trailer park in a Navy staff car.

The dead Seabee's buddies had told us that the wife had some problems, and as we soon discovered, that was an understatement. Most of the inhabitants of the trailer park were military families, so the sight of a Navy staff car with officers in service dress uniforms meant bad news. As I rang the doorbell, I could hear the phone already ringing as the neighbors started calling to find out what had happened. The wife was about eight months pregnant, and there was a little girl of about two tugging at her dress. She looked at us blankly, wondering who we were and why we might be there. I asked if we could come inside as we needed to tell her something. I introduced myself and the rest of the group and told her I had some awfully bad news to tell her. Then I related that her husband had been killed in an accident about two hours earlier. Nothing is gained by trying to ease into this kind of news. We later found out that she had mental issues for which she was receiving treatment.

We asked if there was anyone we could contact to be with her. We offered to take her to the dispensary because we were concerned about the effect of this news on the baby she was carrying. She was struck dumb by the trauma. I turned the conversation over to the chaplain. My staff did a superb job handling this awful event, and not too long afterward, I was at Arlington National Cemetery presenting the folded U.S. flag to the widow with the thanks of a grateful nation for her husband's service and sacrifice; the parents of both the dead man and his widow looked on with the crowd of mourners. The investigation into the accident was yet another distraction and had to be redone since it was done so poorly the first time by the outside command tasked to do it. In the end, the petty officer who had been in charge went to captain's mast and received the severest punishment I could give him, along with a bad evaluation. I saw nothing to be gained by sending this man to a court-martial as he was already devastated.

Inherently Dangerous

The danger involved in operating causeway ferries and small craft in the surf zone in sea state 3 is best illustrated by an example of what can go wrong and the consequences. During the testing of the new SLWT craft while conducting ELCAS operations on a day when the sea was calm, a squall suddenly and unexpected blew up toward the beach changing the sea state from 0 to at least 3. The SLWT was attached to a causeway barge it was ferrying toward the ELCAS when it experienced a failure of the hydraulic system that operated the controls for the water jet propulsion system; this system not only propelled the craft but was also the steering mechanism for turning and maneuvering the craft.

While we watched from the beach with the crew on the SLWT talking to us via radio, the barge spun helplessly toward the beach out of control. There were no other craft that could help, and all I could tell the men on board was to make sure they had their life vests on and that they had attached themselves to the craft so they would not be blown overboard. The only question was whether the barge would hit the ELCAS. Through sheer luck it did not, and no one was hurt when the barge ferry hit the beach on the other side. The maneuverability of a barge ferry in the best possible circumstances during an SS 3 is limited due to the weight of the causeway sections and whatever they are carrying. The new SLWT was an improvement, but the former system of two pusher boats to maneuver the ferry offered a redundancy that the SLWT did not have against a catastrophic failure such as the one I witnessed. This was all pointed out in the incident report we filed as part of the acceptance test for the SLWT.

There were other man-made dangers caused by stupidity when operating barge ferries that were hard to believe. For instance, who would have believed that as a Seabee battalion commander I would be involved in a collision at sea? I received a call during the JLOTS exercise that one of my barge ferries had been involved in a collision with a *Los Angeles*–class submarine, USS *Jacksonville*, in the early morning hours. The investigation proved enlightening as it demonstrated that having a well-trained and experienced barge ferry pilot in charge of our operation was the saving grace for ACB-2 and its CO.

As we prepared for the exercise, one of the key things was to ensure that the barge ferries were properly lighted for night operations since the exercise was a 24/7 affair. My waterfront company commander, a surface warfare qualified female officer, had made a trip over to the local Coast Guard command and received its direction as to the proper lighting to be displayed on the ferry consisting of both bow and stern lighting displays. The only problem was that what they told us to use was incorrect for some reason. As the submarine was proceeding up the Thimble Shoals Channel returning to Norfolk early that morning, the captain and the XO were in their cabins, and the officer of the deck was a junior officer who oversaw maneuvering the submarine up the channel.

Fortunately, being ridiculously detail oriented, submariners make voice recordings of everything that is said on the bridge while underway. In this case, the OOD saw our lights and thought they represented two fishing boats and said he was taking the submarine between them (and out of the channel) for a lark. The submarine struck the 360-ton ferry dead center causing over a million dollars in damage to the sonar dome on the front of the submarine. It was determined that the ferry was right where it was supposed to be, piloted by the most experienced boatswain mate chief barge ferry pilot in the Navy. The submarine's commander, his XO, and the OOD were relieved of duty, and the submariners in turn demanded that my chief be taken to flag mast for a determination of what punishment he should receive (since he was not in their chain of command). When our PHIBGRU commander heard all the evidence, he awarded the chief a nonpunitive Letter of Caution and told him he needed to be more careful when submarines might be around because they were unpredictable. This really pissed off the submariners, as there was always a degree of professional rivalry between surface and submarine officers. In this case, our flag got to twist the knife a little since all the evidence was clearly on my chief's side.

The surface community got a good laugh at the submariners' expense, and both the submariners and the Coast Guard came out with egg on their face.

Integration of Women

Commanding a unit with women assigned (two officers and thirty-eight enlisted) is obviously a different experience for a male officer who had served exclusively in all-male troop units. It was not as novel to me since my wife was a Navy nurse who had female Navy corpsmen working for her; she had related her experiences to me of working with male officers and in supervising females. Lest I be labeled as "sexist" for my nuanced opinion about the role of women in the military, I will state unequivocally that the AVF could not function without women—they play a vital role in the defense of the nation. As mentioned, my wife was a Navy officer, and I had worked with women in the military, both officer and enlisted, throughout my career. However, that does not mean I had blinders on and did not see the problems that arise in mixed-gender units, though many politicians and out of touch four-star officers seem to discount them. Even today I chuckle when I hear the sanctimonious members of Congress, both men and women, talking about women in the military and what they should and should not be able to do. Except for a couple that were in the military, they are clueless about the environment and the stresses that service personnel face. For this reason, it is instructive to relate a few of the incidents I dealt with while I was trying to focus on the mission of ACB-2, as these were all things that would have never come up in an all-male unit.

In a fleet unit, the initials PMS stand for preventative maintenance system, and that is what comes to mind when those initials are used. How that has changed! A PMS incident was illustrative of the inability of the Navy to come to grips with how women's issues affected unit leadership, as well as the necessity for the appearance of evenhanded treatment of men and women. I had assigned a female lieutenant to be the waterfront/craft company commander. She was a good and dedicated officer. She came to me one day to tell me she had placed one of her junior enlisted women on report for malingering and failure to report for her duties, but it was more complicated than that. She said this sailor kept going to the hospital and getting light or no duty passes from working due to PMS (premenstrual syndrome) attacks. These passes were often for more than a week, and when one expired, she would simply go get another. As a woman, this lieutenant was appalled and could not believe the doctors would do this. She had enough of this malingering and had placed the sailor on report but wanted me to know the background. I received a brief tutorial on PMS from my wife, who had been an OB-GYN nurse, and the malingering sailor's story sounded strange.

I called the head of the OB-GYN department at the Portsmouth Naval Hospital and asked him what was going on. After he went through the usual "medicine is not an exact science" spiel, he said doctors make subjective judgments that are not always understood. I told him what I did not understand was that the prefix "pre" suggested that at some point the condition would pass, thereby leaving the sailor free to do her work, but the doctors seemed to be turning this into a permanent disability. How was that possible medically? His response was ridiculous, so I thanked him and consulted a Navy lawyer about what I should do. He recommended that the sailor be ordered to the hospital for a fitness for duty examination (which I did). Before that could happen, however, this sailor went absent without leave (AWOL) and stayed gone long enough to be declared a deserter, so I thought I had seen the last of her. Wrong!

One day I received a call from the sailor's father saying he realized what his daughter was doing was against Navy regulations, but she feared for her wellbeing because everyone at ACB-2 was out to get her, and she was not receiving proper medical treatment. I assured him this was not the case, and I would promise him if she returned I would have her evaluated by the naval hospital to get to the bottom of her medical problem. He brought her back, and she was taken to the hospital for physical and psychological evaluations. At the end of this process, it was found that she did not have any unusual female problems that merited being excused from work; however, she *did* have a manipulative personality. When I asked if there was any reason she should not be held accountable for her actions, the medico responded in the negative. At the captain's mast hearing into her desertion charge, she said she was having a PMS attack and needed to sit down before announcing that she would not accept nonjudicial punishment and wanted a court-martial, which was her right under the UCMJ. I was happy to drop this on the Navy legal system and once again thought I was out of it.

Not too long after this, I received a call from the Bureau of Naval Personnel telling me that this sailor's local congressman had become involved, and my boss would be receiving a call from him directly. I later learned that the congressman had said, "Commodore, you and I both have a problem. I can help you fix your problem, but you can only lessen mine. Your problem is she is in your unit. My problem is she is in my district. What can I do to help you get her out of your Navy as soon as possible and back to her parents?" The commodore said he would investigate the matter and told me to make it happen. I told the commodore to tell the congressman that a call from him to the CNP requesting expedited administrative processing of her release from active duty via an Administrative Discharge might help. The congressman said he would do that, and later that day I received a call telling me that if I would drop all charges against her, I would receive a message to administratively separate her within two days, waiving anything that would take any longer. I said "Great!" and that was that.

On a lighter note, aside from the continuing pregnancies among the assigned women (both officers and enlisted) and the effect this had on just covering the duty sections and critical skills due to light or no duty passes, I noted the fact that young men continued to act like young men in their dealings with women. The classic case involved the construction of a small building to house the duty section that remained in camp overnight. Of necessity it had a section for men to sleep in, with an adjacent toilet and shower facility, and a similar, but smaller, section for women since there were fewer of them. One day, there was quite a commotion, and the XO came in to tell me that one of the men staying in the duty section bunk room had gotten up in the overhead drop ceiling and crawled across the supporting grid. He then removed the panel above the women's shower and was watching one of them take a shower when she saw him and screamed. He was captured as he tried to get down. This led to another memorable captain's mast during which I asked the female sailor how she could identify the individual from the shower episode. She exclaimed, "Those eyes, those eyes!" I made an example of the young voyeur by giving him a severe punishment, and I learned another lesson about how things had changed.

Investigations and Scapegoats

The theft ring episode and the Seabee's death were both followed by investigations and a search for the guilty. The primary target of all Navy investigations is the CO since the ultimate accountability belongs in that office. Withstanding the inquisition and preordained guilt associated with having the ill fortune to be in charge when something bad has happened required a combination of luck and preparation. I had both. The luck manifested itself in my immediate boss, the commodore of the beach group; and his boss, the flag of the amphibious group. Both were fair and understanding leaders who resisted the pressure to produce a scapegoat by ensuring a thorough and unbiased investigation. They drew their own conclusions to be sent up the chain of command.

The preparation had to do with carrying out the responsibilities of a CO to ensure his personnel were adequately trained and qualified for the tasks they were directed to perform. A CO also had to safeguard the resources entrusted to him and be sure they were used in a proper manner. Since I had experienced the results of a bad safety atmosphere in my previous battalion tours, I demanded a tough safety program in the very hazardous environment in which ACB-2 operated. This entailed making sure all those operating equipment not only had received all the required training but also all the required safety briefings. The investigation into the Seabee's death concluded that both he and his supervisor had been professionally trained and had acted in blatant disregard of that training. Accordingly, I was not held accountable for the death.

The theft ring investigation was another matter. I was required to justify how this ring could have existed in my command and not be my fault. Fortunately, since I was the one who had requested NIS place an agent in the supply department even after the Type Commander's Inspection Team had given ACB-2 accolades for its supply department and had previously requested a Management Assistance Visits for the CESE equipment and watercraft to correct deficiencies, I was able to present the case that I had done everything possible to ensure Navy resources were being properly controlled and maintained. This defense did not make the three-star type commander happy. When the investigation reached the four-star level, it was the three-star who was criticized for having an ineffective and unsatisfactory inspection program, and he was ordered to fix it immediately. Despite being exonerated by the investigation, I was called in by the commodore and informed that as a face-saving measure he was giving me a Letter of Caution and Requirement—a nonpunitive letter that would not be part of my record—saying I should be more diligent in carrying out my duties in the future, so he could tell the chain of command I had been disciplined. When I asked what else I should have done, he replied, "I don't know."

One other distraction worth mentioning was ACB-2's involvement in what came to be known as the Wedtech scandal. It became news in 1986, the year after I left the battalion. Wedtech had won defense contracts without competitive bidding under Small Business Administration (SBA) preference programs for minority-owned businesses, even though the owner was not a minority. All that this involved is too lengthy for this account, but

ACB-2 was the recipient of causeway sections manufactured by Wedtech for "testing and acceptance," and they were found to be defective. I would not accept them and provided a lengthy report on the deficiencies we had found that had to be corrected. Significant political pressure was brought to bear to ignore these deficiencies and accept the causeways so that final payment could be made. An independent counsel later charged Attorney General Edwin Meese with complicity in the scandal, as a close friend of his had worked as a lobbyist for the company and asked for Meese's help on Wedtech contract matters, possibly extending to the causeway contract. While Meese was never convicted of any wrongdoing, he resigned. Assistant Secretary of the Navy Everett Pyatt was also involved, the same individual I had first met when I was an aide in the Pentagon. In the end, the responsibility for accepting the faulty equipment continued to move up the chain of command—and that was fine with me.

Not long into my tour in command, I received a surprise phone call from the assignment officer who said, "Have you given any thought to your next assignment?" Of course, the answer was "no," since I had only been in command for six weeks. He said, "I'm preparing the slate of moves to occur two years in the future for approval by the CEC flags, and I need your input on what you would like to do." I said I knew of several jobs in the Tidewater region of Virginia for an O-5 that might suit since Mary and I had just bought a house and gotten her settled with three-year orders from the Nurse Corps. Then he dropped the bomb. "You are coming back to Washington, and it is just a question of your preference between two jobs. I have you down to either be the executive assistant to the chief (Admiral Jones) or the head of CEC officer assignments." I was stunned and unhappy and asked him to call me again after I had been in this job longer. He agreed and about five months later he phoned and said, "The incumbent in the EA job is extending, so you are going to be my relief as head detailer." I asked him how I could get out of this, and he said, "Tell Admiral Jones to go screw himself!" My fate was sealed.

High Visibility

My final hurrah as CO occurred a couple of months before I left the battalion and was the culmination of over a year of work on the doctrine and operating procedures required to meet the CNO/CMC (commandant, Marine Corps)[19] memorandum on the offload of the MPS Squadron in forty hours. The reality was that the manning of the amphibious construction battalions did not contain enough personnel of the correct types to carry out the mission and never would unless it was changed. The problem originated in what are called the "required operating capabilities" (ROC) and "projected operating environment" (POE) that dictate what a unit must be able to do in what type of environment. The major defect that occurred when the new generation of equipment was developed to offload container ships was that the ROC/POE of the amphibious construction battalions had not been changed or even looked at. The ROC/POE drives the manning requirements of the unit, and the one in current use was for the offload of a Marine expedition force (MEF) under the old system, which produced entirely different manning requirements.

The MPS offload requirement had been added to the amphibious construction battalion mission by naval message without any of the required adjustments to the ROC/POE. Once we had completed the development of the operating procedures, we knew what it took to accomplish the MPS offload as required, and we had to send the bad news up the chain of command that without a change in the ROC/POE and subsequent changes in the manning of the amphibious battalions, the initial operating capability promised to the Joint Chiefs of Staff could never happen. I carried this unhappy news through each layer of the chain of command until it got to the four-star who was commander in chief, U.S. Atlantic Fleet. He decided to send a personal message to the CNO informing him of the problem. This was answered by a mind-numbing message saying we were wrong and asking the CINC to send a briefing team to the Pentagon to explain ourselves. I was the briefer and was accompanied by the NBG commodore and the deputy CINC, a two-star. The briefing had nearly a dozen flags with at least five three-stars in attendance. Simply stated, the manning of the ACBs would have to be tripled to carry out the two missions now assigned. Our recommendation was that this be done with a combination of active and reserve personnel. There were questions but no disagreement with the facts. At the end, the three-star in charge of the meeting looked at me and said, "How did you let this happen?" and smiled. He then told our team we were excused and turned to the other flags and said, "Who's going to tell the JCS?"

In due course, I received my orders, and too quickly I was scheduling my change of command. Two days before the ceremony, I received a call from the flag commanding the amphibious group whom I had asked to be the guest speaker. He said that the type commander was exacting his revenge for the theft ring incident by disapproving the award my boss had submitted for me and that he had personally forwarded with his strongest endorsement. He said mine had been a particularly successful command tour and this was not right and that he personally called the three-star to protest, but to no avail. I told him I understood and really appreciated his efforts and the privilege of working for him. On a blustery day I turned over command as a hurricane bore down on the Tidewater and took Mary and the kids to Disney World.

Head of CEC Officer Assignments

I arrived back in Washington, DC, and reported to the Bureau of Naval Personnel conflicted. Any assignment after command that is not another command is going to be a letdown, but that was not the conflict. If I had to come back to Washington, DC, being assigned to run the CEC Officer Assignment Office was a plum job and was somewhat autonomous, so no complaint there. The real conflict was the fact that Mary and the children were not with me, as the Nurse Corps had not seen fit to find her a job in the DC area. Despite there being two major medical facilities in the environs—the National Naval Medical Center in Bethesda, Maryland, and the U.S. Naval Hospital Quantico (where she had previously been assigned), they quibbled. The lame excuse was she was up for promotion to O-5, and they needed to see if she was selected before they moved her. They had no answer for the obvious question: did that mean they would not move her if she were not promoted? These were the days when there were not many married military couples, and colocation was the subject of negotiation more than policy. The Nurse Corps was not particularly military couples–friendly, and I laid that off on the number of unmarried senior nurses who viewed the Nurse Corps as a calling, sort of like being a nun. Marriage indicated disloyalty to, or at least nonacceptance of, "the calling." I would be forced to commute on the weekends back to Virginia Beach. I found a place to stay during the week with a bachelor CEC officer I knew who had an extra bedroom. The experience gave me more insight into the issues surrounding the increasing numbers of women in the Navy and finding an accommodation to the assignment policies this would require.

From my previous tour in BUPERS, I was familiar with the office I would be running. It had a small staff of highly qualified personnel to carry out a particularly important function. The senior detailer (that is, I) oversaw putting together slates or recommended assignments for captains and commanders and then presenting them first to the chief and, after his initial blessing, to the active duty CEC flags at a once a year Flag Detailing Session. These assignments were for all the important jobs, such as command and major staff assignments, while lesser jobs were handled directly through discussions with the CEC flag in whose area the assignment would be. Conflicts between that flag and others over an individual would be brought to the chief for resolution.

Other duties included oversight of all the assignments for lower-ranking officers; oversight of the clerical staff and accountability for the budget of the office; supervision of the education program (primarily post-graduate school) for CEC officers; and managing the sizing of the CEC to include determining the recruiting quotas and sources (along with qualifications for acceptance), together with the proper mix of regular versus reserve officers. There was also preparing the promotion plan for the annual promotion boards for all officer ranks and oversight of women's integration into the CEC. Dealing with all the correspondence that is generated by the emotional area of assignments from all sources (to include congressional), while keeping the chain of command within BUPERS aware of all issues that could potentially impact them, rounded out our tasking.

The remainder of the staff consisted of a lieutenant commander, who handled the assignments of lieutenant commander and more senior lieutenants; a lieutenant, who handled first tour lieutenants as well as those of the more junior officers; a lieutenant commander or lieutenant, who handled force shaping issues such as recruiting planning, promotions planning, retirement and separation planning, and other issues; a lieutenant commander or lieutenant, who handled the post-graduate program; and sometimes another officer for special duties that came up as an additional assignment from NAVFAC. The force shaping issues were always very political within the Navy as all the staff corps were in a continual battle with the line over requirements and numbers. The line always viewed the place to cut the Navy, if so directed by the secretary of defense, was in the Staff Corps to protect itself. This led to massively stupid decisions that had to be fought almost continually. Most of this fighting was done through the chief going directly to the CNP or, if important enough, to the CNO. My job was to be ahead of stupid policy decisions and get our flags involved as early as possible. Additionally, there was a clerical staff of civilians for letter preparations, order processing, and a host of other personnel related issues. My turnover with my predecessor was painless, and I started settling into the job.

Flag Board Recorder

Within a couple of weeks, my first collateral duty was one of the most eye-opening in my CEC career. I was to be the recorder on a flag selection board that was picking two CEC one-star admirals. The administrative part of this job was straightforward and not difficult. I had to review the records of everyone eligible for consideration to ensure they were complete with all performance evaluations, an up to date picture, and all other required information. There were also the logistics arrangements for the boardroom and accommodations for the board members if they wanted assistance. The chief always hosted a dinner for the board, and I would assist with that as required. The members of the board were all CEC flags, including a couple of retired flags who had been recalled to active duty for the board since there were not enough active duty flags who met the requirement of not sitting on two consecutive flag boards. The composition of all boards would be changed later to exert line influence over all Staff Corps boards by requiring a line officer be a member, together with a misguided notion that having a lawyer present would make sure the board did not do anything wrong—that is, wrong as defined by the lawyers. Both were detrimental and negatively affected promotion quality.

What I determined in looking at the records of those eligible was that out of the seventy to a hundred officers above (those who had already been considered once and not selected), in, or below the zone of year groups to be considered, there were not more than half a dozen that were truly competitive for the selection. They had performed well in the required types of assignments—that is, those having survived a winnowing assignment selection process, applied because some assignments are more equal than others. The flag maker jobs: command, key staff jobs, combat assignments, education, professional registration, and others were generally well known by those moving through the ranks unless they did not care or want to be flags. The members of the board knew three things well: the requirements to be a flag officer in the CEC, the professional reputations of all or most of those being considered, and, more importantly, the reputations of the officers who had written many of the evaluations, including non-CEC officers. Their job was to find the best qualified for promotion without preconceived ideas or outside influence in accordance with the directions signed by the secretary of the Navy to the president of the board.

What I learned from this experience was how superbly qualified these flags were, not only intellectually but also in knowledge of those being considered. Their reading of the records only confirmed what they already knew, and I had figured out—there were about six almost equally superbly qualified candidates whom they would have to discuss in greater depth before making their final decision, which had to be unanimous. When these discussions occurred, there was nothing that was out of bounds for discussion about these officers, including their personal lives, families, foibles, quirks, and even stories of adventures during their careers. The point of all this was to make sure everything possible was known about these men so the best could be chosen. As it turned out, the discussions, though thorough, were faster than I thought they would be, and the two selectees were arrived at by unanimous vote. They were the two I had felt would be selected from all I had known before the board and having read their records. Their subsequent performance as flags vindicated their selections.

What was very apparent was, in addition to the record of the individual, the two most important factors in selection were the strength of the competitive group the individual was in and the membership of the board, neither of which could be influenced by the individual. Fate or luck played into this, so I concluded that anyone who said they were following the sure path to flag was delusional since they could not control these key factors. My advice became, "Take the toughest jobs and perform the best you can, and see what happens." This was good advice until lawyers and diversity champions became involved and decided other factors were more important than performance in tough jobs.

Making Assignments and Managing Requirements

Since ostensibly the primary task in this job was recommending the assignments of the senior officers of the CEC to the CEC flags and supervising the staff making assignments to the more junior officers, I will spend a little time discussing what I saw this task encompassing. The first and most important factor in assignments was knowing that the bell-shaped distribution curve of talent was alive and well and a critical factor. Simply said, there were never enough top-quality officers for all the jobs that required them, so assigning them to the critical jobs and allocating risk in assigning lower quality officers to the remaining jobs was really what I did (along with my staff). This involved determining which jobs truly were the critical and most important and then distributing the remainder in a manner that allocated risk and consequences of failure by an officer as best I could. Once I had done this, I briefed the chief and got his concurrence with how I saw the jobs, so I could begin the process of putting the slate together. While command positions were obviously at the top of the critical list, it quickly became apparent that there was going to be risk in filling the O-6 command jobs since my screening told me that there were not enough top-quality O-6 officers to fill all the command jobs. Additionally, there were critical staff jobs, such as the senior CEC advisor to line three- and four-star admirals, that required exceptionally talented and knowledgeable officers who had to be presented as nominees to and accepted by those officers before they could be assigned. The need for talented officers within the NAVFAC command structure was also a competing factor. Command positions at the O-5 level, such as battalion command, were fewer and not a problem to fill with supposedly top-quality officers, although mistakes happened in these assignments.

The above analysis did not consider the desires of the individuals and was a cold-blooded clinical determination. The handling of the desires of the individual was in the process of undergoing a fundamental change in all the armed forces, caused by the new freedom and job opportunities for women and, specifically, spouses. Many of these women wanted careers and were not content with simply following their husband from assignment to assignment at the whim of the military. This was not only a family problem between spouses but also a distribution problem, as officers said they would take themselves out of the running for promotion to stay in a location or even retire or resign from the service instead of moving. This problem has only gotten worse despite attempts to downplay it and craft policies that say staying in the same place for extended periods will not hurt a career. The other factor in personal desires for assignments was the "believing your own press clippings" syndrome that caused individuals to think they were better than they were thanks to the inflated performance evaluations they had received, many times in less-demanding jobs. In their mind, being passed over for promotion was something that happened to others.

It fell to me to disabuse these people of this misperception, and being that messenger was one of the less glamorous aspects of my job. I felt it was especially important for each officer to understand how their record rated against their peers, at least in my opinion, and be prepared for the eventuality of not being selected for promotion. I used to tell audiences that the only officer in the CEC that was never going to get the call saying he was not being promoted was the chief. Every other officer, including flags, was going to be told at some point they were not selected for promotion or the

Ensign Mike Shelton, Civil Engineer Corps, USN, June 1967

The Shelton family in uniform, August 1967.

NMCB 9 sign at the front gate at Camp Hoover.

Camp Hoover, 1967, Cruisebook picture.

Camp Hoover, 1967, Cruisebook picture. View looking east toward contested areas.

View of Camp Hoover looking west, with rice paddies, Dog Patch, Danang Airbase, and the bay in the background. The white blob at top right is the USS *Sanctuary*, a Navy hospital ship.

Detail Echo Camp in Phu Loc, looking west toward the enemy contested area.

Detail Echo Camp, Phu Loc, RVN, view from Viet Cong positions.

Mike returning from a convoy to Liberty Bridge, November 1967.

Mike at Danang, RVN, 1967. The sign says "Make love, not war."

LT Fred Rothermel (Chaplain), Mike, and LT John Nesbitt (the Doc).

Buds John Nesbitt, Ed Timlin (fellow ensign), and Mike.

Mike at the Naval Advisory Detachment Danang, 1971.

AEROVIEW of Operation New Life

APRIL 21

FOCUS ON FOUR   page twenty-four

Operation New Life, the beginning, an abandoned Japanese airfield, Guam.

May 8, seventeen days later, Operation New Life, the end of construction.

THE SECRETARY OF THE NAVY
WASHINGTON. D.C. 20350

      The Secretary of the Navy takes pleasure in presenting the MERITORIOUS UNIT COMMENDATION to

NAVAL MOBILE CONSTRUCTION BATTALION FOUR

for service as set forth in the following

CITATION:

      For meritorious service while participating in Operation NEWLIFE from 23 April 1975 to 1 September 1975. During this period, Naval Mobile Construction Battalion FOUR was directly responsible for the construction of the refugee camp on Guam which accommodated 50,000 Vietnamese at the height of the Operation and through which almost 200,000 Vietnamese passed. Working twenty-four hours a day, seven days a week, the personnel of the Battalion met or exceeded ahead of schedule every assigned task. In addition, personnel not involved in the construction phase of the camp effectively participated in the Vietnamese dispensary, dental clinic, and administrative processing. By their exemplary professional expertise, resolute determination, sincere concern for others, and selfless devotion to duty, the officers and men of Naval Mobile Construction Battalion FOUR reflected credit upon themselves and upheld the highest traditions of the United States Naval Service.

W. Graham Claytor

Secretary of the Navy

Meritorious Unit Award for NMCB 4 for Operation New Life, 1975.

CDR MacDonald promotes Mike to LCDR, 1975.

Mary when she met Mike in Rota, Spain, 1976.

Mike wearing Loafers Loops as Aide to DCNO Logistics on OPNAV Staff, 1976.

Our wedding day, October 15, 1977, at Most Holy Trinity Catholic Chapel, West Point.

Promotion to Commander at Naval War College, 1981.

Dangerous work – unloading equipment at a beachfront via a causeway barge ferry.

ELCAS – the critical facility in off loading of container ships when no port is available.

Citation

to accompany the award of the

Joint Meritorious Unit Award

to the

Amphibious Construction Battalion TWO

The Amphibious Construction Battalion TWO distinguished itself by exceptionally meritorious service, from July 1983 to October 1984. During a period of unsurpassed operational tempo including the support of the Multinational Peacekeeping Force in Lebanon, OPERATION URGENT FURY in Grenada, TEAMWORK 84 in Northern Europe, and OCEAN VENTURE 84 in the Caribbean, Amphibious Construction Battalion TWO was the primary Navy unit responsible for conducting the majority of operations in support of the Navy-Marine Corps phase of Joint Logistics Over the Shore II. In accomplishing this demanding mission, Amphibious Construction Battalion TWO developed and mastered the operating techniques for many new systems, including the Side Loadable Warping Tug, the Roll On/Roll Off Platform System, and the Elevated Causeway System. All of these new systems were required to ensure success of Joint Logistics Over the Shore II and will be centerpieces for future Logistics Over the Shore operations. Outstanding support provided to the United States Army elements of the Joint Logistics Over the Shore II test by Amphibious Construction Battalion TWO contributed significantly to the successful completion of the Army's phase of Joint Logistics Over the Shore II. The extraordinary ingenuity, dedication, and professionalism of Amphibious Construction Battalion TWO, coupled with exceptional attention to safety and seamanship, were major contributing factors in the success of Joint Logistics Over the Shore II. The distinctive accomplishments of the personnel assigned to Amphibious Construction Battalion TWO reflect great credit upon themselves and the Department of Defense.

Given under my hand, this second day of October, 1986.

Secretary of Defense

Joint Meritorious Unit Award for ACB 2 for JLOTS, Greneda, and Lebanon, 1983-84.

THE SECRETARY OF THE NAVY
WASHINGTON

The Secretary of the Navy takes pleasure in presenting the MERITORIOUS UNIT COMMENDATION to

AMPHIBIOUS CONSTRUCTION BATTALION TWO

for service as set forth in the following

CITATION:

For meritorious service while providing outstanding support to a variety of amphibious operations, tests, and exercises from 1 February 1985 to 31 August 1986. During this period, Amphibious Construction Battalion TWO successfully participated in the initial installation, tests, and demonstrations of the Chief of Naval Operations-sponsored Offshore Petroleum Discharge System. The tanker based four-mile long ship-to-shore pipeline was tested in three phases requiring over 1368 man-days of direct support and another 1540 man-days of indirect support. Additionally, assigned personnel played an instrumental role in the successful execution of Commander in Chief, U.S. Readiness Command-sponsored Exercise BOLD EAGLE 86 while conducting the first remote offload of two TAKR/TAKS ships in support of that Exercise. Shortly thereafter, a total commitment in preparation for and participation in the first U.S. Atlantic Fleet Maritime Prepositioning Ship download termed Exercise AGILE SWORD 86 exhibited the continued superlative performance of this unique command. The outstanding leadership, motivation, and desire to excel displayed by personnel assigned to Amphibious Construction Battalion TWO enabled that unit to efficiently function in areas not previously assigned. By their continuous display of professionalism, determination, and total devotion to duty, the officers and enlisted personnel of Amphibious Construction Battalion TWO reflected credit upon themselves and upheld the highest traditions of the United States Naval Service.

Secretary of the Navy

Meritorious Unit Award for ACB 2 for OPDF Development and Testing, 1985-86.

Mary promoting Mike to Captain at LANTDIV, 1988.

Mary and Mike shortly before her retirement, 1991.

Mike with his Seabees in Somalia, 1994.

Mike talking with his Seabees on a deployment in Europe.

Mike giving up command of the 22nd Naval Construction Regiment to CAPT Peter Marshall, August 1995.

Mike's mentor and friend, Jack Buffington, congratulates Mike at the NCR Change of Command ceremony, August 1995. Tom in background.

Change of Command ceremony, 22nd Naval Construction Regiment, 1995. Mary and Jessica are standing right behind Mike.

Future CNO Vern Clark Administers the oath during One Star Promotion Ceremony with Mike's mom looking on, September 1995.

Mike's mom and Mary put the One Star shoulder boards on for Mike's promotion with Jessica in background, September 1995.

Mike and Woody Held, one star promotion, September 1995.

Mike receiving arrival honors as Basic Training graduation, NTC Great Lakes, Spring 2001.

Retirement review with VADM Jim Amerault, CBC Gulfport, July 2001.

The Shelton family at Jessica's wedding, July 2007. Pictured l-r: Michelle, Luke Wilson, Jessica, Mike, Mary, and Tom.

Family photograph, December 2015. Pictured l-r: Michelle, Tom, Mary, Mike, Jessica, and son-in-law Luke; grandsons Mason, Mike and baby Sean. Patrick came 18 months later.

Michael W. Shelton
Rear Admiral, Civil Engineer Corps. U.S. Navy

crowning assignment. Everyone (and their spouses) should be prepared for this. Despite this counseling, human nature proved difficult to overcome, and most did not prepare themselves or, more importantly, their spouse, who assumed their husband would always be promoted. This led to some extremely sad occurrences up to and including divorce when promotions did not come. All of this made me feel like a priest about half the time as officers, and sometimes their wives, told me of their problems, desires, and even martial issues with the expectation that their case deserved special treatment. This is not to say that we did not give special treatment for exceptional cases, such as illness of family members, unexpected deaths, or other tragedies, but that the Navy definition of "tragedy" did not include such things as having to move overseas when their parents were old, not liking the schools in a new place, and so on was hard for many to accept. One of the best stories I heard was, "My dog does not like the weather there." I am not making this up.

The real nonquantifiable issue with making assignments was the subjective opinions of the senior officers involved in approving assignments, from the flags to the commanding officers of commands to usually captains in key staff areas. I called it the "pet rock" syndrome. This is not unique to the military and is a human tendency to form opinions of individuals, good or bad, based upon experiences working with them or knowing them. These thoughts are retained for a lifetime regardless of not working with them subsequently, or in many cases, even being around them, as they did other things. The fact that an officer was an outstanding junior officer did not automatically guarantee they would be an outstanding middle grade or senior officer for many diverse reasons.

The one that worried me most was the officer who had the reputation as one who got whatever was assigned done to meet deadlines that made his boss look good no matter what. Looking down from above, these officers almost always received glowing performance evaluations and became pet rocks of their seniors. Unfortunately, too many of these seniors did not worry about what methods were used to achieve the results they had gotten from their subordinates. I called it making the "how many bodies were left in the wake?" leadership evaluation. Senior officers who are blind to this problem promoted and assigned individuals who destroyed morale and sometimes lives because of the reinforced success of behaving in this way. Surprisingly, finding out how results are achieved and what kind of reputations officers have with their peers and subordinates is not that hard for someone who cares. Throughout my career, I had several senior officers call me and ask what I thought of a contemporary or someone between me and the senior in rank. This started happening when I was a lieutenant, when I supposed my track record provided me a reputation as a straight shooter who could be trusted. I was always careful not to drop a dime on anyone that did not deserve it in my opinion or I did not know well enough, but I did give my honest opinion if asked because as I had observed in Vietnam, bad leaders get people killed. All of this does not mean that there are not times when tough decisions must be made that force subordinates to do unpleasant, dangerous, or even potentially deadly things, as that is a possible situation in the military especially in time of war, but it is not a frequent enough occurrence to warrant the extent it is practiced by some.

Flag "Help"

An example of how all this came together in a flag detailing session will illustrate pet rock blindness. The story starts before the flag session with my discussions with an O-5 who was a pet rock of the chief. He wanted command of a Seabee battalion, but not any battalion—it had to be a specific battalion in a specific location. Initially, it did not look like this would be a problem until a family tragedy caused one of the other candidates for battalion command to drop out. His replacement required assignment to the specific location the pet rock wanted because of a family medical treatment issue. I discussed this with the chief, and he said he knew his pet rock would understand, so I should move him to the other battalion location. When I told the pet rock of this decision, he went ballistic and said this was UNSAT. I told him that all of this was going to be presented at the flag session, and if after that he still felt strongly, he should talk to the chief, but not before.

Flag sessions usually were an afternoon and following morning affair, with the first day spent on O-6 commands and assignments plus O-5 commands if there was time. In this case, by the time the O-6 issues had been determined, one of the flags had to leave for an important meeting and said to the chief, "I have looked at the proposed battalion commanders and think we really need to discuss one of them, so please don't make any decisions until tomorrow when I can participate." When the chief asked who he was concerned about, the flag said he would rather not say until the slate was discussed. After he left, the chief made the comment that he was puzzled by what had been said as he thought the candidates were very qualified. He then proceeded with a monologue talking about his pet rock being the best among them and what a superb officer he was with a great future in the CEC. No one else said anything, and the meeting adjourned.

The next morning all the flags were anxious to hear what was going to be said concerning the list. The flag who asked to be heard described his concern this way: "There is one of the candidates who is arrogant and condescending to everyone including flags. He uses your name frequently to get things he wants that I am sure you do not know about. From what I hear, his contemporaries do not like him for his superior attitude and generally don't want to work with him. I just don't think someone like this should be a battalion commander!" The chief, known for a hair temper, exploded, "Who is that SOB?" The flag replied with the name of the chief's pet rock. The chief's face went white as all the other flags except the speaker simultaneously laughed at this unexpected turn of affairs. When he recovered, the chief asked each flag in the room if they thought what had been said about this officer was true. To his great shock, every single one answered in the affirmative. He was speechless for a while and then said, "He is getting command, but I want him watched, and the first time he screws up, I will fire him." At this point, I brought up the issue of the pet rock not wanting to go to the other homeport, and the chief exploded again: "I don't care what he wants, he goes where I send him!"

As I left the session, the pet rock was hovering outside and said to me, "Did you bring up the fact that I don't want to go to the battalion you have me down for?" I said yes. Then he said, "I guess I'll be going where I wanted, now that the chief knows what I want." I replied, "No you won't." He said, "I'm going to go see him right now and get this changed!" In one of the kindest and most undeserved acts of compassion I engaged in during my entire time as detailer, I said to him, "Although you do not deserve it, I will save your life by telling you that you should avoid talking to the chief for a considerable period and never bring the battalion location up to him again. If you do, I won't be responsible for what happens." Unfortunately, this type of thing did not happen enough, and pet rocks routinely got away with their counterproductive maneuvering to the detriment of the CEC and the Navy.

While many consider these aspects to be the most important part of the assignments job, I did not. Just as in the enlisted assignment job, the profoundly important tasks involved fighting personnel policy battles to protect the CEC from arbitrary and capricious actions, usually generated by the

Navy line in some self-serving, self-important manner. I always marveled at the number of line officers that felt that being able to sail a ship out into the ocean and return it to port without colliding with another ship or running aground qualified them to make decisions on anything and command anything. This mindset led to the conclusion that the last thing to ever be cut in directed personnel cuts was line officers. Another sore point was that highly qualified individuals should have a choice of where they served in the Navy. This manifested itself in policies that forbid midshipmen coming from the Naval Academy or Navy ROTC programs who were qualified to be line officers from being commissioned in any other part of the Navy, regardless of their desire or education. This prevented NROTC graduates with degrees in civil engineering from being commissioned in the CEC. The stated opinion was that the purpose of these programs was to produce line officers; other needs of the Navy for well-qualified officers were of secondary importance. Later there was a policy that surface line junior officers at the end of their initial obligation and desiring to transfer to a Staff Corps would be released from the Navy rather than allowed to transfer; the idea was to intimidate these officers from leaving the surface Navy. This myopic policy resulted in driving many highly qualified officers from the Navy.

Diversity at All Costs

Right at the top of the ridiculous personnel policy directives that came down for the CEC for implementation were the ones regarding minority and women quotas for recruiting and subsequent promotion. Percentage requirements were established without any realistic evaluation of the possibility of attaining them. The qualifications for acceptance into the CEC, as mentioned before, were the same as the nuclear power program, with whom we had already been made less competitive by the prohibition of graduates of the Naval Academy or NROTC being assigned to anything but the line. The number of women and minorities graduating from accredited engineering or architecture programs in the United States as a percentage of total engineering/architecture graduates was below the quotas established by the rocket scientists in BUPERS, who were trying to adjust the imbalance in the Navy overnight. Not only were there not enough women and minorities graduating with the right qualifications but also the competition for the graduates, regardless of quality, was intense, as every major corporation, government agency, educational establishment, and military service had been given similar quotas without regard to the available pool.

This fact did not count for much since no waivers were granted, and we were continuously left wanting when it came to meeting our unrealistic and unattainable goals.

Once again the battle over reserving seats in the basic officers' training program for women and minority accessions that could not be filled had to be fought. Worse yet were promotion quotas that specified 100 percent of women and minority candidates had to be promoted unless they were deemed unqualified (an impossible standard unless there was a disciplinary breech in their record). Since there were a limited number of slots for promotion to each pay grade, giving preference to these groups ensured white male officers would receive fewer slots, and better-qualified officers would be passed over for promotion to meet the unrealistic goals for women and minorities established in the name of diversity. This policy was modified in later years so that these groups competed amongst themselves; that is, if the promotion rate was seventy percent, then seventy percent of the women and seventy percent of the minorities had to be promoted versus promoting seventy percent of the entire group on a best-qualified basis without regard to quotas. It was Navy policy that this was required because reporting seniors and boards would be unfair to these groups (or had been in the past), although I never saw any real evidence of this in the CEC.

A logical corollary to the accession and promotion policies was the desire to put these officers in high-visibility assignments to serve as role models and demonstrate the Navy was doing its part on the diversity front. This put extreme pressure on the officers in these groups, particularly those who were less qualified. I had one talented female officer tell me she would leave the Navy if she was given one more assignment as "the first woman" to do it. She was sick of the pressure and the knowing looks from her male contemporaries that she had not earned the job but had had it handed to her on a silver platter. It also put pressure on the commands, where they were assigned, to treat women and minorities differently to ensure their success. A crisis developed when one of these officers was failing in an assignment because of the stigma attached to removing them. None of this was unique to the military services, but it created a morale problem within the service, and dealing with it detracted from other important aspects of my job.

Understanding the Odds

During the many presentations I made to the CEC community, I liked to use a blackboard or paper chart to illustrate the probability of making captain by taking the promotion percentages at all the pay grades from O-2 to O-6 and multiplying them together. These promotion percentages by grade varied from year to year depending upon the needs of the service, but the learning point was there. For instance, if a hundred ensigns started out in a year group, the number who be selected for O-6 would be: $(100) \times 1.0 \times .95 \times .80 \times .70 \times .55 = 29.26$. From that number of O-6s, one would probably, but not necessarily, be selected to flag for a one percent probability of flag selection. When I was selected for O-6, I regarded that as the limit of my promotions after witnessing what a crapshoot flag selection was.

There are a host of anecdotes I could relate from this assignment, but two had special significance. The first was how my next assignment came about. As the slate for the moves that would include me was being put together, I received a call from the flag in charge of the largest engineering field division (EFD) in NAVFAC, which happened to be located in Norfolk, telling me he wanted me to come work for him as the head of the Acquisition Department responsible for managing a $2 billion military construction (MCON) design and construction program that ranged from the East Coast of the United States to Europe, Africa, the Middle East, Central America, and the Caribbean. It was a great job right where I wanted to be, but I had one concern. The only job I really wanted as an O-6 before I retired was Commander, Construction Battalions, U.S. Atlantic Fleet as my last Seabee job. It would be turning over in two years, and the hitch was that the flag wanted me for three years in his job. When I explained my concern, he said, "Don't worry, I'll make sure you're considered for that job, and I'll support you." That was good enough for me. This time the Nurse Corps was more obliging, and Mary received orders to move with me, being assigned to Naval Hospital Portsmouth to finish her twenty years of service.

The second anecdote was a reinforcement of the lesson I had learned when I left ACB-2, "No good deed goes unpunished." It started the same way it had there—with me being called up to my flag boss's office at BUPERS. He was a line one-star I had a great relationship with, and we had worked through many issues together. He said that he had recommended me for an award, but when it went to the chief for concurrence, it had been disapproved and he was dumbfounded. The chief I had worked for most of the time had retired about six weeks earlier, and a new chief was in place. I thought the new chief and I had a rather good relationship; I had briefed him a few times without any problems that I was aware of. I thanked him and told him I was equally perplexed, but as I had to perform my departing call on this chief the next week, I would ask about it.

I did not have to ask, as the chief told me straight off that he did not like the way I had done my job. He had received complaints from a few officers saying they did not like dealing with me. Accordingly, I did not deserve an award. I should understand that from now on he would be watching me and would control my fate in the CEC. Did I have anything to say? I said I had done my job the way the previous chief had wanted it done and at his direction. The previous chief had personally thanked me for the job I had done in tough circumstances when he retired. The fact that some officers did not like how I did the job was part of the job. It was not possible to make everyone happy doing what needed to be done as I saw it and had been directed to do it. I understood he was the new chief, and I served at his pleasure. I had nothing more to say to him. This put the seal on any thought I had of making flag, but at least I was going back to Virginia Beach. The family was happy, and my new boss had promised to support me for the only job I really cared about in the CEC. After that job, I could leave the CEC and the Navy with no regrets.

Chapter Eight

THE CAPTAIN

If the highest aim of a captain were to preserve his ship, he would keep it in port forever.

—St. Thomas Aquinas

Atlantic Division, Naval Facilities Engineering Command (LANTNAVFACENGCOM, or LANTDIV) was the premier field division in NAVFAC for many reasons, not the least of which being the high quality of the workforce, particularly the senior civilians. I often joked that the senior civilians who worked for me running the design, construction, and project management branches (all GM-15 or O-6 equivalents) were the most military personnel in NAVFAC, as many of them were Virginia Military Institute (VMI) graduates. Over the years, the Navy had hired many graduates of VMI, Virginia Tech, University of Virginia, and North Carolina State. Many had served in the Army coming out of the ROTC program. They ran their functions with more discipline and accountability than I had seen anywhere else in the Navy civilian work force and produced outstanding results. Having these superb subordinates handling the day-to-day issues freed me to deal with the more complex and political problems of dealing with the officials of other countries where we were doing construction. I also had to work with the other service branches, principally the Marines and Air Force, in executing their military construction programs, for which we were responsible, and fighting internal NAVFAC battles over turf. By congressional direction, either the Army or Navy handled all Air Force military construction. The list of high-profile programs/projects that I dealt with during my tour was a Cold War compendium of force-projection facilities to contain the Soviets in the European and African theaters.

The Job

Almost immediately upon reporting, I was running the negotiations with the Icelandic government over the construction of force-projection facilities in Iceland. These included airfield and radar facilities for Air Force F-15 fighters and Navy P-3 submarine patrol aircraft that were to close the GI (Greenland/Iceland)-UK gap to Soviet aircraft, ships, and submarines in event of war. Each year Icelandic government officials met with the U.S. Navy in the form of LANTDIV to negotiate the next installment of the facilities program. Since Iceland had no military forces at all, but was a NATO member, it allowed U.S. forces to be stationed in the country. I say these were negotiations, but they really were not. The Icelandic government representatives read the Congressional Record, and whatever Congress approved for construction of facilities in Iceland had to be done only by Icelandic contractors for the approved amount. On the positive side, the quality of the work done by these contractors was excellent and generally met the time schedules, even if it was overpriced (in our view). The annual meetings alternated between Norfolk and Reykjavik. For the Icelanders, it was a nice shopping trip to the U.S., and generally these meetings were more of a social event with little actual negotiating done. Occasionally, there would be some issue that we would dig our heels in on, and sometimes they would yield to show good faith, but the bases were too important to the U.S. military to risk really alienating the Icelanders.

In Europe proper, we had a subordinate command in Madrid, Spain, headed by an O-6, under the title of officer in charge of construction Spain (OICC Spain). This command had handled our workload in Europe and Africa. It had been in place since the U.S. bases in Spain—principally the two Air Force bases and the naval base in Rota—had been built in the '50s, but its mission had been expanded to cover the adjacent areas. At that moment, the most important task assigned to OICC Spain was the completion of the Ground Launched Cruise Missile (GLCM) base at Comiso, Sicily, for the Air Force. This move challenged the balance of power in Europe because of its proximity to the Soviet Union and its client states. It was nearing completion. There were not only the missile facilities but also personnel support facilities such as housing, commissary, hospital, school, and so on. OICC Spain was also constructing modifications to old, abandoned Strategic Air Command (SAC) facilities in Morocco to serve as divert fields for the Space Transportation System (the space shuttle) and POL storage facilities for the air bridge to the Middle East. There were also many high priority projects supporting the U.S. 6th Fleet, with port facilities in Italy, Spain, Crete, and Sicily. A major expansion of facilities at the Naval Air Station Sigonella rounded out a staggering workload, and each customer felt their project was the highest priority. The political side of negotiating with the foreign governments, especially the Italians and Spanish, was dicey and involved the State Department and the countries' embassy staffs, including the ambassadors.

All the facility requirements for the Navy's Caribbean and Central America bases and operations were handled by LANTDIV. The bases at Guantanamo Bay, Cuba; and Roosevelt Roads, Puerto Rico, were particularly important, as were the underwater ranges (used for submarine training) and the bombing ranges. The ongoing tension with Castro's Cuba made issues in supporting that base a constant problem. Environmental activists protesting the bombing ranges were another thorn in the government's side. The facilities in the Panama Canal Zone that the Navy was responsible for required resources and attention as the United States prepared to turn over this American territory in accordance with President Carter's agreement with the Panamanian government. There was a lot going on that required monitoring.

In the United States, there was a major construction program being undertaken at Camp Lejeune, North Carolina, involving the replacement and expansion of barracks and other facilities for the Marines. Aviation facilities for the Harrier jets were being built at the Marine Corps Air Station (MCAS) Cherry Point, North Carolina, together with an expansion and modernization of the Naval Aircraft Rework Facility there. A new hospital at Lejeune had just been completed but had roofing problems. Norfolk was the biggest Navy fleet concentration in the United States, and there was a constant list of high-priority construction and repair projects on the numerous bases in the Tidewater area demanding attention. All of this was what I saw when I took over the head of acquisition job, and it just continued during my tour, with me acting like an overextended fireman jumping from fire to fire.

Coup

The biggest internal issue that consumed NAVFAC as I reported to LANTDIV was a directed reorganization that made the contracting function independent of the acquisition chain of command. Until this reorganization, the contracting function had been part of the cradle-to-grave acquisition process that included design, project management, construction, and contracting under one overall boss. Owing to some perceived irregularities in contract awards, overblown concerns of undue influence in the contracting process, and lack of adequate paperwork explaining decisions, the powers that be determined that the contracting function had to be independent to assure the "purity" of the contracting process. What this really meant was that a contracting officer, rather than an engineer, would run negotiations and evaluation boards. This was the proverbial sledgehammer being used to crack a peanut, and it has screwed up government contracting ever since. All it really did was change who was making subjective judgments in the contracting process from those that had a clue what was needed to those who did not. As anyone who has read the papers over the last thirty years can testify, it did not stop dumb contracting decisions from being made.

Overnight, "little old ladies in tennis shoes," who had essentially been contracting clerks and processors, were put in charge of critical acquisitions. Many of these individuals had no college education and had worked their way up with internal contracting courses and on-the-job training. Suddenly when the decision was made to put them in charge, a host of senior contracting jobs became available to be filled by, in many cases, nothing more than clerks without management training or executive experience. My kindest observation of this fiasco was the contract files became much better, but the contracts did not. In fact, the *process* became all important while the results became less important, causing delays in awards of critical contracts, awards to the wrong contractors, and a host of other problems all in the name of transparency in contracting. Having worked in the NAVFAC command under both methodologies, it was not hard for me to see almost immediately that this smacked a great deal of "putting the inmates in charge of the asylum." There was an excessive amount of "getting even" by these new power brokers in contracts for the years they had endured as second-class citizens being under the thumb of the engineers.

The government contracting process is still broken without any fix in sight as the subjective judgments of the mostly unqualified continue to dominate this critical function. In addition to the reorganization, Congress shares a huge amount of the blame with its proliferation of pork in the form of set-asides, the grossest of which was the creation of the Alaska Native Program that led to the creation of billion dollar companies that received preference in awards of contracts, while employing very few Alaska natives.

This was to rectify some injustice the Alaska natives had suffered that I never understood since I do not remember the cavalry fighting in Alaska or Wounded Knee-type atrocities being committed against indigenous peoples in Alaska. What I do know is the U.S. taxpayer paid grossly inflated prices for work because there was no competition, and in many cases the price was negotiated after the contractor was selected. These situations made the acquisition job and all my subsequent NAVFAC jobs more difficult.

Being "Higher Headquarters"

Another first-time issue I dealt with was being on a "higher headquarters" staff directing commands in the field that naturally felt they did not need any direction. I had been in the field and resented staff direction from above, so I understood the issue from the other direction. In this case, OICC Spain was our subordinate command, and it was commanded by a highflier O-6 with an impressive reputation and ego. He was very smart, knowledgeable, and had a PhD. He was required to report what was going on in his area of responsibility to my boss, the flag, periodically. I was responsible for monitoring what was going on and to keep my boss advised if I had concerns. This came to a head several months into the job when I sent a trip request to the O-6 who was the flag's deputy for approval of a trip to talk to this CO. The next day, I received a note back with the disapproved request, asking me to come talk with him about it. He said that he had spoken with the CO and that the CO did not want me bothering him. He further explained that briefing me would be a distraction for him and his staff that they did not need. The deputy agreed with the CO, so he disapproved the trip. "Do you have any questions?" I said I had one.

Had he read the monthly progress report this CO had sent two days before saying that a high-visibility project was going to slip several months for some lame reason? He said he sort of remembered that, but what of it? I said that the chief had testified to Congress that this project would be completed on time, and now this CO was saying it would not, in effect, because he did not think it was important enough to worry about. Did our flag know all this? My purpose in making the trip was to confront the CO and educate him on the facts of life. Because of the chief's testimony, the project could not slip without some massive justification that the circumstances had changed *after* the chief's testimony. I further said I did not care about another trip to Europe and would much prefer to stay in Virginia Beach with my family. If he did not have any further questions, I needed to get back to work. He said no, and I left. It was about a ten-minute walk to my office. When I arrived, my secretary told me the flag's secretary had just called, and he wanted to see me immediately.

When I was admitted to the flag's office, the deputy was there and had obviously briefed him on our recent conversation. The flag was visibly upset and said, "You are leaving for Spain as soon as possible. Tell the CO either he gets this project back on track or he will be fired! Tell him he better not ever send a message like that without discussing it with you first and me, if necessary. Furthermore, you can travel anywhere, at any time, if you think it is necessary. In fact, I expect you to, as you are my eyes, and I do not care what people in the field think. Am I clear?" "Yes sir."

I think the deputy subsequently called all our field offices and alerted them of the flag's words, as I never had another issue with traveling. I filed away more lessons on command relationships, staff oversight, and being careful of what is reported up the chain of command and why. This was another step in my leadership/management development. Empathy with peers had entered the equation and would grow in importance in future assignments. The management layer of LANTDIV consisted primarily of CEC captains and senior government service (GS) employees (GM-15) who felt they were their equivalents. Egos and sensitivities were sometimes huge, while professional competency varied. While I felt I knew what my flag boss wanted accomplished, maintaining a good working relationship at the "peer" level while doing this was a new and time consuming challenge.

Unhappiness

About a year into this assignment, it was time for the slate to be assembled for the CEC flags to approve for the following summer's rotations—including the COMCBLANT job that I lusted after. I made an appointment with my flag to remind him of my desires, although I knew he was aware of them. When we met, he looked at me and said, "I have thought this over, and I am not going to let you go to the COMCBLANT job. It is a waste of your talent. You have already had three Seabee tours, and you do not need another one. You should command a public works center, and I will make sure that happens when it is time for you to leave here. Any questions?" Although I knew this was a lose-lose situation for me, I ventured to say that the Seabee job was the only O-6 job I really wanted, and I had been looking forward to it. That just pissed him off, and he proceeded to tell me he did not understand why talented officers (naming several) were obsessed with the Seabees, and if he was around (most people felt he would be the next chief—and he was) he was not going to waste officers with multiple Seabee assignments. I left his office and thought my CEC future was not going to be longer than it took for me to serve the necessary amount of time to retire as an O-6 (three years in grade). I felt I had been deceived. I was very unhappy, and coupled with my encounter with the chief when I left the detailer job, it seemed to me that the CEC leadership and I were not simpatico, so it was probably time to be thinking about doing something else.

Time passed, and I was busy with the design of the new Portsmouth hospital that had reached the concept approval stage. A big meeting was scheduled on a Friday in Washington, DC, at the architect's office with all the players. Over the lunch break, I met with my successor in the detailer job just to catch up. The story he laid on me was a jaw-dropper. The officer who had been selected for the COMCBLANT job that I wanted had submitted his retirement papers and would not take the job. The chief had decided to move the CO of the PWC Yokosuka (Japan) early to take the job. My boss had recommended me to be the CO in Yokosuka, and the chief needed to know by this afternoon if I wanted to be considered for the job. I was stunned for a couple of reasons. First, the stupidity of moving an officer from the other side of the world to the COMCBLANT job when I was virtually right across the street from it made my head hurt. Second, although Mary and I had talked about wanting an overseas assignment and agreed the only command assignment we both would like was PWC Yokosuka, she was within eighteen months of retiring. Even if there was a job for her at the Naval Hospital Yokosuka, she would have to serve two years in it before she could retire if she made the move. Third, there was no way I would make this kind of decision without a face-to-face discussion with Mary. I said that without knowing the possibility of Mary being transferred with me, there really could be no further discussion of this. If he wanted me to consider it, he would have to get back to me, and he said he would. I was called out of the concept review later that afternoon and told the Nurse Corps had a job for Mary that would be open in the right time frame, so what was my decision as the chief, my "buddy," had said I had to decide that afternoon. I told the detailer if this was the condition, the answer had to be that I do not want to be considered. I would not make this decision without talking to Mary and allowing her to talk to her assignment officer (if she were even interested), and that could not happen until the following week. He told me he would get back to me. Later that day, he called me back and told me the chief had relented, and I had until the beginning of the week to decide.

When I discussed this with Mary, she was conflicted. She was ready to retire and become a full-time mom, but she really wanted to go to Japan so she could visit the Far East. The kids were still small, except for Michelle who would be graduating from high school that year and likely be headed off to college. This would be the best time for the kids to experience living in another culture. She called her detailer, and although the job was not great, it was OK since she was retiring anyway. Additionally, as CO of the PWC, I would have an assigned set of quarters, so we would have no issues finding a place to live. After agonizing over the decision, we decided to do it, and I informed my detailer and Mary hers so they could work out the timing, and we were issued orders to move in September.

Before September rolled around, I was called to NAVFAC headquarters for the rest of the story about the expectations of what I should accomplish in Yokosuka. A significant and emotional change in the fiscal accounting system of the PWC was going to take place during my watch to bring the PWC in line with all the other PWCs in the Navy. It could not be screwed up. This change would entail moving the funding of the PWC from the operations and maintenance (O&M) funding line to the Navy Industrial Fund (NIF). These terms are Greek to most people, and I am not going bore you with an explanation of the nuances. Suffice it to say, this was a major change and would not make our customers happy—especially the U.S. 7th Fleet commander—as it would raise the cost of the PWC services while there was supposedly going to be an increase in funding to the customers through their chain of command that smacked of the "trust me" jokes.

This change would require the extensive training of the Japanese workforce of more than a thousand people with the computerization of the accounting and work processes. Having heard all the talk about how technologically advanced the Japanese were supposed to be, it came as a shock to learn this really was not universal in the country. There were still many businesses and processes that were done by stubby pencils as opposed to sophisticated computer systems, and the PWC's was among them. Just to add to the fun, I was also informed there had been some internal problems with the PWC's U.S. government civilian supervisory workforce. There were around thirty senior civilians who augmented the small number of CEC officers assigned to the PWC to manage the thousand-odd Japanese employed by the PWC. I was expected to straighten this out quickly so this would not interfere with the fiscal conversion.

A few more observations are in order before moving on to my next assignment. The first was that I was involved in many meetings and negotiations with foreign military, government, and contractor personnel during this tour, which built on my previous experiences in Vietnam and the UK. The takeaway for me was most of these people were very competent and working hard for their countries as we were for ours. It was especially important to understand the political constraints they were working under and try to operate within them and the ones our government was imposing on us. It was usually possible to find a win-win solution to most issues, but arrogance on our side would have been a death knell. There was great sensitivity to being thought a pawn of the Americans or caving in too quickly to what might be considered dictation by the United States. Sovereignty was important to all, and that had to be recognized. Second, the same was very much true of dealings with the other U.S. military services. The cultures of the various services often conflicted and were aggravated by the continual battles over defense budget share and the need to show one service was more valuable than the others. Funnily enough, many times the engineers of the services joined together to convince their line masters of the right thing to do. And third, doing the right thing was in the eye of the beholder, despite all the lawyers and other self-appointed experts on ethics and law. In the end, it was the individual's conscience that ruled, not outside oversight. Trust and the determination of that quality was the benchmark by which I came to view everything in relationships from superiors to peers to subordinates. What you see is not always what you get.

Land of the Rising Sun

The fact that Japan was culturally different was brought home to us, and particularly our six-year-old son Tom, from the outset of our arrival. As small children are prone to do, as soon as we got off the plane at Narita Airport near Tokyo, Tom announced he had to go to the bathroom. I took him to the closest one, and while we were at the urinals, a grandmotherly Japanese woman came in the men's room and started to mop the floor to include pushing the mop between Tom's feet as he stood there. When he looked around and saw her, he yelled, "Dad, there's a woman in our bathroom!" I told him to finish his business (now impossible for him), and I would explain this to him when we got outside. He could not wait to tell his mother of this strange happening. When I tried to explain that in Japan women often cleaned men's rooms with men in them and this was normal for them and no one cared, it went nowhere, so I decided he would get used to it by experiencing it. Indeed, we all did our utmost to experience as much of the Japanese culture as we could during our time in Japan, learning doing things differently does not mean they are being done wrongly or badly—just being done from a different perspective. This was an important lesson in dealing with my large Japanese workforce and the Japanese defense officials, community officials, contractors, and military, which was a significant part of my job.

Since Japan is twelve time zones away from the U.S. East Coast, just getting our body clocks adjusted was a big deal, so the turnover week with my predecessor seemed like it took forever. I listened a lot and did not share the information regarding how his senior civilian supervisors were viewed by NAVFAC since he obviously did not see it and thought they were doing a great job. In a déjà vu happenstance, the XO of the PWC was the same officer that had been the XO of ACB-2 when I took over, and by yet another coincidence, he had orders to leave just as he had when in ACB-2. His grasp of what was happening in the PWC was about the same as it had been in ACB-2—not much. The plan was for the production officer (the operations officer responsible for PWC operations) to be moving up to replace the XO, and a new production officer would be arriving. I had two different staffs reporting to me as there were two different commands that I had at the same time. In addition to the PWC that reported up through the U.S. Pacific Fleet chain of command, I was the officer in charge of construction (OICC), Far East, reporting through Pacific Division, NAVFAC (PACDIV) to NAVFAC and had a contracting warrant for signing contracts for construction and services that were required for the Navy and Marine Corps, not only in Japan (Yokosuka, Misawa, Sasebo, and Okinawa) but also in Korea. There was an O-5 deputy OICC and a small staff to oversee this contracts function.

The principal lessons learned during the turnover were that the "Big Dog" at Yokosuka was the three-star U.S. 7th Fleet commander whose fleet was homeported there with a carrier; his quarters were located there. My boss was the commander, Naval Forces Japan (CNFJ), a two-star submariner; and the joint commander in Japan was U.S. Forces Japan, an Air Force three-star that was also the 5th Air Force commander located in Yokota. He led all negotiations with the Japanese government and military. These were the outside worlds that I would be dealing with, while managing the PWC and OICC inside worlds, while transitioning the PWC. The principal outside issue in negotiations with the Japanese was the Japanese Facilities Improvement Program (JFIP) through which the Japanese paid for improvements to U.S. bases in Japan as their share of the cost of American forces being in Japan. It was very political as one of the Japanese rules was none of the funds could be used to increase war-fighting capabilities. The projects had to be for support such as utilities, housing, roads, and so forth. The division of the annual JFIP funding between the three U.S. services was, of course, a big deal, as was preparing proposed projects for approval by first the U.S. chain of command and then by the Japanese government. The principal thing the Japanese wanted was to reduce the American footprint in Japan by consolidating American forces on the fewest bases possible and having excess bases returned to them. This had been going on for many years and had been successful. The major remaining issue as of this writing is the relocation of most of the Marines from Okinawa to Guam. The Japanese are eager to see this change of base, but the tsunami that damaged a nuclear power plant resulted in major funding diversion, thus stalling the move.

While I do not want to get too technical relative to PWC operations and technology, there is one thing I do want to mention. It is another lesson I learned from the Navy direction on the above-mentioned shift from O&M to NIF accounting for PWCs. This meant the PWCs acted as stand-alone businesses. All their funding was drawn from a system in which the total cost of operations, major repairs, equipment, new projects, and the like was paid for from a fund that collected payments from the PWCs' customers based upon rates that were set and approved at the Washington staff level. These rates included the costs and a surcharge to provide funds for investment in facilities and infrastructure. In this regard, the NIF concept was supposed to be like operating a commercial business.

While this is all sounded well and good, the Navy line customers did not understand it, and worse, they thought NAVFAC was gouging them for some self-serving reason. The common complaint was that the rates were too high, it cost too much to get anything done through a PWC, and they could find it cheaper commercially or through civilian contractors. Most line officers had no idea at all what the cost of anything really was since everything was just delivered to their ship, submarine, or aircraft from ordnance to fuel to repair parts and so on. They paid for nothing and did not worry about the costs of their support yet expected it to be there when they needed it. Paying for it was someone else's problem; however, when they left the fleet and got promoted, many suddenly were experts on what things should cost because they had owned a house once and had someone fix their plumbing or something else. Really?

In-Depth Knowledge Not Required

The lesson I learned from this perception issue was that a solution that was worse than the problem comes when it is directed by people with little to no understanding of the problem, how a business is run, the effect of government regulations and laws, and recruiting from private industry to meet vague requirements. It was always interesting to hear people who had been appointed to jobs in the office of the secretary of the Navy (or of the secretary of defense) from private industry talk about applying commercial practices to the military, where there are volumes of regulations and rules—mostly the result of congressional interference, auditors, and lawyers—that do not apply in the commercial world. Doing what is smart in the commercial world in the military is generally impossible because it would, many times, greatly restrict which firms get the work and make it extremely hard for small businesses and preference programs to be competitive. Once again, the talk comes from both sides of the political mouth.

Politicians talk about efficiency and holding down costs while they earmark vast amounts of government work to firms that will cost more to do it than large businesses in the name of helping these groups that are less competitive. That is a worthy objective, but it gets lost in the shuffle because these same politicians want to control how the military tries to run its business. The case in point relative to PWCs was that the secretary of the Navy decided the way to make PWCs more businesslike was to require them to engage business managers to help the COs make better business decisions. These individuals would be at the GM-15 level (comparable to an O-6) and senior to all the other military officers in the PWC except the CO. It sounded like the Soviet concept of having a political commissar in every military unit to ensure the CO of the unit was toeing the Party line. Since the compensation for such a person would be significantly higher in the private sector, the question of why anyone who had the right qualifications and experience to do this job would *want it* apparently never occurred to anyone. The prevailing wisdom suggested that high-quality individuals were readily available and could be recruited by COs with no commercial business experience to guide them on the requirements of the job or what to look for.

Another idea was to create a PWC corporate board, composed of the COs and business managers, to create policy, solve problems, and manage the business. This had been underway for several years when I took command. What I saw was despite the desire for commercially experienced business managers, several of them were former government employees who had been promoted into these jobs for reasons I never really understood. As I met those business managers who came from the commercial world, it was not clear to me what expertise they brought that made any of them a valuable contributor to the enterprise. It short, I thought the board was dysfunctional. Each PWC pretty much did what it wanted, while mouthing whatever was necessary to be left alone.

I just did not get it, but I knew this group was not going to be of any help to me in completing my tasks with the exception, perhaps, of selected individuals who were made available for their expertise. The political machinations and infighting between the COs and the business managers were an unnecessary distraction, as was the requirement to meet with the frequency dictated from on high to discuss PWC issues. The elephant in the room was who really ran the PWC, the CO or the business manager? The presumption was that since the business manager had been created expressly for the purpose, he must be in charge because the CO was not qualified to do this job. Add personalities to this mix, and you have a recipe for disaster.

One other significant occurrence took place two weeks after I arrived in Japan that required me to fly all the way back to Washington, DC, two days after the change of command. The chief that chewed me out as a detailer was retiring, and my boss from LANTDIV was being installed as the new chief. These NAVFAC changes of command cause numerous meetings to be scheduled so that attendance would be appropriate without trips just for the event. A PWC corporate board meeting was scheduled. Given my discussion with the new chief about the Seabees, this pretty much settled my future in the CEC and made being twelve time zones away a good thing.

As I became familiar with the PWC and its staff, the Japanese culture came through from top to bottom. The senior Japanese supervisors were all lifelong U.S. employees who spoke at least passable, if not good, English. They were technically very competent and handled their staffs in the Japanese fashion, expecting obedience because of their age and experience and brooking no dissent. The quality of the work produced by the staff was particularly good and sometimes led to the charge that it was *too* good and *too* expensive. The workers always built a Cadillac when a Chevy was needed. Over-engineering was a problem that we worked on as well as overstaffing. It was not like we had control over the number of Japanese employees, as any significant reduction in the workforce was a political issue since the Japanese government paid their salaries. Reductions had to be obtained through attrition. Lifetime employment was a feature of Japanese industry, and it carried over to the PWC. The performance of the American civilian supervisors ranged from generally competent to outstanding, as was the performance of the CEC officers and the few enlisted on the staff.

Business Manager

The real turmoil in the PWC was who really ran the PWC, the CO or the business manager. The initial briefings that were given to me on the status of the conversion to the NIF accounting system, the computerization of the PWC, and the training of the Japanese workforce did not give me a warm fuzzy feeling. The same applied to the comments of the business manager, who assured me that he was managing these things, and I did not have to worry about them. What I could see was his relationship with the other supervisors, both military and civilian, did not appear to be a good one. We had several one-on-one meetings to discuss what was going on and to determine in what direction the PWC should move. Finally, I told him that he needed to understand that I ran the PWC and was accountable for it, not him. I was the one who needed to know what was going on to decide whether I was happy with it. The "trust me" approach did not cut it. The feedback I required was not negotiable nor was my prerogative to discuss any issue directly with anyone I chose in the PWC. He did not like this and said so.

The business manager was from private industry and assumed the business manager position with no prior military experience and no understanding of how the military functioned. It was clear he had read much more into his position than I did, and that was going to be a problem. The discussion I had in NAVFAC was now crystal clear to me, as was the course of action I would have to take. I will not belabor how all this played out, but it did not have a happy ending. Since there was a fundamental difference of opinion in how the PWC should be run that was not going to be resolved in the business manager's favor, he decided to leave to pursue other opportunities after a lengthy period of unhappily trying to accommodate my directions.

I then went through the process of hiring a new business manager that was not concluded until shortly before I left the PWC.

Despite the problems associated with who was in charge, the conversion was accomplished, as was the computerization and training of the workforce. The PWC received a secretary of the Navy commendation for this effort. While this was going on, I was involved in substantial negotiations with the Japanese government in the execution of the JFIP program that centered around two large undertakings: the provision of additional military housing to include replacement of senior officer housing (which is always an emotional issue) and the upgrading of the utilities systems on base that included building utilities tunnels under the waterfront to place the steam lines, water, electricity, and other utilities underground. Both projects were complicated and expensive. From an operational point of view, placing tunnels under a port area that had been in use for nearly a hundred years as an Imperial Navy port and then as a U.S. Navy port (not to mentioned being bombed during the war) while maintaining operations for the U.S. 7th Fleet was exceedingly difficult and complex and required exceptional coordination and planning.

Providing additional "American-style" housing was the number one morale issue for families of the U.S. 7th Fleet and base personnel; the waiting list for housing on base was almost two years long. This required most families arriving to spend at least that long living in Japanese off-base housing, which proved to be an adventure because of the lack of heating and utilities, not to mention the general construction of the houses. This also required a fleet of school buses to travel through the communities to pick up school-age children to attend school on base. These negotiations were completed, and the projects were constructed while I maintained a good working relationship with my boss, CNFJ, and the commander US Forces Japan. I had several direct dealings with the commander of the U.S. 7th Fleet and more often his chief of staff that were pleasant and professional. We were able to resolve issues, including the conversion to NIF funding, to their satisfaction with the PWC being looked upon as a team player.

OICC Far East

On the OICC Far East side of my job, I traveled to the four subordinate offices in Sasebo, Misawa, Okinawa, and Korea and met with the local commanders on a regular basis. Since the JFIP program in Japan and a similar program in Korea provided most of the project funding, the construction, maintenance, repairs, and services contract loading on these bases was relatively small as was the staff. Unfortunately, I had the same problems with the contracting function that I had at LANTDIV dealing with senior contracting personnel at PACDIV who thought they were autonomous and could just direct me to do what they wanted. They were wrong, and I spent significant time dealing with the PACDIV CEC flag putting them back in their boxes. It helped that for most of the time the CEC flag was a longtime friend of mine with a large measure of common sense and a dislike for bureaucratic infighting.

I enjoyed this tour and learned a great deal, especially reinforcing what I had learned previously in negotiating with foreign government officials, this time Japanese and Korean. Our family enjoyed Japan, and we took every opportunity to travel around not only there but also around Southeast Asia, Hong Kong, and Korea. Mary was able to retire after two years at the hospital, but not without suffering Nurse Corps intransigence. It disapproved her retirement request and told her she could not retire for another year despite her orders saying the opposite. That required me calling in a flag favor from a three-star I had dealt with, who happened to be the chief of Naval Personnel.

Mary and I particularly enjoyed the social side of the job, as the Japanese military and civilian officials kept up a continuous stream of official parties, dinners, receptions, and other events to which we were invited. A good deal of business was conducted at these "social" functions. Many of these affairs were quite lavish and put the U.S. Navy's efforts to reciprocate to shame. One group that we developed friendships with was the Japanese-American Association. This group regularly sponsored events for the American military personnel and their families. The Japanese who ran it were mostly very wealthy individuals who did this out of their own pockets. One of them told me that the reason they did this was that these men had all been young children after World War II ended, and they and their families were facing starvation. It was the kindness of the sailors stationed in Yokosuka (who gave them food, clothing, and treated them so well) that made the difference in their lives, and they could never repay or forget this generosity. This was the same kindness that I had witnessed worldwide as our young Seabees adopted kids wherever they went and did much the same thing.

One evening after Mary and I had returned from a Tokyo U.S. Chamber of Commerce Christmas dinner dance and had just gotten to bed, there was knocking on the front door. A young petty officer from base security was standing there. He said, "Sir, I believe your car is on fire." I told him I had not driven all day but would look. The garage for the house was located above it on the side of a hill and required walking up a flight of about fifty steps to see it. As I arrived at eye level with the top step, I saw a wall of flames pouring from the garage and the car. I said, "You're right. I assume you have called the fire department?" He responded in the affirmative, and I told him I was going back to bed since there was nothing else I could do. I had just gotten back to sleep when there was again knocking on my front door. The same petty officer informed me that our family had to leave the house because they believed there were terrorists on base that had set fire to my car, and the Navy security forces were making a sweep of the hill where the quarters were. I asked him if these security forces were armed, and he said they were. I told him we were not leaving our quarters. The last thing I was going to do with my family was have them standing in the open while armed individuals were wandering around.

I went back in the house and shortly heard another knock. This time it was the petty officer; his boss, an E-6; and my O-6 medical doctor neighbor. The doctor informed me that I had to leave my quarters immediately because the E-6 said so. I told him I was not leaving, and the last time I looked an E-6 didn't outrank an O-6; while I appreciated the petty officer's counsel, I could make my own decision. This really set the doctor off for some reason. He informed me that the wives of all the senior officers who were deployed with their ships had been ordered out of their houses and were standing just down the path from my place waiting for further instructions, so my family had to go too. I said, "You're kidding me!" I told him to get lost and then went down the trail to find the wives standing there in their nighties and robes. I addressed the group: "Go back into your houses and get under your beds as there are scared young sailors out in the bushes with weapons looking for people they have little information about. If a raccoon startles them, they will fire, and this whole hill could become a shooting gallery. Don't open your doors and stay inside until morning." The group dispersed, and I went back to bed.

The next morning the base security officer, accompanied by a Japanese police detective, came to my door and asked me to come up and look at what was left of my car. It was a burned-out hulk sitting on its rims. They told me they caught one of the terrorists, a right-wing extremist who had intended to blow up the radio tower that sat atop our hill. It proved to be too secure, so as they descended the hill, they cooked up the idea to couple their incendiary device with the propane tank from my barbeque grill and set it off in my garage. The date was December 8, 1991—the fiftieth anniversary of the Pearl Harbor attack (because of the international date line, December 7th in Hawaii was already December 8th in Japan). They told me the attack on our base was designed to commemorate this Japanese victory. I said I thought that was ironic since my father had been at Pearl Harbor during the attack, and now they were after me. The Japanese police were extremely embarrassed by the affair and asked me to provide them with an estimate of my losses so they could reimburse me promptly. The perpetrators were both ultimately apprehended, tried, and sent to prison, and the incident was downplayed in the Japanese press.

During the beginning of my last year of this three-year assignment, the new chief made a visit to the Pacific and came to Yokosuka. He was there several days calling on the appropriate flag officers, including the U.S. 7th Fleet commander and my boss, the commander Naval Forces Japan. We held the expected social events so all the officers and their wives could socialize with the chief. We briefed him on all our issues, including the status of the conversion of the accounting system, and he was pleased. On the last day, we had a meeting in my office before he departed for the next stop of his tour. After thanking me for the hospitality, he said he was surprised that I had not talked with the detailer about my desires for my next assignment, as I would be moving the next summer. I told him that I really did not care since I would be doing the mandatory one-year upon returning from overseas and then retiring. He was stunned. "Why would you do that?" He had several top jobs in mind for me and really had wanted my input on what I wanted to do. I told him the same thing I had told him when we talked in his office two years earlier—I wanted to be with the Seabees. Since he had decided that was not to be, I did not see any reason to take on a job that I was not interested in. It seemed to me that I should try to get settled in the civilian world before my two youngest kids finished with grade school. He was concerned; he said, "You should really think about this decision. I will talk with you sometime later about all of this." That is where we left it, but my mind was made up.

My last year in Yokosuka was moving along, and I still had no orders for a new assignment. The detailer told me that the chief was handling my case personally. He had no idea what that meant. One day, my secretary buzzed me and told me the chief's office was on the line, and he wanted to speak to me. From our conversation when he visited, I figured the time had come for a showdown. He started by asking me what I had heard about the Seabees' participation in Desert Shield/Desert Storm, to which I replied not much. Was I aware there had been issues with the call-up of the reserve Seabee units and with their command structure? And had I heard that there had been political fallout from all this? To all of this, I responded in the negative. He then dropped the bomb: the Seabees were being restructured, with the active and reserve Seabee units in each fleet being integrated into one command—the 2nd Naval Construction Brigade (2 NCB). The largest Seabee command, 2 NCB would be located in the old COMCBLANT headquarters in Norfolk since the latter command was being disestablished. CBLANT was being replaced by a recommissioned Naval Construction Regiment (NCR), the 22nd. This regiment would control the active-duty construction battalions under the 2 NCB, which would also be responsible for overall command of the reserve construction regiments and the training regiment in Gulfport, Mississippi. He said, "Mike, I want you to do two jobs for me. Take command of the 22nd NCR and run it. But more importantly, I want you to be the deputy commander of the 2 NCB. The commander will be a reserve CEC two-star, who will not be there on a day-to-day basis. You will need to run the brigade and make sure this integration works. I think this is the kind of job you asked for, right?" What could I say? I was all but speechless, but I managed to stammer out "Yes, sir!" and asked when this was going to happen. Mary and the kids were excited since we were going back to our home in Virginia Beach and the school the kids had left. I could not have scripted a better ending to the tour in Japan.

Back to the Seabees

Welcome to the culture wars! Nothing could be a better descriptor of the environment I was to operate in. The reserve CEC/Seabees felt they had been disrespected during the call-up for Desert Shield when they were treated as second-class resources, unfit to command in a real war. Active-duty officers replaced the leadership of a reserve regiment just as the regiment was being mobilized and sent to the war zone. Active-duty officers had consistently looked down on the reserves and made disparaging remarks about their lack of preparedness for the real thing. For their part, the active-duty CEC officers who had been involved with the reserves during the call-up were disgusted by what they perceived as a highly political reserve program, where connections rather than merit were important in job assignments and promotion. They felt there were too many incompetent "weekend warriors" in key positions, and that was a recipe for disaster. The general levels of training, particularly military and tactical training, were thought to be low. The reserve Seabee battalions were not ready. The result was that the participation of the Seabee reserves in the war was not what the reserves felt it should be. They used their considerable political clout to complain, forcing the restructuring I was slated to manage. It was a Rodney Dangerfield meets the Seabees movie, and I was the director. My only command guidance was, "Make it work!"

There really was no turnover for this new job except the briefings on the current operations and readiness of the active-duty battalions that would report to me (the old CBLANT role). I was once again relieving the same officer I had relieved at PWC Yokosuka, who was retiring from the Navy. The decommissioning of COMCBLANT and the commissioning of 2 NCB and the 22nd NCR was a big affair carried out on the parade ground at the Construction Battalion Center Gulfport, Mississippi, the homeport of the Atlantic Fleet Seabee battalions, with the commander in chief U.S. Atlantic Fleet as the presiding official. Even though the ceremony started mid-morning, it was July in Mississippi—which is to say it was extremely hot and humid, and it only got worse as the speakers droned on. Seabees were collapsing on the parade field from the heat when the ceremony finally began to wrap up and 22nd NCR was officially commissioned, and I read my orders as its first commander. My speech was about thirty seconds long; I said, "I'm glad to be back with the Seabees and looked forward to working with you again."

This job really required a split personality since commanding the operational regiment involved supporting U.S. forces in the Caribbean, Europe, Africa, and the Middle East in real time. This was entirely different from the job of integrating the active and reserve Seabees into one brigade that was prepared to operate as a unit and meet wartime tasking. There was also the touchy job of integrating the reserve CEC flag into the Atlantic Fleet staff thinking, which did not include reserves as a rule or have them in command of active-duty naval units. This had been given a lot of lip service, but not a lot of practical thought. I had an active-duty O-5 assigned as the chief of staff of 2 NCB. He had been a battalion commander and was in the holding pattern waiting for the O-6 board. He would hold the fort when I was gone—which was often, as the 22nd NCR job and the

2 NCB job required significant travel visiting units and operational sites. The reserves met monthly for their weekend drills and had two weeks of active duty in the summer. There were, of course, homework assignments for the principal staff officers, who had to juggle their civilian jobs with their reserve assignments. These people were dedicated and put in long hours. Tasking and follow-up became the key, along with accountability as I saw it, which was sometimes different from what many were used to.

Continuous Engagement

During the three years I had this assignment, the 22nd NCR's battalions were continuously engaged in not only their scheduled deployments but also numerous contingency operations, such as Hurricane Andrew recovery operations; Haitian refugee camp construction at Guantanamo Bay, Cuba; Operation Uphold Democracy in Haiti; Operation Restore Hope in Somalia; support for the U.S. Army and UN forces in Bosnia and Croatia; and nation building in such diverse places as Tunisia, Albania, Columbia, Trinidad, and Guatemala. As with other things I have referred to, I will not spend time talking about these operations, as that would require a lengthy discussion. Suffice it to say, the Seabees performed magnificently and provided invaluable support to these efforts. Use of the Seabees in these types of operations always involved the same problems. First, there was always the infighting within the Navy because the Navy did not want to share Seabees with anyone, including the Marines, and resisted requests for their use even though it reveled in the publicity the Seabees received executing these missions. All this resistance was usually to no avail as the joint commanders and the JCS would overrule the Navy and direct the use of the Seabees. It did, however, place our staff in a difficult position, as we were continually being questioned about volunteering for things we wanted to do that the Navy did not want us to do.

Second, there was the continuous fight to make sure my men were able to defend themselves and not placed in hostile environments with ridiculous rules of engagement, like those that had been the bane of tactical operations the entire time I had been in the Navy. We were generally successful in this when it was pointed out that we would be on record requesting adequate self-defense capability. Someone would have to sign direction overruling this request, which would be an uncomfortable position should something bad happen. Third, there was logistics support to include not only personnel support in the form of water, food, fuel, and the like but also construction materials to carry out the tasking. These issues were assumed away by the planners of operations because they were too hard, but they did not go away and many times led to extremely expensive fixes. Fourth, transportation of the Seabees and their equipment was a major issue since construction equipment is heavy and bulky. It generally required sealift and port facilities plus adequate roads to get it to the contingency sites. Although there was airlift-capable construction equipment, it was of limited capacity and required extensive aircraft to move.

Since the overall airlift capacity of the U.S. forces was finite and all the services were competing for that precious asset, coordination and scheduling was a major issue. The operators wanted the facilities the Seabees would be building as soon as possible but did not want to devote the required airlift. The brigade and regimental staffs worked all these issues behind the scenes, and to the outside, things just sort of happened. Unfortunately, decision makers did not learn the lesson that engineer support for joint operations is usually the long pole in the tent, mainly because they did not want to admit it or resource the fix.

Active/Reserve Integration

At the 2 NCB, the integration of the active and reserve staffs was successfully, if painfully, carried out. The pain mostly was derived from the cultural issues referred to earlier. There were some extremely talented and dedicated reserve CEC officers, but there were some incredibly incompetent ones as well. An illustration will help clarify this and explain part of my role in making the sausage.

The issue was that a troubling number of reserve officers had a loose interpretation of "discretionary" orders. This was exacerbated by an informal, but powerful, "old boy" system of mentorship that was relied upon to get out of trouble. The integrated staff was stood up with a combination of active-duty officers and reserve-component officers in key billets. To spread the billets between active-duty and reserve personnel, some of the senior billets were filled with either an active-duty or reserve officer, with the representative of the other component serving as the deputy. Shortly after the stand-up, an issue arose: I directed the reserve officer in charge of a function to perform some duties, but he did not feel like he should have to do them. When this officer's deputy asked him about the plan I had directed, he was told it was not going to happen because he did not care what I wanted, as this was *his* function to run as he saw fit. Unfortunately for him, the deputy was an ex-enlisted LDO who happened to agree with me. He gave me an off-the-record call to let me know what was happening and his concerns about it.

I allowed an appropriate period of time to go by to let the reserve officer hang himself and then sent a message asking for the status of the tasks I had directed him to perform. His reply constituted so much waffling and dodging, so I told my reserve flag boss I was relieving this officer (who was one of the flag's pet rocks) and finding someone who knew how to obey orders. The timing was perfect because it sent shock waves around the leadership of the reserves. The flag asked me not to relieve the man, saying he had been chastised; he assured me that what I wanted would be done without further insubordinate behavior. I let it pass. I did not have any further issues with this officer, but I did encounter this attitude with other officers. This added a layer of nuance to my understanding of empathy of "peers" and "superiors." Ensuring the integration without antagonizing the reserve flag and captain community was critical. Again I found that once expectations were understood and agreed upon, the problems assumed the character of background noise. To be fair, I had one or two similar occurrences with active-duty battalion commanders that required some action to correct, but these seemed more personality issues than outright defiance.

The relationships that I developed with the two reserve flag officers I worked for during those three years were generally good ones, as they were both talented officers, though with different personalities. My job was to make them look good both inside the brigade and out. This involved briefing them extensively for their trips and meetings, particularly with line flag officers. They both understood that I knew the Seabees and the active-duty culture (both CEC and line) and had been selected by the chief for this job, so they usually took my advice.

Aside from the operational requirements and the reserve integration issues, another time-consuming and overly micromanaged tasking came down: assigning women to the naval mobile construction battalions. None of the problems with assigning women to NMCBs that I had briefed when I was both the enlisted and officer detailer had gone away, but the pressures to find more billets for women had finally overcome the resistance and commonsense arguments against doing this. The biggest problem was there were not enough CEC women officers and enlisted Seabee chief petty officers to provide leadership and role models for women in all the battalions, so only some of the battalions would have women initially. A shocker to many senior officers was a significant number of the junior CEC women officers did not want to be in the Seabees. It was still a bad idea to have the only women officers in a battalion be non-CEC officers who generally did not want to be in a battalion. The same was true of non-Seabee chief petty officers. We worked the tasking and made it happen.

There were women CEC and other staff and line officers on the brigade staff, and that led to some interesting issues. I had, after all, read *Men Are from Mars, Women Are from Venus*. I understood the concept that women do not necessarily want a man to offer a solution to a problem; rather, they just want a man to be a good listener. Still, I could not see this working in a command relationship. The TMI (too much information) factor in that situation is real. A precursor of the male/female time bomb that has entangled not only the military but also all aspects of social interaction, brought this home to me, when a female lieutenant filed a sexual harassment complaint against a male lieutenant in a different department. After a distracting investigation, it turned out that these two had been in a relationship, and the male decided he was no longer interested and moved on. The female apparently felt this constituted harassment and the problem could be rectified if he just came back to her. It came as a shock to her that the legal system found that if there was any harassment, it was on her part. While this episode was unfolding there was a steady stream of Navy training on sexual harassment for all hands intended to educate the males on how to deal with females without stepping over the line. This has gone on from then until now without huge success judging from all the media coverage of sexual abuse.

Higher Headquarters, Redux

Commanding a higher headquarters with subordinate unit commanding officers reporting to me was a new experience, but the issues I faced were not. My experience as an officer detailer, aide, and staff officer working with flag officers had already delivered a large dose of dealing with officers with more ego than common sense. While every effort is made to pick the right individuals for command, mistakes are sometimes made because true personality traits can be hidden until the individual is placed in command. Arrogance breeds a feeling of invulnerability that is at odds with reality. The media has made everyone vulnerable, even those who have done nothing. The dichotomy is that while almost all COs do things that could be viewed negatively by the public at one time or the other, those who are respected by their subordinates and supported by their chain of command do not tend to get into trouble. Those who are not respected or are disliked are frequently ratted out for the most insignificant of things and are even relieved of command because of them. I would almost guarantee that over ninety percent of the incidents that are reported in the press concerning perceived abuses of authority or privilege come from "insider" knowledge within the command. I have seen some very colorful, but admired, COs do some amazing things that flew under the radar.

Esprit de corps and morale are not hard things to discern in a unit if one has any feel for what to look for. I have said many times that I could tell the state of a unit within an hour of arriving for a visit. This was usually confirmed by my command master chief from his own wandering around and talking to the chiefs and enlisted chain of command. It is the little things such as the appearance of the troops, the cleanliness of their facilities and berthing areas, the military courtesy they extend, and the pride they exhibit in their unit and what they are doing. How the officers get along in the wardroom and the chiefs in the chiefs' mess are big indicators as well. In short, despite the pedigrees the COs who worked for me may have brought to the job, it was not difficult to rank them. I was forced to relieve one CO for bad personal conduct that could not have been predicted, but that did not make it any easier. Others I had to chew out and give specific guidance for improving their performance on pain of relief. The principal trait leading to these officers' troubles was almost always arrogance and an inflated opinion of themselves versus others, including their boss.

I visited units throughout my assignment, both active and reserve, in homeport and deployed, to size them up and keep a warm fuzzy that they were prepared, well taken care of, and doing their tasking in the best manner possible. This led to some great experiences, a couple of which I will relate, as they demonstrate the quality—good and bad—of the officers and enlisted personnel we have in the Seabees. Visiting a deployed Seabee camp always involved an inspection of the barracks, in addition to the job sites. My usual routine was to go to the barracks and walk around until I found a room with the names of the two or three lowest-ranking enlisted men on the door and then inspect that room and two or three similar ones from other companies. My reasoning was if these rooms were good, it meant the chain of command had worked; if not, it had not. While I would have thought the word would have gotten out on what I did, I was amazed that it did not travel between battalions, which led to some interesting results.

On several occasions, as I started to walk around looking for the rooms I wanted to inspect, I was told that rooms had been determined for me to inspect, and I should follow the chief master at arms to those rooms. I told the CO I did not want to look at those rooms, as I knew they were squared away or they would not be taking me there. I was interested in seeing if the other battalion rooms were in the same condition. One CO started arguing with me and told me this was not fair, whatever that meant, and I told him I thought he needed to bring that up with the chaplain, as I was going to do what I wanted. The rooms I chose were not prepared and were, in fact, a mess, much to the CO's dismay. This just confirmed what I already suspected about the state of the battalion.

I believed it was important to visit the Seabees who were in harm's way since I was the one who sent them there. While these visits were necessarily brief, they did subject me to the same dangers the Seabees were facing daily. The message was still there. Visiting Somalia, where there were two battalions supporting the Marines and coalition forces, was informative, depressing, and exhilarating at the same time. Those who only see the Third World and its abject poverty on television really have no idea what they are looking at. One of the most eye-opening experiences for our Seabees and other U.S. forces is to operate in these areas and realize how great we have it back home. The lack of the most fundamental resources, such as water and food, are a huge problem, as was the provision of construction materials to a place that I deemed "the end of the world." There were skulls on highway markers, skeletons and half-buried corpses just off the roads, and filth everywhere. There were also lots of starving Somalis, the most pathetic of which were the children.

My favorite anecdote from the visit was flying out to a Marine operating base that was about an hour by CH-53 west of Mogadishu. I was to visit a Seabee water-well drilling team that was there to sink a well for the Marines. As we landed, a red silt cloud rose up from the rotor wash; it covered us completely and I marveled that the pilot could see anything. We went to the Marine camp and met the O-5 in charge. We were then shown the well site where a chief was running the team drilling the well. The lieutenant colonel bragged about how great the team was, saying he was sure we would have water very soon. After a while, before the helicopter picked us up for the return flight, the chief pulled me aside and said, "Commodore, there ain't no water here. I told the Marine CO that the water is over there, pointing to a location maybe five hundred yards away, but he said we had to drill the well inside the perimeter, so it could be protected!" (You can't make this stuff up!) I told the chief we would resolve this from a different direction as quickly as possible, so he would not get in trouble and the Marines would get their water. Why his chain of command did not know this issue I didn't know, but I got the information to the right people to get it resolved.

A very high-visibility, dangerous, and political assignment we received was to insert a detachment into the jungle about two hundred miles south of Bogotá, Columbia, to build a riverine base for the Columbian marines. This was right in the middle of narco gang territory, where drug plants were cultivated and harvested for transport down the river. After some incredible negotiations regarding being able to have weapons for our Seabees to defend themselves, the compromise was a company of Columbian army rangers would be colocated with our Seabees to protect them, so they would keep their weapons in the armory and only issue them if they were under attack. We sent the det in and the CMC and I went to visit them; my "pucker factor" was extremely high, indeed. It did not get any better when we arrived at the local airport and were met by our escort of Columbian soldiers to ride down to the project site on river boats. The local natives glared at us in the same manner both the CMC and I had seen in Vietnam—they viewed us as part of the Columbian government's effort to deprive them of income. Our escort included many noticeably young troopers armed to the gills with a variety of small arms and grenades—they did not instill confidence of high levels of training. The hair on the backs of our necks stood up as we pressed on to the site.

What I saw when we arrived was gratifying. The defensive positions around the camp were skillfully built with cleared fire zones that would make any attack costly. The Columbian army rangers were alert and well positioned. I was met by the lieutenant and senior chief who oversaw the Seabee det, and they walked me around the project and defenses. When we were finished, we sat down for a status briefing, and I was praising the lieutenant and senior chief for what I had seen. The lieutenant said,

Commodore, I hope you don't mind, but I was concerned about our security and the senior and I thought about what we could do about it. We noticed that these rangers don't get supplied very often with food, and when they do, it was pathetic. They watched us eat and were drooling. The ranger captain speaks some English, and I asked him if our security could be improved if we helped them out with some food. He said, "For sure!" Since then, I have significantly increased our provision orders for the C-130 resupply flight. We also let them watch our movies and use our washing machines. There was an immediate increase in our security with the positions you saw, and the captain went to the local villages and told them that the Seabees were not to be messed with as they were "for real" going to defend them, and the narcos had better understand that. Is that OK, sir?

I could hardly suppress a laugh and I said, "That's just perfect!" They completed the base without incident to the delight of the country team, and the ambassador himself did the ribbon cutting. Once again Seabee ingenuity had won the day.

I also got to fly in a Columbian army UH-1 Huey that looked like a maintenance disaster with doors that could not close. I was told cheerily that the last Huey that took this trip had crashed. Det visits were not for sissies (despite the ribbing I got for my travel schedule—or as my kids used to call my trips when they were smaller, my "vacations").

I knew all along that the last year I was in this job I would be in the promotion zone for flag. I well understood the luck required to be selected and felt there were at least six real contenders for the two spots that were being filled. I was happy to have gotten my Seabee job; I could accept not being selected and retire feeling I had done all that I wanted to do in the Navy. I was making a visit to the deployed battalion in Europe and visiting its detachment in Souda Bay, Crete, when I received a call from the chief, Jack Buffington, a career-long friend who had relieved the one who sent me to the Seabees. He gave me the good news that I had been selected for flag. He did not know anything about my new assignment, but he counseled me to enjoy the moment, as it would probably be the best of my flag career. After a couple of months, I was told I would be getting my choice of jobs, which is to say, I was being assigned to LANTDIV in Norfolk. The family would not have to move, and I would be going to a job I knew well. An old friend, Peter Marshall, would be my relief as the commodore and deputy 2 NCB, so the whole plan came together well, and I closed out what I thought would be my last Seabee job contented.

Chapter Nine

THE FLAG DECK

Damn the torpedoes, full speed ahead!
—Admiral David Farragut

My promotion to rear admiral (lower half) occurred at 2 NCB headquarters shortly before I left the Seabees to go to LANTDIV. The presiding official was my old friend Vern Clark, who I had served with as an aide on the E-ring when we were both lieutenant commanders and who would end up as the CNO in the future. He was the deputy commander, U.S. Atlantic Fleet. My cow roommate from West Point, Woody Held, and his wife, Sally, were there, together with my family, friends, and fellow Seabees. The astonishment of my classmates that a West Point graduate could be selected as a flag officer in the Navy was palpable. The small number of classmates selected for stars in the Army, compounded by memories of me as an indifferent cadet who abandoned the Army for the detested Navy, fed this feeling. Obviously, it was a red-letter day that I realized had more to do with luck than skill, but I remembered Jack Buffington's admonition that it would probably be the best day I spent as a flag, which was not far from the truth.

Two flag acculturation events took place before and after the promotion ceremony and reporting to LANTDIV. The first was what was laughingly called the one-week flag "Knife and Fork School," or "What's Expected of Navy Flag Officers" course, for selectees (all line and staff corps) and their spouses in Washington, DC. Each service has a similar course for their flag and general officer selectees, during which the senior service leadership congratulates them on their selection, admonishes them on their expected conduct (both the selectee and the spouse), and welcomes them to the rarified air of wearing stars. As the adage "truth in advertising" suggests, there was also some frank talk about how being a flag may mean sometimes being treated shabbily, like being given orders on truly short notice to take on a job you don't want with no discussion, as the needs of the Navy are supreme, so get over it. The CNO, Adm. Mike Boorda, told us that from where we sat, we could all see the "light at the end of the tunnel" on our Navy careers, some of which would end earlier than others. We should understand that only half the people in the room would be selected for two stars, and those not selected would be out of the Navy within four years. Most of the rest would make two stars and serve six years or so, and a handful would make three or four stars and could stay for up to ten years or so. I do not think many in the room looked at this promotion in that manner. It was sobering for some, but given the extraordinary egos involved, many thought they would be in the select group to last ten years. This could not include me; six years was the longest I could be around since there are no three- or four-star billets in the CEC.

Boorda then said, "You have made flag, and no one can take that away from you. To your family and friends, you will forever be the 'admiral' regardless of how many stars you end up getting. You should all remember that and feel proud of the accomplishment." This was not entirely true, since three of the selectees in the course were subsequently removed from the flag list after investigations into their conduct revealed abuse of their position or improper sexual adventures with subordinates. This was yet another illustration of giant egos causing a view of invulnerability that just does not exist. While there was a great deal of comment this day about flag and general officer conduct, I would posit it has always been about the same and will always be, egos being what they are. My principal takeaways from this course were meeting my contemporaries, who would prove helpful in the future; not being overwhelmed that I was in the company of people who were much smarter or better qualified than me; and identifying a few people to watch out for.

The second course was six weeks long and a requirement of a law that all flag and general officer selectees must attend for their promotion to take effect as part of the forced "jointness" of the Goldwater-Nichols Act. This course was called "Capstone" and was conducted at the National War College at Fort McNair in Washington, DC, as a joint course with the class including selectees from all branches of the services plus some government agencies, such as the CIA. The purpose was generally an expansion upon the individual services' indoctrination and focused on bringing us up to speed on U.S. foreign, military, and government policy plus indoctrination into the capabilities of each of the services.

We visited Fort Bragg and flew with airborne troops as they jumped from the aircraft with full combat equipment; sat in a pitch-black room into which Delta Force operators silently entered and fired their weapons, taking out targets before we even knew they were there; and witnessed demonstrations of airmobile assaults and other impressive Army capabilities. We visited Nellis AFB and Langley AFB, where we watched a perfectly coordinated B-1 bomber attack on one of the bombing ranges (the bombers had flown from North Dakota to arrive at a precise time); a demonstration of the "Aggressor Squadron" advanced fighter training, in which Soviet air tactics were employed to attack Air Force F-15 pilots and Navy F-14 pilots; and briefings on the Air Force missile and space intelligence programs.

The Navy visit took us to Norfolk and U.S. Atlantic Fleet. The high point was being flown out to a carrier at sea and landing on it, touring the ship, and then being launched off the ship. This was a real thrill for me. There were demonstrations of Marine amphibious capabilities as well. The point was for us to appreciate what each service brought to the fight, so we could better do our jobs in the future. The briefings on potential adversary capabilities were interesting as were the observations of many important political and think-tank types who spoke to us off the record. Newt Gingrich was one of the speakers.

A major benefit of this course was meeting the classmates who participated from the other services and getting to know my fellow Navy selectees better. Mike Mullen, who was to become a beer-drinking and golfing buddy, was a seatmate on a Western Hemisphere tour; he would later serve as the chairman of the JCS under President Obama. There were some very impressive Air Force and Army officers in the course, who reminded me of the ones I had met at the Naval War College. Of course, West Point graduates gravitated to each other thanks to their common experience, as did the Corps of Engineers officers, the Air Force engineers, and the CEC selectees. This again proved useful down the road. All in all, I found the course a good one and useful for future reference.

Returning to LANTDIV, a few "ghosts of Christmas past" were waiting for me. The OICC Portsmouth Hospital had been stood up, and the construction of the replacement hospital was well on its way. Our team had compiled a substantial list of lessons learned from the construction of the other replacement Navy and Air Force hospitals that led to mock-ups being built and tested to prevent roof and window leaks and equipment installation problems for the mechanical systems. Full-scale mock-ups of patient rooms and operating rooms ensured the right equipment was ordered, while the doctors and nurses who would be using these facilities were able to offer their input directly to the designers after seeing what the completed facilities would look like. The results were outstanding.

A bad ghost that was still haunting LANTDIV, as well as the rest of NAVFAC, was the continuing conflict between the operators and the contracting function. Fortunately, this time they all worked for me, and I called them together and told them they had to play nicely, and I would not tolerate the finger-pointing and power trips that served no purpose. Generally, this happened, although there were some ugly incidents with the NAVFAC headquarters SES contracting types who tried to say I could not tell the contracting people what to do. Eventually, these issues were resolved; they just instilled in me how ridiculous this division of responsibilities was.

Finding an Aide

In my new position I was authorized an aide, so one of the first orders of business was to find a good candidate. Since I had served as an aide myself, I knew what characteristics I wanted, and the detail office sent me some candidates to interview. They asked if I minded if they included a female officer as a candidate, and I said I did not. After interviewing all the candidates, it was clear that the female was the most outstanding, and I decided to select her because she answered the tough questions I had asked her professionally and directly. These questions could not be asked today because of the mindless PC mentality regarding females that precludes facing real issues head-on. Suzanne Fiori was a Naval Academy graduate who had served in ACB-2 and had been awarded the Seabee Combat Warfare pin. She was married to a classmate who was a surface warfare officer stationed on a destroyer in Norfolk. I asked her what her husband would think about her traveling with me in close quarters all over my area of responsibility. She said he understood that was part of the job and had no problem with it. I then asked, "How will you react when we go to hotels in Europe and Latin America, and the management assumes we are sleeping together and tries to give us one room or two adjoining rooms? Middle-age executives in those countries often have young assistants traveling with them." That was the question she had not anticipated, but to her credit, she said, "I will react professionally and thank them for their attempt to anticipate such an arrangement but note that the admiral is happily married and would prefer not to give any other impression." Great answer and it sewed up the job.

When I called her to my office and told her she was my selection, she was flabbergasted. She told me when she left the interview, she was convinced she did not have a chance and had told her husband so. She proved to be an outstanding aide and officer.

There were a host of important projects that LANTDIV was responsible for that filled my time. I have already mentioned the construction of the Portsmouth Naval Hospital, but an equally important and emotional project was the construction of the personnel support base near Naples, Italy, for those serving at the myriad of commands supporting the U.S. 6th Fleet, the NATO headquarters, hospital, and airfield in that area. For a host of reasons, a complete support base was needed. The chief two among many were the earthquake frequency, coupled with the substandard construction of some of the places available for renting locally; and the increasing concerns for the security of the servicemen and their families. Not much had changed since I had lived there except the locations for the leased facilities that were being used for the important support facilities, such as the hospital, schools for the dependent children, commissary and exchange, recreational fields and activities facilities, and the administrative spaces. What had changed was the crime and terrible traffic issues as more and more Italians were able to have their own cars. The solution to this evolved into a two-phased plan. The easier of the two phases was the use of U.S.-funded military construction projects to build facilities on the portion of the commercial airport that served Naples that was owned and controlled by the Italian Ministry of Defence and was used as a naval air facility. There was enough space to build administrative, operations, and unaccompanied barracks together with parking structures. The area was small, however, and required an extraordinarily complex daisy chain of demolition and construction while operations were carried out. The more political and complex project was to complete a leased construction and operation of support facilities for dependents away from Naples that could be secured and provide the necessary level of acceptable support.

The decision was made that the support base would be built through lease construction, a process that required a contractor to acquire the land for the base, finance the construction of the desired facilities, maintain them, and be reimbursed by lease payments over a long-term contract. This was not a new idea, but political issues (U.S. and Italian, local and national) had blocked it for years. Finally, the pressure became so great, an accommodation was made, a competition held, and a contract awarded.

The groundbreaking was held on a rainy day when the U.S. ambassador, the four-star, Italian dignitaries, and I (representing NAVFAC) did the honors. This undertaking took years to complete in phases with the housing, school, childcare, and exchange/commissary being completed first, followed by the hospital and other facilities.

I spent a good deal of time traveling, not only to visit our far-flung customers but also to attend a multitude of endless meetings on a host of issues. The extent of the geographical area for which I was responsible had me traveling as far as Oman and Bahrain in the Persian Gulf, Central America and the Caribbean, as well as all over Europe and Iceland, not to mention the Marine bases in North Carolina, where there was an extensive building program going on since the size of the Marine Corps was being increased. I went to the weekly four-star flag meeting at the Atlantic Fleet compound when I was in town. These gatherings were always entertaining, as the line flags vied for the CINC's attention, and some were caught short by his questions. Occasionally, there was a question in my area, but not too often. Most of my interface with the CINC was through specific briefings he asked for on topics of interest. I had more meetings with the two-star deputy and the staff than the CINC personally.

There were numerous meetings within the NAVFAC world and attendance at conferences to discuss and strategize issues. In addition to this, there were many direct meetings and phone discussions with the new chief, Dave Nash, who had been a lifelong friend since we were lieutenants together in Europe in the early '70s. I provided a sounding board for his ideas to deal with the constant attacks by the bean counters against NAVFAC, the Seabees, and the CEC. These took the form of directed cuts with no basis other than the arrogance of some line flags who understood little and cared less for the requirements of the shore infrastructure in their quest to protect ships, aircraft, and submarines at all costs. Even potential dire consequences to the facilities vital for the support of their beloved toys and the sailors who manned them were of little interest. "They did not know what they did not know," had no interest in learning, and generally knew that the consequences of their decisions would not happen on their watch, so they felt no accountability for those consequences. The bureaucratic infighting and positions of the power brokers that I had seen as an aide had not changed at all, nor has it to this day. As a result, success is dependent upon relationships in many cases, as opposed to data, to the detriment of the service.

Selection Boards

One thing I spent considerable time on was sitting on selection boards. As one of the five CEC flags, I shared the role of board president of various boards on a rotating basis with the other flags. We could not sit on the same board two years in a row, and all the boards met every year except the flag board. What had changed since my days as a recorder on the flag board and sitting on the lieutenants' board was that now a lawyer had to be present during all deliberations; add to that the pervasiveness of specific quotas for the promotion of women and minorities and the requirement that line officers had to be part of the board. The lawyer was there to ensure that nothing that was not written into the record was discussed about anyone being considered. This meant no personal negative knowledge of the individual could be shared—no matter how pertinent it was to the promotion—on the misguided belief the individual had a right to know what was being considered and to refute any negative observations that might be made. This requirement struck at the core values of the officer community. It implied that officers sitting on boards could not be trusted to behave ethically without a lawyer present to monitor them.

To believe that all the information necessary to evaluate an individual for promotion is contained in their service record is ridiculous; it ignores the fact that service reputation is a key to success. Rarely does immoral behavior, although known, end up being recorded in a fitness report, but it usually comes out in some form. In one case, we were voting on an individual whose record was spotless, but I knew from personal dealings with him during my detailer days that he was unethical. Since it was not in his record, I could not say anything about it; I simply voted 0 while the others all voted 100 percent confidence in this selection. Engineers being engineers, when the composite score was shown, the other members quickly determined that one member had voted 0 and were dumbfounded. After they had wasted time trying to figure out who had done it and why, I admitted that I had cast the black ball but could not tell them why because of the rules, and there was nothing they could say that would make me change my vote. If they wanted to change the percentage required for selection on this one individual, they could, but I would not be a party to it. The lawyer was pissed, but there was nothing he could do. It did not matter; the board did change the percentage, so the unethical officer was selected without my vote. I would add that he went on to prove he was the unethical officer I knew him to be.

What made this all a joke was that it did not apply to the selection of three and four-star admirals, since no service record was reviewed by a selection board. Selection was by the CNO, passed up to the secretary of the Navy and later to the secretary of defense, based upon his preferences and relationships with these individuals. This led to some extremely poor choices of officers with both questionable ethics and morals that have played out when these officers were subsequently relieved for conduct that had been overlooked, though in many cases well known, in the selection process. I have already discussed the effect of quotas on selecting the best-qualified officers, but the inclusion of line officers on the board was another pernicious attempt by the line to influence selections for pet rocks and to intimidate the CEC for no good reason since the value added of these officers was nil. The net result of these changes compromised the selection process; I became disgusted with it and have remained so. My general officer classmates in the Army told me these restrictions on discussion do not happen in the Army selection boards. Additionally, these "protections" were nowhere to be seen in corporate America, hence the charges of "glass ceilings" and so on. I found this interesting since it was the civilian appointees from the business world who had driven the implementation in the Navy. These issues seemed to be handled by "back room" decisions on senior promotions in the corporate world.

Seabee Command

An unhappy story was playing out in the leadership of the 2 NCB. For numerous reasons that boiled down to the lip service the line had given regarding the integration of the active and reserve Seabees, it was decided that the Commander of the 2 NCB had to be an active duty CEC flag. Since the line was not about to give the CEC another flag billet, the only solution was to "double-hat" the flag at LANTDIV as the Commander 2 NCB. When the incumbent reserve flag retired from 2 NCB, I was given orders to assume command—which suited me fine, as I was back where I wanted to be. This increased my travel and the number of Seabee balls I attended as a guest speaker, but it also gave me a chance to visit Bosnia during the conflict there since we had a Seabee battalion supporting the Army. This offered a perfect example of the stupidity of the thoughtless cuts the services made, as the Army trigger-pullers cut their construction engineer battalions and placed most of the remainder in the reserves, so they could no longer support themselves when they needed engineers. This gave me an opportunity to observe how the idea of supporting combat forces with contractors was going to play out. The short answer was it was awfully expensive and limited in scope; everything had to be paid for à la carte. Where military units could be tasked as required, contractors generally could not because the contract spells out specifically what the contractor will do.

There was also the problem that contractors are not combatants, so they could not carry weapons and defend themselves. A perfect example of the problem with contracting for support was an audit finding that one contractor was overcharging the Army for meals because some bean counter took the number of meals the contractor said were being served and divided it by the number of troops and came up with more than three per day. The reality was the mess halls were open 24/7, and the troops came in whenever they had time to eat, leading to more than three meals a day. The metric for payment was meals served, so the contractor was happy to oblige. I never saw troops fed so well in all my experience, but the bean counters went crazy. In the AVF, the leadership apparently had trouble restricting meals to three a day or forcing one or more to be MREs (Meal, Ready to Eat), a packaged ration. The Army division commanders loved the Seabee support, and the Seabees loved being in the mix.

Final Promotion and Assignment

The time passed quickly, and it was soon time for my next and final promotion board—two-star, or rear admiral (upper half). There were two one-stars competing for one slot, and I was fortunate enough to be selected, giving me the bonus three years as a flag officer before I had to retire. Not long after that was the competition between me and the other two-star to see which of us would be the chief. This would be the CNO's choice based upon what he wanted in the job. It was a clear choice between the two of us since I was a field guy, having had many commands in every area of the CEC and Seabees but no Washington staff jobs as an O-6 or O-7, whereas the other officer was a Washington guy, having spent over a decade in key Washington staff jobs, and had no Seabee command on his CV. Given the track record I had observed, it was no surprise to me that the Washington guy was chosen; he was a known quantity inside the Beltway. I was to replace him as the senior CEC officer on the CNO's staff, which would make me responsible for getting resources for the Seabees (among other things). This was something I really wanted to do. On the personal side, this caused me to commute to Washington and spend the week staying at my brother-in-law's place since my youngest daughter and son were nearing the end of high school; it would have just been too traumatic to move the family. The hours of the job were impossibly long anyway, so I would not have seen much of them through the week even if they had moved. I worked out an arrangement with my three-star boss, allowing me to take off for important events like sporting contests, school events, and so forth, and we made the best of a less than desirable situation.

When I completed my tour at LANTDIV, I was ready to leave due to yet more organizational changes within the Navy designed to put line officers with no knowledge in further controlling positions in the infrastructure roles. Ambitious, self-promoting, business manager types in key jobs without any real knowledge supported them. This led to the same issue I had at the PWC; that is, who oversaw advice on the infrastructure—the CEC flag or a civilian SES know-it-all on the line flag's staff?

CNO's Staff

Apart from the personal inconvenience of being in Washington, DC, without my family, I was in a good position on the CNO's staff to do what I wanted when I reported for duty, for several reasons. First, I was fortunate enough to have a superb line three-star as my boss, the deputy chief of naval operations (Logistics)—the same position I had served as an aide to—Jim Amerault, who was a surface warfare officer. We hit it off immediately when he told me he was relatively new to his job and knew absolutely nothing about the things I was responsible for. This differentiated him from many line flags I had known who never wanted to admit what they did not know and wanted to posture their brilliance all the time. He told me my job was to keep him from looking foolish to the CNO and secretary of the Navy in the areas I was responsible for and to use him to make things better for the Navy in those areas. He promised to support me if I came to him for help since he had been promoted from being the comptroller of the Navy as a two-star and knew the budgeting process inside and out. As a bonus, Don Piling (USNA '65), vice chief of naval operations, the four-star responsible for the day-to-day management of the Navy, was his good friend and classmate. Second, I was promoted to two stars almost immediately upon reporting. This limited the number of people who were senior to me on the CNO staff to the three-stars (plus the two four-stars on the staff), although there were misguided two-stars who thought a more senior date of rank as a two-star would have some influence on me. Third, in addition to having enough rank to be a player and a supportive boss, there was no one on the staff who knew more about my areas than I did, so I was not worried about a "gotcha" from the line bubbas. And fourth, but extremely important, I had a superb staff working for me, plus access to the NAVFAC staff to handle the myriad of tasking, congressional inquiries, and so on that bureaucratic staff must deal with.

Simply stated, the function of the CNO's staff, or OPNAV as it is called, is to determine the policies, plans, and doctrine necessary to carry out its part of the national defense strategy, the requirements for the Navy to carry out that mission, and the resources necessary to meet those requirements. To do this, the Navy must continuously monitor the readiness of its forces to execute the strategy. Reporting requirements were promulgated through its chain of command for this purpose, specifying four levels of readiness from C-1 (the highest) to C-4 (the lowest, or unable to execute). It must also use the intelligence resources available to it to continuously monitor the capabilities of potential adversaries to compare against its capabilities in the requirements determination. All of this seems straightforward, but the fly in the ointment is there are numerous places where subjective judgments are required, starting with the individual unit commanding officer's determination of his unit's readiness level. Reporting one's unit as C-4 is a good way to have a short career.

Since there are never going to be enough resources to satisfy all the requirements in a finite defense budget whose size is, after all, a political decision made by the administration and the Congress, what is important and where risk can be taken is a subjective judgment of the CNO as advised by the OPNAV staff. Here is where finding the honest broker is difficult because the prejudices of a lifetime of service in the surface, air, or submarine forces tends to color one's views and minimize the importance of the other parts of the mosaic of capabilities required to execute the Navy's part of the national strategy. It also causes problems with supporting the Marine Corps, which falls under the jurisdiction of the Department of the Navy. The Navy supplies many support services to the Marine Corps (grudgingly, at times), such as medical and dental support in the form of doctors, dentists, nurses, and corpsmen; chaplains and their assistants; Seabees; amphibious support, including the ACBs; and a host of other supporting services. It is fair to say taking Navy budget dollars to support the Marine Corps is resented in many circles since the Marines are viewed as resource drainers that detract from the Navy's capabilities.

The Seabees constitute a prime example, as they provide the main construction support for the Marines in contingencies and wartime but are supported entirely out of the Navy's budget. Hence, cutting the number of Seabees is not seen as impacting the Navy while it has a direct effect on the mission of the Marine Corps in that it has no resources to offer. All the above is included in the constant infighting on the OPNAV staff between hardware and infrastructure/logistics requirements, line and support personnel requirements, and Marine Corps support. The upshot was the Navy budget that had to be defended against the other services in office of the secretary of defense battles and then in the Congress until the final defense budget was approved. This was my world for the next three years.

As the director of the Facilities and Engineering Division, I was responsible for resourcing and managing the Navy's military construction program, facilities maintenance, bachelor and family housing, and the Seabees' activities, while NAVFAC served as the technical advisor on these issues, and I, therefore had access to that staff. The budget slice of these items was about $6 billion. While I was there, another shore infrastructure directorate was created that would eventually morph into the commander of naval installations (CNI) under a line three-star, with many of my functions subsumed into it. My billet shifted to include the CNI deputy duties for a while and was then eliminated entirely in a flag billet cut. Fortunately, this happened after I had retired, but it completed the unqualified line officer and SES civilian assumption of control of the shore infrastructure. That arrangement continues its fast track of making the lousy condition of the Navy's infrastructure an acceptable risk in the line mania to buy more line toys in the form of ships and aircraft at the expense of the shore establishment, Seabees, and other things they consider unnecessary or someone else's problem. Since the MCON program and funding of maintenance of facilities translated into major pork for the Congress, it led to lots of help from the various congressional committees in the quest of the members to secure more contracts for their states or districts. This drove a significant amount of correspondence to answer endless questions about this or that project or facilities issue, together with preparation for testimony before congressional committees on the proposed budget in these areas.

My number one goal during my final tour was to reorganize the Seabees while recapitalizing their equipment to increase their effectiveness. The reorganization was necessary to overcome the duplication of policies, doctrine, and inconsistent oversight caused by the Atlantic and Pacific Fleets each having their own Seabee commands and resourcing those commands as they saw fit. This had led to inconsistent training of the battalions and endless disputes as an Atlantic Fleet battalion relieved a Pacific Fleet battalion at deployment sites and vice versa. The way project materials were ordered grew out of this lack of unity of command. The integration of the active and reserve Seabee units further exacerbated the already significant problems. All of this begged for one central Seabee command to provide the policy and doctrine oversight with a unity of command and control so vital to effect operations. My idea was to create a Seabee division, like the Army and Marine Corps divisions, that had all Seabee units assigned, both active and reserves. The staff would be integrated with active and reserve officers and commanded by a CEC two-star. I would get my opportunity to make this happen—against the heavy odds of fighting the entrenched line bureaucracy. But I had double-barreled secret weapons in my boss, Jim Amerault, who wanted what was best for the Navy, and my old friend from lieutenant commander days, Vern Clark, who had been selected as CNO. Over the course of my tour, I laid the groundwork for this reorganization and then got approval to spend my last six months in the Navy finalizing it, briefing it to the unified commanders to win their support, and making a final presentation on the plan to the CNO for his approval.

One of the key aspects of the justification for the restructuring was using data to show how badly the lack of unity of command had affected the equipment the Seabee battalions had in their inventories and, worse yet, the large stocks of equipment sitting in warehouses for the reserve battalions in case of mobilization. Simply stated, the equipment the Seabees had on hand was worn out. They had warehouses full of Vietnam- and Desert Storm-era equipment, and active-duty battalions were only receiving a trickle of the replacement equipment they desperately needed. Desert Shield/Desert Storm had revealed how poorly prepared the Seabees were, as equipment was pulled from everywhere to properly outfit the four battalions that were sent to the Gulf. The sad part was having to seek the necessary funds for the project, even though the dollars required to properly outfit the Seabees was not even a rounding error in the Navy's budget. Research and development had come up with improved equipment, and the Navy could tag on to the larger procurements of the Army and Marine Corps to procure certain common equipment such as trucks, humvees, and the like. This would allow the Navy to get them at the best price possible. Having Jim Amerault's expertise and contacts in the budgeting area made putting together a workable recapitalization plan possible; he was also instrumental in gaining the critical approvals as the budgeting process for the coming years took shape. Once Jim understood the rationale and need, he became a solid supporter of this effort and made sure it got through the budgeting process virtually intact. The result was the Seabees were ready when the U.S. military went into Iraq in 2003.

While the Seabee efforts were in train, there were a host of other high-priority issues to address that kept the staff and me busy. One of the continuing issues was completion of the previously mentioned BRAC base closures that had become a cash cow for communities all over the United States. Given that the original publicized intent of BRAC was to get rid of unneeded military bases by selling them at a profit to help with the peace dividend occasioned by the fall of the Berlin Wall and the demise of the Soviet Union, I found that the reality was that local communities did not want to pay for these bases; they wanted them for free, so they could sell them at a huge profit. They also expected them to be pure as snowdrifts, with zero environmental problems despite having been military bases for years. This, coupled with the Congress giving up sovereign immunity on environmental laws, led to a feeding frenzy by local communities, who pushed local, state, and EPA officials to fine the military for environmental issues, real or imagined, to be paid out of the services' budgeted funds. It seemed ironic that these same communities who had benefited immensely from the presence of these same bases as employers now argued they were a burden that they should get environmentally pure and free of charge. The local congressmen jumped on this bandwagon for their political purposes, and the cost of the BRAC program grew with little offset of revenue from sales. The process took much longer than necessary as the standards demanded by the communities became more unrealistic, while generating an unending stream of correspondence, lawsuits, hearings, and so forth as the self-righteous vilified the services for their handling of this program. It was truly disgusting and not for one with a weak stomach.

Aviation support issues were another continuing problem, particularly on the environmental front. Most military airfields had been built before or during WWII in the middle of nowhere, without communities near them. Over the years, communities encroached on the airfields by building homes and offices all around them and then amazingly complained about the noise of the aircraft operating out of these bases. Congress finally started acting by authorizing the purchase of land around bases to preclude encroachment, but too little, too late. More amazing nonsense surfaced as environmentalists sought to restrict flights over bombing ranges because it bothered the creatures living there, such as tortoises. The Navy was sued for trying to practice antisubmarine tactics because environmentalists were worried about the effects of sonar on dolphins and whales. The list was endless of things that were more important than national defense in the eyes of self-proclaimed saviors of nature and the planet. This caused yet more dilution of services' resources and manpower, while impeding efforts to defend the country and causing endless paperwork and legal battles.

This does not mean that the services were blameless; they routinely developed weapons systems that could cause environmental concerns, while doing a poor job on their Environmental Impact Statements (EIS). The EIS is supposed to outline the impact of the actions and whatever mitigation there will be for a decision-maker to evaluate and render a decision. Such a determination might be that the needs of national defense override the EIS concerns, so the weapons system should be developed in spite of them. If the process is followed as specified by the law, national defense needs are protected. The lawsuits and delays come from challenges to the process versus attacking the final decision, as it is a difficult thing to argue that someone outside the defense establishment knows more about the needs of national defense.

A classic case was the EIS for the F-35 Joint Strike Fighter (JSF), the next-generation manned fighter for all the services. While there are a host of sound reasons for the capabilities built into this fighter that I will not go into, its basing was an afterthought that did not receive much thought until late in the process. The noise generated on takeoff and the pollution from the engines made using Navy bases on the U.S. coasts a practical impossibility. This creates a huge problem for the Navy, which was trying to have its squadrons based near its carriers. There were other problems for the Navy—such as the noise on carrier decks and the heat of the exhaust on the deck—that were slow in being addressed.

Military Family Housing

There is no denying that the state of military family housing in the late '90s was appalling. Since the family housing maintenance funding was one of those discretionary pots of money that the services could steal from relatively easily, they had done so over the years to the point that housing was in sad shape. While there was a great deal of data to support this, the requirement for family housing at all kept morphing to fit the latest rationale to get more money. What should have been brought out was that military family housing was a vestige of the days when military bases were located far from urban areas, where there was no housing for the military families that could be provided by the local community, nor were the communities likely to invest money in building any. This was no longer the case for the Navy within the United States since most Navy bases were more worried about encroachment by the communities than lack of housing. The argument then morphed into providing appropriate housing since all military members were paid a housing allowance that was not taxable to offset their housing costs in the community; the amount of this allowance was based upon surveys of availability and price performed every few years.

The catch that I brought up many times—to no avail—is that housing is discretionary, in that everyone has a different view of what is "appropriate" for enlisted personnel. Those same enlisted personnel, given the choice of where they want to spend their money, will many times choose accommodations of poor quality that some might say are not appropriate. The leadership then adopted the position that it must dictate where and how housing allowances should be spent, no matter what the individual wanted. One of the laughable conversations that arose from this policy was when these do-gooders would say we needed to provide housing for sailors comparable to that of their civilian counterparts. I would point out that an eighteen-year-old civilian with comparable education and training, sometimes with a spouse and small children, was either living with their parents, squatting in a slum or very low-quality housing, or renting a trailer with broken windows since they could not afford a single-family residence that our leadership would consider to be "comparable housing." Further, a significant percentage of recruits came from single-parent homes and had never lived in a single-family home in their life, so to attempt to define what was "comparable" was ridiculous. These arguments went nowhere because these folks were bound and determined to educate these poor benighted sailors about what they wanted them to be as opposed to what the sailors wanted.

There were only three solutions to the problem. First, the Navy could keep the housing it had and fund its complete renovation. This was never going to happen since Congress had continuously funded the maintenance for the military housing already, and this would be double-funding the same thing a great expense. Second, it could get completely out of the housing business by disposing of the housing and reverting to paying allowances that put the onus on the sailors to find their own housing. Finally, it could come up with some combination of these two that made sense. One further wrinkle that exacerbated the housing problem was the services' recruiting and retention of single parents, thereby accepting the responsibility of not only housing them but also providing all the associated support in the form of childcare, healthcare, and so on. The entitlement mindset hit the services big time with sailors looking to the Navy to provide everything for their families at little or no cost, plus all the time off they felt they needed to raise their kids while being paid to perform their military assignment. I really could not get my head around how this squared with the mission of the military services, but then again, I was not a "new-generation socialist" like the ones who seemed to be running the Department of Defense and saying all this was necessary for an AVF.

What was ultimately decided was the worst of both possible worlds because, once again, the businessmen who came into the administration and Congress decided contracting out the housing function could solve all this. Fine, but the payback required to recover the investment needed to fix the problem would take a long time. No problem—we'll let the services sign fifty-year contracts that turned housing funding from discretionary to a bill in the form of housing allowances that must be paid and escalated to meet the contractor's cost formula. The result was that some genuinely nice (some would say too nice) housing and community facilities were built, while older housing was either upgraded or demolished. Supposedly, the services were protected from the contractor renting these former government quarters to civilians by the military having first preference, but what happens when the military members decide they do not want them? The contractor can rent them to whomever they wish. Wow, that is great for morale and esprit de corps. How about when the size of the services shrinks (which was inevitable and is happening now)? What does this do to the entitlement mentality embraced by those being recruited?

My biggest problem with all of this was it took the responsibility away from the service member to provide housing for their dependents and made it the services' responsibility for no good reason. From a budgetary perspective, it was a disaster. The housing dollars became "must pay," and the ability of the services to move money was further restricted. When this happened, the fate of the shore infrastructure was sealed; it was now the largest discretionary account left from which everything would have to be stolen for pet rocks (and it has been). The state of the infrastructure is appalling, but according to the service leadership and the secretary of defense, the risk is acceptable. Right!

"Too Hard" Problems

Over the years, I had seen that a favorite method of dealing with "too hard" problems was to "assume" them away in some manner. For instance, since recruiting and maintaining an AVF is an awfully expensive proposition, there is a continuing drumbeat from the administrations and the Congress to reduce the manpower costs and requirements. This in turn led to the concept of minimum manning in the design of new ships, relying on technology to replace manpower. I sat in a briefing on the new DD-21 replacement destroyer where the program manager discussed the capabilities of the ship and the fact that it would have a highly trained crew of fewer than a hundred, as I recall. The crew would be composed of senior petty officers who seemed to need the equivalent of at least a master's degree to function as expected. The number of junior enlisted was minimal. Having watched ships being loaded out by working parties of junior sailors throughout my career, together with the assignment of these same sailors to collateral duties such as security and shore patrol, not to mention damage control during battle, I could not understand how these functions were going to be carried out with such a small crew. Additionally, the priority for the best-educated and most intelligent recruits was already going to the submarine force, so where were all these new highly trained and ultra-intelligent sailors coming from? I asked the program manager at the end of the brief and got the usual assumed away response.

Someone else would be responsible for the tasks that had been standard in the Navy before. A favorite fallback was contractors. The loading of the ship would be performed by an automated system that allowed the ship to order what it needed over a computer from the warehouse, where it would be deposited in some sort of conveyer system and transported to the pier, where it would be automatically loaded into the correct part of the ship. When I pointed out there were no piers in the Navy that could do this, nor were there any plans to place these kinds of systems on existing piers, I got the "not my problem" response. The fact that requirements are expensive does not mean they can be ignored, but in too many cases they were.

One of the persistent bait and switch games played in the Pentagon was placing funding in the budget based on justified requirements and, once the budget had been approved by Congress, moving that funding to what the service viewed as higher-priority areas. Even the members of Congress can see this happening—which makes for some interesting testimony before the various committees. A favorite ploy was to show the problem being addressed in the out years, or the budget years after the current one under consideration for approval. Everything is wonderful in the nirvana of the out year where all issues are appropriately funded. While I was testifying in that vein one year, a member of the committee said to me that he had been on that same committee for years, and every year the services said the same thing, but the out years never seem to yield the expected fixes. "Why is that?" he asked. All I could say was the same old pap about higher priorities for the limited budget dollars. The truth is that priorities are in the eyes of the beholder with an expectation that nothing terribly bad will happen if budget items have their funding removed. Congress will just raise the budget total if it is really worried about the issue. Neither of these outcomes is a certainty and they only rarely occur, but having discretionary power over the limited available funding is a good thing, if the leadership is held accountable for its decisions. Moving issues from the discretionary category to a "must pay" bill in an already shrinking discretionary pot causes huge problems as in the case of the privatization of military housing.

Another major issue I dealt with that was a continuing problem was the relentless conversion of flag billets to SES billets, with the selection of supposedly smart individuals who were either narrowly experienced or had no real experience in the job function. With the diversity pressures building, this was no surprise. The idea of converting a billet that had been filled by a flag officer of many years' experience (hopefully including the handling of contingencies or even combat) into one held by a generally younger, less experienced, civilian did not seem to bother anyone but the military. We kept being told how smart these people were, implying experience was not important. It made my head hurt. The results are visible in the continuing poor performance that has resulted. These people tended to do the politically correct thing rather than the right thing since they were political animals who were more interested in maneuvering themselves into the next higher job in the department or perhaps in the administration. The role of the military officer as the honest broker was on a fast track to extinction. When a senior military leader disagreed with a political appointee, it caused serious political issues. The best way to deal with this is not to let the military liaisons express themselves or to pick individuals for these jobs who could be controlled. By the time I left my last job, it was hard not to look at every selection in the SES community with equal cynicism since political correctness versus best qualified was the order of the day; diversity was a driving factor, regardless of experience or real qualifications.

This was my last lesson in empathy while serving in the Navy. It was more a matter of understanding that my empathy should be directed to my superior military leaders rather than to the SES community. Whereas I understood the flag and general officer community and knew how to successfully deal with them, dealing with the SES community was a different proposition altogether. Status and position were everything to most SES personnel, and any indication they did not have the requisite qualifications for their job caused serious organizational problems and time-consuming infighting. Choosing one's fights and getting concurrence from the military chain of command became key. Even then, the political consequences of "winning" often overruled the "right thing" being done.

My last important strategic input to the nation's defense came not long before I retired but two years before the next major contingency—the invasion of Iraq. I was selected to lead the engineer section of the first-ever joint logistics war game held at the Naval War College in Newport, Rhode Island. I was to look at the war plans and determine whether the current armed forces logistics resources could be supported. The short and easy answer was "no," as it had always been—if logistics resourcing remains the constant bill payer for the pet rocks and toys the political and military leadership are constantly seeking to fund. The results are predictable. In this case, the top five concerns that came out of the war game were all engineer issues, with the number one issue being "contractors on the battlefield." Those who would have to make it work viewed this as a huge problem. The expense, together with the difficulty of writing a contract to cover the myriad circumstances that arise in combat coupled with the Geneva Conventions' prohibitions on armed civilians made this an intractable problem. The results of the war game were briefed to the JCS, but nothing was done since the issues were in the "too hard" category and not connected with political correctness. I enjoyed working over the issues with my staff and Jim Amerault, but I was happy to move into my last six months on my Seabee project.

Seabee Reorganization

The major activity during my last six months was putting the final touches on my brief and scheduling that brief to key decision-makers in the fleets and the unified commanders prior to my final briefing for approval with the CNO. This involved working through the staffs so that the principal or his deputy was brought up to speed on the issues before I gave him my brief. The major angst was with the Pacific Fleet since the creation of a Seabee division under the Atlantic Fleet appeared to remove Seabee asset control from the Pacific Fleet, which would be a nonstarter. This was solved by retaining a Seabee command element with the CEC flag who was double-hatted on the Pacific Fleet. The unified commanders were strong supporters of the Seabee division; they were, after all, mostly Army or Marine generals who were extremely comfortable with the concept and understood the advantages to them in command and control with resource allocation. Everything came together on several levels to make this series of briefings go smoothly with the requisite approvals from all the key players. Old friends from the past held several of the key positions, such as Adm. Tom Fargo, who was the unified commander in the Pacific and had been a friend since we had been aides together years before, and Lt. Gen. Mike DeLong, USMC, who was the deputy commander of Southern Command. He had been a high school classmate and graduated from the Naval Academy at the same time I graduated from USMA. Armed with the endorsements of the unified and fleet commanders plus the strong support of Jim Amerault and his connections on the OPNAV, particularly the VCNO, I was set to brief my old friend Vern Clark, the CNO.

What a surprise—the briefing was a "love-in"; Vern liked the idea on its merits and trusted my judgment. The Seabee division concept was approved, along with the plan for standing it up. The officer selected to stand it up and be its first commander would be Rear Adm. Chuck Kubic, whom I had known since he worked for me as a lieutenant (jg) and company commander in NMCB-4. He had been a White House fellow and CNO fellow and was just the man with the intelligence and drive to make this happen. Not only did he make it happen (with Vern Clark presiding as the commissioning officer a year later), but he also led the division during the 2003 Iraqi Freedom Operation. The performance of the division under Chuck led to the division being the recipient of a Presidential Unit Citation. The division's performance in the real world fully validated the concept. That was the exclamation point on my involvement with the Seabees, which had started thirty-four years before as an ensign in NMCB-9.

I retired from the Navy on the parade field at the Construction Battalion Center, Gulfport, Mississippi, in July 2001. It was a great send-off as I had done everything that I wanted to do and more, and I was now ready to try my hand in the business world that I had heard so much about. I left with no regrets other than concern for the future of the services since choosing the best-qualified person was rendered obsolete in the quest for meeting social goals. My concern has since been confirmed. I was lucky enough to serve when I did; I had a great deal of fun with great people along the path of my career. I doubt that those currently serving can have much fun because the atmosphere in the military has become so stiflingly politically correct that joking around, camaraderie, and esprit de corps have become victims. Good officers are forced to confront whether they want to command in an atmosphere where any malcontent can cause them to be investigated for anything and the chain of command is increasingly spineless and ruled by lawyers and political know-nothings. Timing was everything and my timing had been good!

EPILOGUE

Thanks for the Memory
—Ralph Rainger and Leo Robin

B ob Hope's theme song title seems appropriate when I look back on my life experiences. I had fun throughout my adolescence and my military life. One of the oft-heard refrains of my friends and colleagues who served in the military is, "I'm glad I served when I did and not today." Political correctness and the tyranny of the various "entitled" groups whose sensitivity has decreed the death of having fun for fear of saying or doing something someone might not like is rampant and uncontrolled. The judicial branch's imaginative interpretations of the Constitution, the laws passed by Congress, and its own increasingly politically motivated decisions have made a mockery of the concept of majority rule and the "reasonable person." Lawyers and political hacks have gutted the long cherished Honor Code at West Point with the cynical pronouncement that the vast majority of young Americans lie and cheat, so they cannot be held to rigid standards.

Congress and the DOD have turned the military profession into just another job, killing the camaraderie, compromising the promotion and assignment systems to ensure politically correct outcomes (as opposed to merit or capability), and isolating ninety-nine percent of the U.S. population from military service through the All-Volunteer Force. Particularly mind-blowing is the notion that discrimination in promotions and assignments against one group by giving unearned preferences to another group will somehow balance the scales for alleged prior injustices. The "how" has never really been answered, unless one is prepared to believe there is no value in promoting the best-qualified candidates for jobs.

The result of this new philosophy is a military atmosphere that is a sterile, humorless, and underfunded world of repeated stressful deployments, unequally shared by increasingly smaller portions of the population of the United States. During these deployments, the traditional outlets for young service members of R&R, alcohol, and sex are vilified and host nations' religious concerns, which were not considered in the past, dictate military personnel policy. Young people in the military are subjected to endless indoctrination lectures designed to change human nature or to alter our definition of it. Military clubs have been closed or restricted to the point they are not utilized. Sexual preferences have become a right to be accommodated by the military without regard to mission accomplishment, good order and discipline, and merit, when the right to serve in the military is not guaranteed and never has been. Telling someone to simply "get over it!" when they don't like something is cause for charges of insensitivity from an educational system that has chosen to adopt the *Animal Farm* ideology that some groups are "more equal than others". Empathy for subordinates, peers, and superiors appears to have been a principal casualty of the new philosophy. Observing this in the current military makes me cherish my time in the service even more.

I do not regret my service nor what it has done for me. Using the experiences I gained growing up and over my military career, I went into the private sector and had a fourteen-year career running two corporations as President/CEO. When I retired as the Chairman/CEO of the last, I had grown the revenues from $70M to over $400M per year and expanded its operations many fold. This would not have been possible without my military experiences and challenges, and I will forever be indebted to those I served with.

ENDNOTES

1 Louis Barthas, *Poilu: The World War I Notebooks of Corporal Louis Barthas, Barrelmaker 1914–1918*, trans. Edward M. Strauss (New Haven, CT: Yale University Press, 2014), xxi.

2 Daniel E. Rice and John A. Vigna, *West Point Leadership: Profiles of Courage* (n.p.: Leadership Development Foundation, 2013), 4.

3 David McCullough, *The Wright Brothers* (New York: Broadway Books, 2004), 5.

4 Michael Montgomery, "Scotch-Irish or Scots-Irish: What's in a name?" *The Ulster-Scots Language Society,* http://ulsterscotslanguage.com/en/texts/scotch-irish/scotch-irish-or-scots-irish/. From this essay, one can conclude Scotch-Irish is correct.

5 David Halberstam, *The Best and The Brightest* (New York: Ballantine Books, 1993), xvi.

6 Theodore Crackel, *Mr. Jefferson's Army: Political and Social Reform of the Military Establishment, 1801–09* (New York: New York University Press, 1989), 73.

7 "Honor Concept," United States Naval Academy, https://www.usna.edu/About/honorconcept.php.

8 www.westpoint.edu/military/simon-center-for-the-professional-military-ethic/honor

9 Tom Carhart, *Sacred Ties* (New York: Penguin Group, 2010), 29.

10 Carhart, *Sacred Ties*, 4.

11 *Merriam-Webster Dictionary*, s.v. "journeyman," https://www.merriam-webster.com/dictionary/journeyman.

12 Not to be confused with the Lockheed SR-71 Blackbird reconnaissance jet.

13 Thomas E. Ricks, *The Generals* (New York: Penguin, 2013), 248.

14 Acton's pithy aphorism is drawn from a letter to Bishop Mandell Creighton in 1887. J. N. Figgis and R. V. Laurence, *Historical Essays and Studies* (London: Macmillan, 1907).

[15] Lt. Cdr. Michael W. Shelton, "Who Are the Heroes?" (United States Naval Institute *Proceedings*, August 1978), 41.

[16] Shelton, "Who Are the Heroes?" 45.

[17] Report of a Board of Decorations and Medals, serial 105B (April 7, 1947), 4.

[18] "Lord Emerich Edward Dalberg Acton," Acton Institute (July 20, 2010), https://acton.org/lord-emerich-edward-dalberg-acton.

[19] Note that the acronym CMC is also used in the Navy to represent command master chief.

GLOSSARY

ACB	Amphibious Construction Battalion
ACU	Assault Craft Unit. A unit of NBG with small craft used in logistics movement from ships at sea to shore.
AFRTS	Armed Forces Radio and Television System
ARG	Amphibious Ready Group. A MEU plus a squadron of amphibious ships to carry them and their equipment, together with the NBG detachment to land them.
AOR	Area of Operations
AOT	Army Orientation Training. Summer training with an active-duty Army unit.
APWO	Assistant Public Works Officer
AVF	All-Volunteer Force
BEAST BARRACKS	Two-month summer training period for new cadets before plebe year.
BEAST DETAIL	Upperclassmen at West Point who supervise the new cadets during the Beast Barracks phase.
BEEP	Basic Equipment Evaluation Program
BMU	Beachmaster Unit. A unit of the NBG responsible for control movement of logistics from ships to shore and controlling the beach.
BOQ	Bachelor Officers' Quarters
BUH	Builder (Heavy)
BUL	Builder (Light)
BUPERS	Bureau of Naval Personnel. Senior Navy organization charged with personnel management.
CAP	Combined Action Platoon. A Marine squad stationed with local South Vietnamese militia to defend their hamlet.
CBLANT	Construction Battalions, Atlantic

CBPAC	Construction Battalions, Pacific
CBU	Construction Battalion Unit
CEC	Civil Engineer Corps. The military facilities engineering and contracting specialists for the Navy and Marine Corps.
CECOS	Civil Engineer Corps Officers School
CESE	Civil Engineering Support Equipment
CINC	Commander In Chief. Four-star officer in charge of a major military command.
CINCPACFLT	Commander In Chief, Pacific Fleet
CINCUSNAVEUR	Commander In Chief, U.S. Naval Forces Europe
CMC	Command Master Chief, an E-9 who is the senior enlisted advisor to the CO. Also, commandant of the Marine Corps.
CMHCN	Construction Mechanic (Construction)
CNO	Chief of Naval Operations. The senior active duty naval officer.
COMCBLANT	Commander, Construction Battalions, Atlantic Fleet
COMCBPAC	Commander, Construction Battalions, Pacific Fleet
COMNAVACTSUK	Commander, Naval Activities, United Kingdom
COMSUBRON 14	Commander, Submarine Squadron 14
COW	A third-year cadet at USMA, a junior
CP	Command Post
CUMSHAW	Defined as a noun (a present, gratuity, bribe, payoff), the verb form is the act of obtaining the item or items.
DCNO	Deputy Chief of Naval Operations
DSC	Distinguished Service Cross. Second-highest Army award for valor.
EFD	Engineering Field Division
EIS	Environmental Impact Statement
ELCAS	Elevated causeway raised from the beach via piles with a jacking system; it is fitted with a mobile crane and turntable so trucks can be loaded and turned around.
EONCN	Equipment Operator (Construction Equipment)

EOD	Explosive Ordnance Disposal
E-RING	The outer perimeter corridor of the Pentagon where the executive offices of the senior military and civilian leadership of the services and DOD are located; that is, a place of immense power.
F-4	Twin-engine jet fighter-bomber, a mainstay of the Air Force, Marine, and Navy air campaign in North and South Vietnam.
FIRSTIE	A fourth-year cadet at USMA, a senior
GOM	General Order of Merit. Composite class standing of academic grade point, athletic grades, and aptitude standing at the USMA.
IOC	Initial Operational Capability
JAG	Judge Advocate General, a military lawyer
JCS	Joint Chiefs of Staff
JFIP	Japanese Facilities Improvement Program
JSF	Joint Strike Fighter
KIA	Killed in Action
LSO	Landing Signal Officer
LST	Landing Ship, Tank. A vessel used to move personnel and large equipment and capable of landing on beaches meeting certain gradient requirements.
MACV-SOG	Military Assistance Command, Vietnam – Studies and Observations Group. Cover name for an ad-hoc military command, primarily composed of Special Forces troops and special operations support personnel that carried out clandestine missions of various types in denied territory.
MARG	Mediterranean Amphibious Ready Group
MCON	Military Construction
MEB	Marine Expeditionary Brigade
MEF	Marine Expeditionary Force. Usually two or more Marine divisions.
MEU	Marine Expeditionary Unit
MARINE RECON	Marine reconnaissance battalion charged with special operations missions.
MOH	Medal of Honor
MOS	Military Occupational Specialty

MPS	Maritime Prepositioned Ships
MTT	Mobile Training Team
NBG	Naval Beach Group. Amphibious command charged with supervising the units required to land the Marine units. It consisted of the BMU, whose duty was to mark the landing areas, control the beach, and supervise the flow of the offload; and the ACU, which consisted of the landing craft of various types for specific offload requirements. The ACB provided ship to shore movement of large equipment, containers, and POL. The NBG was in overall charge reporting to the Amphibious Ready Group commander.
NCB	Naval Construction Brigade
NIS/NCIS	Naval Criminal Investigative Service the follow on command after NIS Naval Investigative Service name was changed.
NCO	Noncommissioned Officer
NCR	Naval Construction Regiment
NJP	Nonjudicial Punishment (Article 15, UCMJ)
NMCB	Naval Mobile Construction Battalion
NROTC	Naval Reserve Officers Training Corps
NVA	North Vietnamese Army
NWC	Naval War College
OCS	Officer Candidate School
OPDS	Offshore Petroleum Discharge System
PDA	Public Display of Affection. Any action deemed improper/inappropriate by a TAC or USMA staff between a cadet and a date.
PE	Professional Engineer license
PHIBCB	Amphibious Construction Battalion, used synonymously with ACB
PLEBE	First-year cadet at USMA, a freshman
PMS	Preventive Maintenance System (as opposed to the female hormonal condition)
PTSD	Post-traumatic Stress Disorder. A medical disorder that involves reaction to traumatic experiences (generally related to combat in a military context) and can cause behavioral issues.

PWO	Public Works Officer
PT BOAT	Patrol Torpedo Boat
QUONSET HUT	Expeditionary constructed structure composed of corrugated sheet metal over arched girder supports with a concrete deck whose interior could be built out to serve numerous purposes.
RFP	Request for Proposal
RECONDO	Training module at Camp Buckner during yearling summer training based on the Ranger School.
REMF	Rear-Echelon Motherfuckers
ROC/POE	Required Operating Capabilities and Projected Operating Environment. Description of what a unit is supposed to do and under what conditions.
ROE	Rules of Engagement
RORO	Roll-on/Roll-off. The concept of driving vehicles on to specially built ships with discharge ramps in the stern that allowed vehicles to be driven on to piers or barge ferries.
ROTC	Reserve Officers Training Corps
S-2	Intelligence/Training Staff Section; also, the officer assigned to direct that shop
S-3	Operations Staff Section; also, the officer assigned to direct that shop
SEA	Southeast Asia
SEABEES	Members of the Naval Construction Force, amphibious battalions, and underwater construction teams that principally support Marine Corps units in various contingencies
SEA STATE 3	Wave heights ranging between one foot eight inches and four feet one inch (abbreviated SS 3)
SES	Senior Executive Service. Government employee rank equivalent to flag or general officer.
SLWT	Side-Loadable Warping Tug
SITREP	Situation Report
SOF	Special Operations Forces
STAND UP/STOOD UP	Military speak for establish or create
TAC	Tactical Officer. Army Officer assigned to cadet companies to monitor and enforce discipline.

TET	The Lunar New Year celebrated in Asian Countries
UCMJ	Uniform Code of Military Justice
UCT	Underwater Construction Team
UDT	Underwater Demolition Team
USAFA	United States Air Force Academy
USMA	United States Military Academy
USNA	United States Naval Academy
VCNO	Vice Chief of Naval Operations. Four-star responsible for the day-to-day operations of the Navy.
VC	Viet Cong insurgents during the Vietnam War
YEARLING	Second-year cadet at USMA, a sophomore

SUGGESTED READING

Betros, Lance. *Carved from Granite: West Point Since 1902*. Williams-Ford Texas A & M Military History Series, no. 138. College Station, TX: Texas A&M University Press, 2012.

Brady, Patrick Henry. *Dead Men Flying*. New York: WND Books, 2012.

Carhart, Tom. *Sacred Ties*. New York: Berkley Caliber, 2010.

Crackel, Theodore. *Mr. Jefferson's Army: Political and Social Reform of the Military Establishment, 1801–09*. New York: New York University Press, 1989.

Gillespie, Robert M. *Black Ops Vietnam: The Operational History of MACVSOG*. Annapolis, MD: Naval Institute Press, 2011.

Goldstein, Gordon M. *Lesson in Disaster*. New York: Times Books, 2008.

Grant, Zalin. *Over the Beach: The Air War in Vietnam*. New York: W. W. Norton, 1986.

Halberstam, David. *The Best and The Brightest*. New York: Ballantine Books, 1997.

Kyle, Chris. *American Sniper*. New York: HarperCollins Publishers, 2013.

Marlantes, Karl. *Matterhorn*. New York: Atlantic Monthly Press, 2010.

McChrystal, Stanley, Tantum Collins, David Silverman, and Chris Fussell. *Team of Teams: New Rules of Engagement for a Complex World*. New York: Portfolio/Penguin, 2015.

McKim, Keith. *US Navy SOG Seals: The MACV-SOG Medal of Honor Recipients Series Book 2*. Yucca Creek Records LLC: audiobook, Audible, 2000.

Miller, Jeffrey R. *U.S. Navy Seabees: The First Fifty Years*. Dallas, TX: Taylor Publishing Company, 1993.

Peter, Dr. Laurence J., and Raymond Hull. *The Peter Principle*. New York: Bantam Press, 1969.

Peters, Tom. *The Little Big Things: 163 Ways to Pursue Excellence*. New York: HarperCollins Publishers, 2010.

Peters, Thomas J., and Robert H. Waterman Jr. *In Search of Excellence.* New York: Harper & Row, 1982.

Plaster, John L. *Secret Commandos: Behind Enemy Lines with Elite Warriors of SOG.* New York: Simon & Schuster, 2004.

Rice, Daniel E., and LTCOL John A. Vigna. *West Point Leadership: Profiles of Courage.*
N.P.: Leadership Development Foundation, May 20, 2013.

Ricks, Thomas E. *The Generals.* New York: Penguin Books, 2013.

Russ, Ted. *Spirit Mission.* New York: Henry Holt & Co, 2016.

Shelton, Michael W. "Who Are the Heroes?" United States Naval Institute *Proceedings*, 104/8/906: five pages, August 1978)

Sommers, Christina Hoff. *The War Against Boys: How Misguided Feminism is Harming Our Young Men.* New York: Simon & Schuster, 2000.

Tregaskis, Richard. *Southeast Asia: Building the Bases; The History of Construction in Southeast Asia.* (Superintendent of Documents, U.S. Government Printing Office: Washington D.C.)

Webb, James. *Born Fighting.* New York: Broadway Books, 2004.

———. *Fields of Fire.* New York: Bantam Books, 1979.

Zumwalt, Jr., Elmo R. *On Watch.* New York: New York Times Publishing Co., 1976.

ABOUT THE AUTHOR

Mike Shelton grew up in a Navy family and received a competitive appointment to West Point. He graduated in 1967, was commissioned in the Navy Civil Engineer Corps, serving thirty-four years on active duty, and retired as a Rear Admiral in 2001. He spent the next fourteen years in private industry, first as President of Burns and Roe Services Corporation. He then moved to EMCOR, a multibillion dollar specialty construction corporation, running its government facilities services subsidiary, EMCOR Government Services. He reorganized and expanded it, building annual revenues to over $400 million. He retired as Chairman and CEO in 2015.

Mike graduated from the US Military Academy (BS), University Of Illinois (MS Civil Engineering), University of Arkansas (MS Management), Naval War College, and Stanford University Executive Program.

He is most proud of his units that received awards, which include a Presidential Unit Citation (Army MACV SOG RVN), two Joint Meritorious Unit Awards, two Navy Unit Commendations, four Navy Meritorious Unit Commendations, and Navy Best of Type (Naval Mobile Construction Battalion, Pacific Fleet 1975). NMCB 4 won the Peltier Award from the Society of American Military Engineers as the best NMCB in the Navy in 1975.

He has many professional affiliations, including: Registered Professional Engineer (Pennsylvania), 1974; Outstanding Young Men of America, 1977; Distinguished Graduate Naval War College, 1981; Distinguished Alumnus Award, Department of Civil and Environmental Engineering, University of Illinois, 2005; Fellow, Society of American Military Engineers, 1996; and Fellow, American Society of Civil Engineers, 1997.

Mike's wife, Mary, is a retired Navy nurse Commander who raised their three now grown children—Michelle, Jessica, and Tom—while dealing with her assignments, family relocations, and Mike being frequently gone. They have four grandsons and reside in Virginia Beach, Virginia.

Mike Shelton

INDEX